REGNUM STUDIES IN MISSION

Mission in Secularised Contexts of Europe:

Contemporary Narratives and Experiences

Series Preface

Regnum Studies in Mission are born from the lived experience of Christians and Christian communities in mission, especially but not solely in the fast growing churches among the poor of the world. These churches have more to tell than stories of growth. They are making significant impacts on their cultures in the cause of Christ. They are producing 'cultural products' which express the reality of Christian faith, hope and love in their societies.

Regnum Studies in Mission are the fruit often of rigorous research to the highest international standards and always of authentic Christian engagement in the transformation of people and societies. And these are for the world. The formation of Christian theology, missiology and practice in the twenty-first century will depend to a great extent on the active participation of growing churches contributing biblical and culturally appropriate expressions of Christian practice to inform World Christianity.

Series Editors

Paul Woods	Oxford Centre for Mission Studies, Oxford, UK
Paul Bendor-Samuel	Oxford Centre for Mission Studies, Oxford, UK
Tony Gray	Words by Design, UK

A full listing of titles in this series
appears at the end of this book

REGNUM STUDIES IN MISSION

Mission in Secularised Contexts of Europe
Contemporary Narratives and Experiences

Edited by

Marina Ngursangzeli Behera
Michael Biehl
Knud Jørgensen

First edition published 2018 by Regnum Books International

Regnum is an imprint of the Oxford Centre for Mission Studies
St. Philip and St. James Church, Woodstock Road
Oxford, OX2 6HR, UK
www.ocms.ac.uk/regnum

09 08 07 06 05 04 03 8 7 6 5 4 3 2 1

British Library Cataloguing in Publication Data
A catalogue record for this book is available from the British Library

ISBN: 978-1-506477-74-9

Typeset by Words by Design
Cover design by Words by Design

regnum

The publication of this volume is made possible through the financial assistance of the Areopagos Foundation and Evangelisches Missionswerk.

Distributed by Fortress Press in the US and Canada

Contents

Editorial Introduction
Mission in Secualrised Contexts of Europe: Contemporary Narrative and Experiences

Marina Ngursangzeli Behera, Michael Biehl
and Knud Jørgensen

Secular and secularity derive from the Latin word *saecularis* meaning "of a generation, belonging to an age". The Christian doctrine that God exists outside time led medieval Western culture to use secular to indicate separation from specifically religious affairs and involvement in temporal ones.

This does not necessarily imply hostility to God or religion, though today some use the term in that way. The reformer Martin Luther used to speak of "secular work" as a vocation from God for most Christians. Secularity may be understood, not as being "anti-religious", but as being "religiously neutral" since many activities in religious bodies and institutions are secular themselves, and most versions of secularity do not lead to irreligiosity.

For believers, by its very nature religion calls for a response since it relates for them to that which is most profoundly human. Seen in this light one may argue that especially in Europe many people today are not so much religiously neutral as religiously illiterate. The 'secular' media, for instance, in general have difficulties making sense of religion. So, they choose sometimes to ignore it in their analysis, focusing on purely socio-economic and political explanations for events unless religion can be identified as the factor fueling conflicts.

Secularism is often understood as the principle of the separation of government institutions from religious institutions and religious dignitaries. Secularism asserts the right to be free from religious rule and teachings. Another aspect of secularism is the view that public activities and decisions, especially political ones, should not be influenced by religious beliefs and/or practices.

Secularism as a philosphy draws its intellectual roots from Greek and Roman philosophers such as Epicurus and Marcus Aurelius; from Enlightenment thinkers such as John Locke, Denis Diderot, Voltaire, Baruch Spinoza, James Madison, Thomas Jefferson and Thomas Paine; and from more recent freethinkers and atheists such as Robert Ingersoll and Bertrand Russell.

The purposes and arguments in support of secularism vary widely. In European laicism, it has been argued that secularism is a movement toward modernisation, and away from traditional religious values (this is also known as secularisation). This type of secularism has often occurred while maintaining an official state church or other state support of religion. In the United States, some argue that state secularism has served to protect religion from governmental interference, whereas secularism on a social, day-to-day level is less prevalent.

In the West a number of writers have focused on the collapse of Christendom, often evidenced by the separation of state and church and the remarkable decline in church membership especially in the Northwestern European countries. A challenging alternative may be for Christians to use this opportunity to explore again and more deeply the relationship of the kingdom of God and the State.

Secularism literally refers to 'belonging to the age'. In this light this book may explore more deeply the way in which the church in 'secularised' contexts has indeed adopted the spirit of the age.

Some of the articles published here are papers that have been inspired and developed further from presentations made at a conference "Mission in secularised Contexts" which took place in February 2016 in Berekfürdő, Hungary. Representatives of the World Council of Churches (WCC), the World Communion of Reformed Churches (WCRC), Council of World Mission (CWM) and Evangelisches Missionswerk (EMW) had agreed to study the topic reflecting on a gap in the WCC mission statement "Together towards Life. Mission and Evangelism in Changing Landscapes". The shared impression was that this document does not pay the necessary attention to the rapidly changing context for mission and evangelism in Europe, tagged with the label secularism. The papers presented there were not published at that time and hence the plan to enlarge the selection and publish them in this volume.[1]

For this book we have invited authors to look at secularised contexts in Europe. Some have called Europe 'the Exceptional Case' in terms of secularism and faith. Even so it was here that the thesis of secularisation in the sense of a disenchantment (Weber) of the world into a place ruled solely by inner worldly laws was developed. In a postmodern context the thesis may be critiqued. Rather it would seem that we live with a tension between global processes of rationalism and secularisation, and regional forms of cultural

[1] Meanwhile a study paper of the European Ecumenical Mission Councils was submitted and discussed in the World Missionary Conference, which took place in Arusha, Tanzania in March 2018. Christoph Anders, Michael Biehl, Gerrit Noort, 'Called to Transforming Discipleship in North-Western Europe. Some Reflections on Witnessing in Secularised Contexts', in *Resource Book; Conference on World Mission and Evangelism, "Moving in the Spirit – Called to transforming Discipleship", 8-13 March 2018, Arusha, Tanzania*, ed. by Jooseop Keum (Geneva: WCC, 2018), 84-101.

specificity. Then Europe may be seen not so much as an exception but a region where secularity and resurgence of religion take different and specific forms.

All the European countries exhibit a significant drop in religious belonging as well as in practice, yet religion is not disappearing. This is a possible starting point for talking about mission in a 'secularised' context. In several countries, it implies that the established church structures are less attractive and often less able to communicate with new forms for spirituality and religious longing. Yet new groups and emerging communities have grasped the paradigm shift and are struggling to find avenues of hospitality in a multi-context (which is more religious than explicitly secular).

We believe that a book like this with essays on the diverse contexts and challenges could be helpful. It is not too heavy on theories and missiological deliberations; rather sharing contemporary narratives and experiences from various settings, but with relevant insights from Scripture. Secularism is a global phenomenon, but too much of a globalisation perspective may lose sight of the European contexts. Focusing on Europe may help the church in other places learn lessons that enable it to avoid the decimation of faith we have experienced in recent decades.

Our purpose is to describe our contexts from a missiological perspective and in that way lay the ground for a broader conversation about religion and church in today's Europe.

The book opens with some 'General Perspectives: An Overview of The Diverse Contexts of Europe', followed by Grace Davie's chapter on 'Religion in Modern Europe: Stabilities and Change'. It was Davie who coined the term 'Europe – the exceptional case'. Raag Rolfsen's challenging chapter on 'Secretes of the Secular. On the Conditions and Possibilities of Faith in and Beyond the Secular Age' is different, but still pursuing the same line of thinking (secular/secularisation/secularism) but in in a more philosophical manner.

In the second part, Perspectives on the Secular Formation of Culture, Hielke Wolters writes from an ecumenical (and Dutch) perspective about 'The Search for Identity in Secularised Contexts'.With Michael Biehl we enter Hamburg and get A West-German Perspective: Believing in a Secular Way'. This is followed by a rather different 'Perspective on Secularisation in Eastern Germany' by Martin Reppenhagen & Thomas Schlegel. Daniel Buda has an essay on 'Mission in Secularised Contexts of Europe. An Orthodox Perspective, with Special References to the Romanian Context'. The Roman Catholic contribution comes from Annemarie C. Mayer, 'Mission in Secularised Contexts of Europe'. Cathy Ross provides an Anglican 'British Perspective: Exploring the Five Marks of Global Mission'. Gerrit Noort's chapter is a 'Dutch Perspective: Emerging Churches as Survival of the Fittest? Some Reflections about the Search for Missional Procreation in the Dutch Secular Context', quite different from the German and British perspectives, but at the same time highlighting the ambiguity of 'secular'. The Swedish/

Norwegian Lars Dahle focuses on 'Cognitive Dissonance as a Missiological Challenge. An Evangelical Perspective on Western Europe'. Paul Bendor-Samuel brings the second part to a close with his chapter on 'In Search of Mission in a Secular Europe'.

One of the observations on secularisation in Europe is that it intensifies over the generations as several contributors point out. Therefore, we have included papers with 'Perspectives among Youth' from Zuzana Bąbicova and Pawel Pustelnik who write about 'Ecumenical Youth Organisations and their Mission in Secularised Contexts', and Tijana Petkovic who writes about Serbia and orthodox youth.

The final part includes some views from 'Europe – and Beyond': Harvey Kwiyani has an insightful article on 'Migrant Churches in a Secular Europe', followed by two perspectives from the global south – one from Marina Ngursangzeli Berhera, with a focus on India, and one from Esther Mombo, with a focus on East Africa. Both highlight the provinciality of Europe in the global context and add insights to the discussion whether Europe is the exceptional case.

The book closes with a brief epilogue, 'Thinking Two Thoughts'.

Our purpose has been to describe our contexts from a missiological perspective and in that way lay the ground for a broader conversation about religion and church in today's Europe. To lay the ground we have expanded our European context. At the same time, we have made it clear that this European context is diverse and that the concept of 'secular' has many facets.

Part 1

General Perspectives

The Diverse Contexts of Europe

Knud Jørgensen

I grew up in the northwestern part of Europe. My peers and most of my teachers focused on the collapse of Christendom and often referred to Dietrich Bonhoeffer's letters from prison[1] where he raised tantalising questions about the role of Christianity and the church in a "world come of age", where human beings no longer need a metaphysical God as a stop-gap to human limitations; and where he mused about the emergence of a "religionless Christianity", where God would be unclouded from metaphysical constructs of the previous 1,900 years. Bonhoeffer witnessed the failure of the German Protestant Church as an institution in the face of Nazism and saw this challenge as an opportunity of renewal for Christianity.

Years after Bonhoeffer's death, some Protestant thinkers developed his critique into a thoroughgoing attack against traditional Christianity in the "Death of God" movement, which attracted the attention of the mainstream culture in the mid-1960s – at a time when I was studying theology in Copenhagen and my professors made me read Paul van Buren's *The Secular Meaning of the Gospel*[2] and Harvey Cox's *The Secular City*.[3] My faith was shaken, so I went to my professor K.E. Skydsgaard to solicit counsel and advice. He helped me and made me realise that the radical interpretations of Bonhoeffer's insights amounted to a grave distortion, that Bonhoeffer did not mean to say that God no longer had anything to do with humanity and had become a mere cultural artefact. Instead he turned my young attention to Bonhoeffer's earlier book on *The Cost of Discipleship*[4] (original German title is simply *Nachfolge*). It is centred on an exposition of the Sermon on the Mount, in which Bonhoeffer spells out what he believes it means to follow Christ. It was first published in 1937, when the rise of the Nazi regime was underway in Germany, and it was against this background that Bonhoeffer's theology of costly discipleship developed, which ultimately led to his death. One of the

---

[1] Dietrich Bonhoeffer, *Widerstand und Ergebung* (Munich & Hamburg: Siebenstern Taschenbuch Verlag, 1951); *Letters and Papers from Prison* (New York: The Macmillan Company, 1962).

[2] Paul M. Van Buren, *The Secular Meaning of the Gospel* (New York: The MacMillan Company, 1963).

[3] Harvey Cox, *The Secular City* (New York: The Macmillan Company, 1965).

[4] Dietrich Bonhoeffer, *The Cost of Discipleship* (New York: Macmillan, 1966).

most quoted parts of the book deals with the distinction that Bonhoeffer makes between "cheap" and "costly" grace. According to Bonhoeffer,

> cheap grace is the preaching of forgiveness without requiring repentance, baptism without church discipline. Communion without confession. Cheap grace is grace without discipleship, grace without the cross, grace without Jesus Christ.[5]

Cheap grace, Bonhoeffer says, is to hear the Gospel preached as follows: "Of course you have sinned, but now everything is forgiven, so you can stay as you are and enjoy the consolations of forgiveness." The main defect of such a proclamation is that it contains no demand for discipleship. In contrast to cheap grace,

> costly grace confronts us as a gracious call to follow Jesus, it comes as a word of forgiveness to the broken spirit and the contrite heart. It is costly because it compels a man to submit to the yoke of Christ and follow him; it is grace because Jesus says: "My yoke is easy, and my burden is light."[6]

Bonhoeffer argues that as Christianity spread, the Church became more "secularised", accommodating the demands of obedience to Jesus to the requirements of society. In this way, the world was Christianised, and grace became its common property. But the hazard of this was that the Gospel was cheapened, and obedience to the living Christ was gradually lost beneath formula and ritual, so that in the end, grace could literally be sold for monetary gain.

But all the time, within the church, there had been a living protest against this process: the monastic movement. This served as a place where the older vision was kept alive. Unfortunately, monasticism was represented as an individual achievement that the mass of the laity could not be expected to emulate; the commandments of Jesus were limited to a restricted group of specialists and a double standard arose: a maximum and a minimum standard of church obedience. This was dangerous, Bonhoeffer says, because whenever the church was accused of being too worldly, it could always point to monasticism as the opportunity of a higher standard within the fold – and thus justify the other possibility of a lower standard for others. So, the monastic movement, instead of serving as a pointer for all Christians, became a justification for the status quo.

Bonhoeffer remarks how this was rectified by Luther at the Reformation, when he brought Christianity out of the cloister. However, he thinks that subsequent generations have again cheapened the preaching of the forgiveness of sins, and this has seriously weakened the church: "The price we are having to pay today in the shape of the collapse of the organised church is only the

[5] Bonhoeffer, *The Cost of Discipleship,* 2.
[6] Bonhoeffer, *Costly Grace,* 3.

inevitable consequence of our policy of making grace available to all at too low a cost. We gave away the word and sacraments wholesale, we baptised, confirmed, and absolved a whole nation without condition. Our humanitarian sentiment made us give that which was holy to the scornful and unbelieving… But the call to follow Jesus in the narrow way was hardly ever heard."[7]

Here is my framework for looking at Europe – the secular Europe with a world come of age and the call to costly discipleship. I am caught between this contrast. I cherish the secular freedom from the bondage of Constantinian Christendom and the ensuing freedom of religion. It is like a breath of fresh air after centuries of imprisonment under the state-church tyranny. At the same time, I long for a call (back) to costly discipleship and faith and obedience: only the obedient believes; and only faith leads to obedience.

This means that I am *not* sure that 'secular' always signifies the opposite of faith.[8] Secularisation may, in part, also be the fruit of the Christian tradition. Secular (northwestern) European society has also been shaped by the Christian tradition; the secular Europe cannot be understood apart from Christianity and its impact on society and culture. Therefore, I am not sure that the solution to a church in decline is a revivalism à la the eighteenth century.

In other words, there are *blessings and challenges* of secular culture. One such blessing is freedom of religion, because of the separation between the religious and the secular realm – between ecclesiastical and political power. Freedom of religion means I can live in a multi-religious world rather than the Christendom world. This also allows space for *the private sphere and personal opinion.*

This implies *an emancipation process of Gospel and church* compared to the Christendom era of the former centuries in Europe. True, there is a growing religious illiteracy: when I speak of God as creator, saviour and liberator, people might not know what I am talking about because they lack the background of the Small Catechism and the Apostles' Creed. I need in new ways to explain and expound. That is a growing challenge to church and Christians – and it challenges us to speak of discipleship in new ways. That is what 'transforming discipleship' in new contexts is all about: how do we in new ways contextualise our call to discipleship? *How may the very idea of discipleship be transformed?* – into what Pope Francis calls "missionary discipleship" – evangelising in Christ's way?

And how may we in new ways *encounter others in a secular culture and context* – through evangelism, advocacy, prophecy?

---

[7] Bonhoeffer, *Costly Grace*, 12.

[8] Christoph Anders, Michael Biehl, Gerrit Noort, 'Called to Transforming Discipleship in North-Western Europe. Some Reflections on Witnessing in Secularised Contexts', in *Resource Book. Conference on World Mission and Evangelism, "Moving in the Spirit – Called to transforming Discipleship", 8-13 March 2018, Arusha, Tanzania*, ed. by Jooseop Keum (Geneva: WCC, 2018), 84-101.

Contrasting Diversity[9]

Interaction between people of different faiths in Europe has become part of everyday life. This raises the question of how churches should shape interreligious and interchurch relations and how to view such relations theologically. The Muslim presence in many European countries is part of the picture, but Eastern religions also attract the attention of many people. Since the Second Vatican Council, the Roman Catholic Church has issued several documents on these of questions,[10] whereas many churches of the Reformation in Europe are still in the process of establishing their position. This is for both historical and practical reasons.

The historical–practical reasons have to do with the fact that Protestant Christianity has for centuries been located mainly in countries of Central and Northern Europe, as well as the US. There was little inclination to engage in interreligious relations. The encounter with Islam took the form of defending Vienna against the Ottoman Empire. The contact with churches in the East was largely nonexistent. During the past decades, the situation has changed significantly for all churches and for their view of mission: the centre of gravity of Christianity is shifting from the North to the South – to sub-Saharan Africa, Latin America, South-East Asia, where it finds itself involved in intensive relationships with other religions. Europe, on the other hand, is becoming more and more multi-religious, because of immigration and secularisation.

It is a challenge to speak of Europe and religion. The continent has never been and is even less today a homogeneous set. The high diversity of the situation and of the historical journeys of each country makes it complicated to give a general survey. Rather we will speak of Europe in its common understanding: that is, we do not focus on a political (the European Union), economic (EEA), or mythical ("Mother Europe") definition, but rather on a broad geographical understanding.

It is also difficult to give a general picture of religious belonging in Europe.[11] A number of surveys provide information concerning the religious affiliation of the European population.[12] For instance, the European Values

[9] See for the following *Protestant Perspectives on Religious Plurality in Europe*, Edition released by the Community for Protestant Churches in Europe Council, summer 2016.

[10] Francesco Gioia (ed.), *Interreligious Dialogue: The Official Teaching of the Catholic Church from the Second Vatican Council to John Paul II, 1963-2005* (Boston: Pauline Books & Media, 2006).

[11] Grace Davie, *Europe: The Exceptional Case* (London: Darton, Longman & Todd, 2002). Grace Davie, Paul Heelas and Linda Woodhead (eds.) (Burlington: Ashgate Publishing Limited, 2003).

[12] Sources of information on religious belonging in Europe are mostly results of the major European studies: *European Values Studies, European Social Survey, International Social Survey Programme, Eurobarometer*. *Pew Research Forum* also

Survey carried out in 2008 in 47 countries shows that more than three quarters of the population in Europe identify with a religion even though this may well represent very different commitments and practices in each country; the Pew Research Center claims that there are in Europe some 18% of non-believers (in 2015). According to the European Values Survey, globally speaking, more than a third of the religious Europeans (36.7%) are Roman Catholics, less than a third (30%) Orthodox, Muslim (15%) and Protestant (14.5%) believers are found nearly in the same numbers, while Jews, Hindus and Buddhists each represent less than 1% of the population. This information provides only a rough picture and a starting point. Depending on the countries taken into account, one can find very different results. From a religious point of view, the unity of contemporary Europe is nonexistent since it covers countries with very different contemporary settings and historical backgrounds.

The Protestant Reformation began in Europe. In a nearly entirely Catholic part of the world, there were some preparatory movements with Peter Waldes (Italy), John Wycliff (England) and Jan Hus (Chechia). However, the writings of Martin Luther mark the start of the Reformation, which quickly spread in parts of Germany, France and Switzerland, and then to the rest of Europe. The history of the propagation of the Protestant ideas and the gradual establishing of Protestantism in different trends and institutions is a long and complex development, marked by theological disputes, persecution and brutal wars. As a result, Protestantism finds itself these days in very different situations, depending on the country. One can find some countries in Europe that have remained mainly Catholic (Ireland, Portugal, Spain, Poland and, to some extent, France), others that have become predominantly Protestant (Finland, Denmark, Sweden, Iceland, Norway), and those that have established, smoothly or painfully, the coexistence of both traditions (Germany, The Netherlands, Switzerland). The Eastern part of Europe was mostly under the influence of Orthodoxy, and Greece, Serbia, Romania, Russia and Bulgaria are predominantly Orthodox, although from different origins. In southeastern Europe, because of the historical spread of the Ottoman Empire, some regions have a longstanding Muslim tradition (such as in Bosnia-Herzegovina), or are predominantly Muslim (Albania). However, Islam is a minority in most European countries.

Each European country is thus different. The importance given to religion also varies, with some countries being very 'secular' whereas others remain deeply religious. Many European countries are experiencing troubled times as a direct result of undergoing years of Communist regime, which others never went through. This regime tended to control religion, and even tried to destroy the religious institutions (e.g. Albania after 1961). The sudden freedom of religion that followed the fall of the regime led to an important rise in religious

---

provides data. For further information on sources concerning religion in Europe, see the Eurel website: http://www.eurel.info/spip.php?rubrique573.

practice in several countries (Ukraine, Bulgaria, Hungary). This surge may also be caused by the economic crisis and the difficulty of making a living, which could be leading young people to turn back to religion (as in Albania). In other countries the Communist regime seems to have been somewhat successful in eliminating religious life and church membership (East Germany, Estonia, Chechia).

Migration trends are bringing to Europe people from Africa, Asia, America and the Middle East, causing the European countries to become a place of encounter between people who express and experience their individual religion in very different ways. This evolution of Europe does not facilitate comparative studies of its recent history: since Europe has not throughout the years always meant the same group of countries, *general conclusions are difficult to draw*. Among the recent entrants to the European Union, one can find the most religious country of Europe (Poland) and the least religious (Estonia).[13]

Status and Place of Religion in European Societies

There are major variations from one country to another; nevertheless, all the countries of Europe share a *common reference point and a similar situation*. The common reference point is the legal affirmation of *the freedom of religion*. The similarity between the countries of Europe is that *their religious setting is changing*, and often changing very quickly. Similarity, however, stops there: the change does not affect all the countries in the same way, or at the same speed. It is not expressed in the same way and does not always have identical causes or consequences. General tendencies affecting several countries may, however, be described. First, *a change in the religion–politics relation* is noticeable. This affects mainly the part of Europe previously under Communist regime: in many of these countries, the presence of religion is now accepted, and the religious groups have recovered. In other places, the relationship of the state to religion has changed because of a major political upheaval. Elsewhere, the relationship of the state to religion has developed at a slower pace. Several nations have experienced an important change concerning the place that religion used to hold in the political landscape. In Sweden, the (Lutheran) Church of Sweden used to be the state church but has not been since 2000; the same applies to Norway from January 2017; the situation in Denmark is moving in the same direction – separation of church and state and thereby the decline of Constantinian Christendom; in Italy, the Catholic Church no longer has a specific social status. Another change is the fact that in many European countries, believers now do not represent the main part of the population. The term "plurality" describes a situation in which more than one entity of a certain

---

[13] For further information, see reports by *Religionsmonitor* (http://www.religionsmonitor.de/ english.html) or *Pew Forum* (http://www.pewforum.org/).

category exists in the same space. "Plurality" is often used synonymously with "diversity", referring to differences between the diverse entities. Nowadays, "plurality" is often used to describe the diversity, whereas the term "pluralism" implies a conceptual dimension. "Pluralism" gives a perspective on how that diversity should be dealt with, i.e. the notion "pluralism" presupposes a reflection and a normative judgement on how the different entities should relate to one another. Today, "pluralism" is used to describe acceptance of plurality and arrangements for respecting diverse entities within that plurality. There are varying degrees and varying ways of acceptance, thus different concepts of pluralism.

The Christian reference is challenged, with Christianity nowadays far from being the only reference with regard to religion. This is, as indicated above, another common feature of European history: the plurality of cultures and religions. Cultural differences, because of the process of globalisation, can be found within European societies. Moreover, mobility (because of tourism and migration), as well as the quick and easy dissemination of information, brings individuals to encounter and learn about many cultural universes different from their own background. Europeans have thus discovered new religious cultures.

Although the numbers may display meaningful and great differences, all the European countries exhibit *a significant drop in religious belonging as well as in practice*. For a long time, scholars have explained that drop by the loss of the belief in the existence of God. Our civilisation was becoming more technological, and this modernity would necessarily come with a growing rationality. This modern thought was considered incompatible with beliefs understood as proceeding from a less advanced way of thinking. However, the multiplication of new religions in the 1970s (the "New Age") came as a major surprise to most of us, also in Northwestern Europe, and led observers to admit that it was more an evolution of beliefs than a drop (some even claim an increase in religious beliefs among youth). Religion was not disappearing, 'secular' was much vaguer than expected. One must admit, however, that the major change concerns *the intertwined dynamics of the relation between institutions and individuals*. 'Belonging' and 'believing' were not synonymous. To belong, or to remain, in a religious group less and less depends on the social birth group of the individuals. On the contrary, people are in search of meaning, move from one group to another, cobble together their own ideas, and change. All this is best expressed as *a development in the relation to institutions*. The caving-in of religious practice most probably demonstrates a reorganisation of traditional affiliations/institutions more than the disappearance of beliefs. Most individuals no longer rely mainly on church institutions to provide the frames for the way they think religion and spirituality; they tend to set the borders up for themselves. Recent European surveys reveal that a majority of Europeans believe more easily in a vague supernatural power or force than in a personal God. The decline in prestige of important religious traditions also discloses new forms of reference to religions: *spirituality becomes an individual matter.*[14] People feel free in their relation to religion and create new structures of faith (a kind of *buffet religion*). It is a risky task to try to provide a general explanation for this development. The changes in the religious landscape can be described quite easily; they are more difficult to explain. The religious change in Europe may be expressing *secularisation, or pluralisation, or the return of religion, or the transformation of religion, or even a combination of these ideas*. All these trends can be challenged, however. Since we actually belong to this historical moment, nobody can really be in a position to provide proper theories, and the explanations given remain narratives. They can inspire our thoughts, but they fall short when we come to a specific country. *It is a challenge to speak of Europe and religion.*

Recent Statistics from Pew

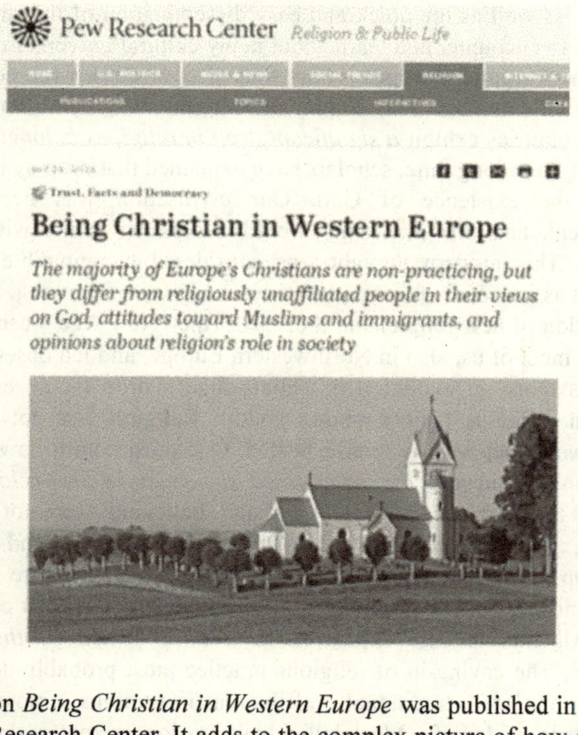

A report on *Being Christian in Western Europe* was published in June 2018 by the Pew Research Center. It adds to the complex picture of how church and Christian faith live and survive in Europe. The picture is increasingly complex, culturally, sociologically and missionally. It is like watching a mosaic: 71%

[14] See Gordon Lynch, *The New Spirituality. An Introduction to Progressive Belief in the Twenty-first Century* (London: Tauris, 2007).

declare they are Christian – in the middle of a post-religious and post-Christian continent. The Pew figures (based on 24,000 interviews) announce that that the death of God in Europe is strongly exaggerated. 71% say they are Christian. 18% attend church. 46% are 'non-practising Christians'.

Denmark 64%, Sweden 52%, Norway 51%.

Germany has a high score with 71% calling themselves Christian. In Austria and Italy, the figure is 80%. France is known to be a secular society; 64% say they are Christian – the same as in Denmark. The figures for Sweden and Norway are surprisingly low. Has Mammon taken over in the oil country Norway? How do we interpret these findings?

Dialogue and Diapraxis

Dialogue has against this background become an essential concept. Dialogue, rather than mission, has now become the paradigm for determining the relations to other religions. That change of paradigm has posed various practical and theological questions in answer to which individual churches, communions of churches and the ecumenical agencies (WCC, Roman Catholic Church and World Evangelical Alliance (WEA)), have issued statements.[15]

Among those who engage in dialogue there is a great variety of motivations for entering dialogue. Some of them are:

- Trying to understand how people of other faiths describe their faith journey;
- Looking for reliable information regarding other faiths;
- Seeking to clarify misunderstandings between people of different faiths;
- Participating in religious celebrations and rituals together;
- Sharing your faith experiences with others;
- Responding to theological challenges that are triggered through other faiths;
- Listening to other faith experiences;
- Establishing good neighbourly relations with people of other faiths; and
- Jointly advocating for people in need.

The shared challenges faced by religious communities in Europe are multifaceted and call for creating spaces of *diapraxis* in many areas: religious education and teaching dialogical attitudes among young people, social care for asylum seekers and refugees, care for elderly people, and other activities known in the churches as diaconal work. Through acknowledging shared

[15] World Council of Churches, Pontifical Council for Inter-Religious Dialogue and World Evangelical Alliance, *Christian Witness in a Multi-Religious World: Recommendations for Conduct,* https://www.oikoumene.org/en/resources/documents/wcc-programmes/interreligiousinter-religious-dialogue-and-cooperation/christian-identity-in-pluralistic-societies/christian-witness-in-a-multi-religious-world.

challenges in these areas, diapraxis may develop from the dialogues and strengthen the sense of community across religious boundaries. The future will bring more multi-religious families and interfaith marriages, as well as people with an experience of multiple religious belonging for various other reasons. The creation of a shared humanity across religious and non-religious affiliations is possible and will empower Europe's Protestants to emphasise an openness in a multi-religious Europe.

Whatever the interpretation, one idea can definitely be turned down for good: *religion is not disappearing*. At the same time as the relation of individuals to religious institutions moves towards a diminution of the political importance of churches in some countries, the highly religious historical base of Europe is being acknowledged or rediscovered. In all the countries, public institutions and their structure, social values and even the cultural framework often have their roots in religion: items as diverse as hospitals, chaplaincies, human rights, or the end-of-the-week rest, originally had a religious dimension. Christian perspectives and practices have significantly influenced many cultures in Europe, and Jewish, Muslim, pre-Christian and Enlightenment traditions also had an impact on Europe throughout history. Although their religious dimension is sometimes lost, such explicit value-orientations are deemed important by people and they refuse to part with it.

Making Disciples

The only imperative in the Great Commission is 'make disciples' (*mateutete*) – not 'go out' or 'baptise' as I was told while growing up. My parents' generation thought of mission in terms of going – from the West to the rest; the clergy of my youth – and even today – talk about the Great Commission as a command to baptise. Both have got it wrong: the focus is to make disciples. This was also the concern of Bonhoeffer in the 1930s – to find or rediscover the link between discipleship and faith in new contexts where grace was costly and not cheap. Wherever I go I call for 'discipleship training', not just among children and youth, but among us adults. In Africa my friends talk about the Christian faith being as broad and as thin as a pancake – great growth, but often quite shallow. Like in my part of Europe, many who are baptised, confirmed and married according to Christian traditions are lacking more depth in their Christin faith and commitment. There have been attempts such as the Alpha courses, but we need a much larger and more broadly based (and less charismatic) focus on discipleship training – combined with a renewed proclamation of costly grace. It is not enough always to talk about the love of God if we do not lift up the cross of Christ.

Religion in Modern Europe: Stabilities and Change

Grace Davie

Introduction

This chapter considers the situation pertaining to religion – and in particular to Christianity – in modern Europe.[1] It is written on the assumption that a careful analysis of context is the starting point for effective ministry, including mission. Specifically, it examines a series of factors that must be taken into account in order to understand the ongoing changes taking place in the religious life of the continent. The crucial point to grasp is that these factors push and pull in different directions: some point firmly in the direction of greater secularisation; others lead to a more nuanced picture as the topic of 'religion' rises rather than falls in public discussion. The latter was not anticipated in the mid post-war decades but has accelerated since the 1990s.

A short conclusion draws the threads together, underlining the persistent paradox concerning religion in this part of the world. At one and the same time, Europe is becoming both more secular and more religiously diverse. The former leads to a diminution of religious activity overall; the latter leads to the

---

[1] The chapter draws largely on my own work – in particular Grace Davie, *Religion in Modern Europe* (Oxford: Oxford University Press, 2000); 'Religion in Europe in the 21st Century: The Factors to Take into Account', European Journal of Sociology 47.2 (August 2006), 271-96; Grace Davie, *Religion in Britain: A Persistent Paradox* (Oxford: Wiley Blackwell, 2015). A considerably expanded version can be found in Grace Davie, 'Christianity in Europe', in Jens Holger Schjørring and Norman A. Hjelm (eds.), *History of Global Christianity, Vol.III: History of Christianity in the 20th Century* (Leiden: Brill, forthcoming). Additional overviews exist in Timothy Byrnes and Peter Katzenstein (eds.), *Religion in an Expanding Europe* (Cambridge: Cambridge University Press, 2006); Effie Fokas, 'Religion: Towards a Post-secular Europe?' in Chris Rumford (ed.), *Sage Handbook of European Studies* (London: Sage, 2009), 401-20; Francois Foret (ed.), *L'espace public européen à l'épreuve du religieux* (Bruxelles: Editions de L'Universite de Bruxelles, 2007); Philip Jenkins, *God's Continent: Christianity, Islam, and Europe's Religious Crisis* (Oxford: Oxford University Press, 2007); Detlaf Pollack et al. (eds.), *The Social Significance of Religion in the Enlarged Europe: Secularization, Individualization and Pluralization* (London: Routledge, 2012); Helena Vilaça et al. (eds.), *The Changing Soul of Europe* (Farnham: Ashgate, 2014); Jean-Paul Willaime, *Europe et religions: Les enjeux du XXIe siècle* (Paris: Fayard, 2004); and Jean-Paul Willaime, *Le retour du religieux dans la sphère publique* (Paris: Olivétan, 2008).

growing prominence of religion in public debate. Both tendencies have implications for mission, but in different ways.

The Factors to Take into Account

There are six factors, which – taken together – contribute to a better understanding of the place of Christianity in twenty-first-century Europe. These factors are present in most parts of the continent, but they are differently weighted in different places. Their mutual accommodation continues producing distinctive formulations in different parts of Europe, some of which are unexpected. The six factors are:

1. The continuing role of Christianity in shaping European culture.
2. An awareness that the historic churches still have a place at particular moments in the lives of modern Europeans, though they are no longer able to discipline the beliefs and behaviour of the great majority of the population, nor – for the most part – would they want to.
3. An observable change in the churchgoing constituencies of the continent, which operate increasingly on a model of choice, rather than a model of obligation or duty, though more so in some places than others.
4. The arrival into Western Europe of groups of people from many different parts of the world, who bring with them very different religious aspirations from those seen in the host societies, noting in addition a later movement of people from the east and central parts of the continent to the west.
5. The reactions of Europe's more secular constituencies to the increasing salience of religion in public as well as private life, brought about largely – but not entirely – by new arrivals.
6. A growing realisation that the patterns of religious life in this part of the world should be considered an 'exceptional case' in global terms – they are not a global prototype.

Each of these factors will be taken in turn in the paragraphs that follow.

Cultural Heritage

The starting point reflects the enduring role of Christianity in shaping European culture, despite growing evidence in favour of secularisation. One example will suffice: the Christian tradition has had an irreversible effect in determining the most basic categories of human existence (time and space) in this part of the world. For example, both week and year continue to follow the Christian cycle, even if the major festivals of the Christian calendar are beginning to lose their resonance for large sections of the population. They are retained nonetheless as a framework for public holidays in most parts of Europe. Such durability is easily taken for granted. Its significance, however, is sharpened as Europe becomes at one and the same time both more secular and more diverse. Take, for example, disputes about the working week or the working day: to what extent can these be modified to suit the changing situation, and who should decide? The answers are frequently disputed.

A similar resilience can be found in terms of space, keeping in mind that the dominant patterns of religion in Europe are, and remain, territorial – finding expression in the institutional forms that have framed European life for centuries (most obviously the parish). It is hardly surprising, therefore, that Christian churches predominate, some of which retain huge symbolic value for the populations that surround them. From the largest city to the smallest village, Europeans continue to orient themselves with reference to religious buildings even if they seldom enter them for worship. That said, in some parts of Europe (notably the larger cities) the skyline is altering rapidly, an indicator in itself of growing religious diversity. The citing of new religious buildings can, moreover, be contentious – see, for example, the protracted controversies surrounding the construction of a mosque in Athens.[2]

In short, Europe is evolving fast, but the legacies of the past remain deeply embedded in both the physical and cultural environment – an inheritance that can be reactivated for political as well as religious reasons.

The Historic Churches

Physical and cultural presence is one thing; a hands-on role in the everyday lives of European people quite another. Commentators of all kinds agree that, with very few exceptions, the latter is neither a realistic nor a desirable aspiration for the historic churches of Europe in the new millennium. This is hardly surprising given the convincing evidence for secularisation revealed in a variety of European-wide statistical enquiries. Two examples will suffice: first, the material emanating from the European Values Study (EVS), which began in 1981 and in which religion is a central theme; second, the findings from the International Social Survey Programme (ISSP), which started in 1984 and in which religion was foregrounded in 1991, 1998 and 2008.[3] The data in each of these covers a wide range of variables, not all of which tell a similar story, but the overall trends are downwards – without doubt.

That does not mean, however, that the historic churches have entirely lost their significance as markers of religious identity in Europe. In my own work, I have developed two concepts to understand their current position rather better: first, the notion of 'believing without belonging',[4] and second, the idea of

---

[2] More detail about the debates surrounding the building of a mosque in Athens can be found in Constantine Danopoulos, 'Religion, Civil Society, and Democracy in Orthodox Greece', *Journal of Southern Europe and the Balkans,* 6.1 (2004), 41-55 and Anna Triandafyllidou and Ruby Gropas, 'Constructing Difference: The Mosque Debates in Greece', *Journal of Ethnic and Migration Studies*, 35.6 (2009), 957-75.

[3] Full details of each of these projects can be found on their respective websites – http://www.europeanvaluesstudy.eu/ and http://www.issp.org/. Both websites accessed 20 January 2018. Religion will be foregrounded once again in 2018 in the ISSP cycle.

[4] Grace Davie, *Religion in Britain since 1945.*

'vicarious religion'.[5] Both draw on the statistical material already introduced, noting in particular the mismatch between 'hard' and 'soft' measurements of religiousness. There exists, firstly, a set of indicators that measure firm commitments to (a) institutional life and (b) *credal* statements of religion (in this case Christianity). These indicators, moreover, are closely related to each other in so far as institutional commitments – in the form of regular religious practice – both reflect and confirm religious belief in its 'orthodox' forms.[6] The believing Christian attends church to express their belief and to receive affirmation that this is the right thing to do. Conversely, repeated exposure to the institution and its teaching necessarily disciplines belief.

No observer of the current religious scene disputes that these dimensions of European religion are both interrelated and in serious decline. Fewer Europeans go to church than they used to and fewer 'believers' sign up to the Christian creeds in their entirety. As a result, the idea of a common narrative (of Christian liturgy or of Christian language and metaphor) becomes more and more tenuous almost by the day. There is, on the other hand, considerable debate about the consequences of this situation. The complex relationship between belief in a wider sense and practice is central to this discussion, for it is abundantly clear that a manifest reduction in the 'hard' indicators of religious life has not, in the short term at least, had a similar effect on rather less rigorous dimensions of religiousness. For the time being, the latter remain relatively strong in most – if not all – parts of Europe. Between two-thirds and three-quarters of Europeans assent to 'belief in God', and roughly similar proportions touch base with the institutional churches at some point in their lives, often at times of crisis. It is precisely this state of affairs that is captured by the phrase 'believing without belonging'.

The connections between emergent patterns of belief and the institutional churches are, however, complex. Not only do the latter continue to exist but they also quite clearly exert an influence, both direct and indirect, on many aspects of individual and collective lives – even in Europe. The notion of 'vicarious religion' is helpful in this context. By vicarious, is meant the notion of religion performed by an active minority but on behalf of a much larger number, who (implicitly at least) not only understand but also appear to approve of what the minority is doing. The first half of the definition is relatively straightforward and reflects the everyday meaning of the term 'vicarious' – that is, to do something on behalf of someone else. The second

---

[5] Grace Davie, *Religion in Modern Europe*; 'Vicarious Religion: A Methodological Challenge,' in Nancy Ammerman (ed.), *Everyday Religion: Observing Modern Religious Lives* (New York: Oxford University Press, 2007), 21–36; 'Vicarious Religion: A Response,' *Journal of Contemporary Religion*, 25.2 (May 2013), 61–67; and *Religion in Britain: A Persistent Paradox*.

[6] 'Orthodox' in this context implies mainstream doctrine in the church in question.

half captures the legacy of the historic churches of Europe and is best explored by means of examples.

Religion can operate vicariously in a wide variety of ways. For example, churches and church leaders perform rituals on behalf of others (at the time of a birth or a death, for instance); if these services are denied, this causes offence – the more so among those who do not attend regularly. Church leaders and churchgoers also believe on behalf of others and incur criticism if they do not do this properly. Once again it is, very often, the occasional churchgoer who articulates this disquiet most clearly, and the more senior the church leader, the worse the problem gets.[7] Third, church leaders and churchgoers are expected to embody moral codes on behalf of others, even when those codes have been abandoned by large sections of the populations that they serve. This is true particularly with respect to family life and is one reason for the widespread disgust that many Europeans (and indeed others) have felt regarding the disclosures of child abuse among religious professionals. Churches, finally, can offer space for the vicarious debate of unresolved issues in modern societies. If the latter were not the case, it is hard to understand the persistent scrutiny of their positions on a wide variety of topical issues, from changing views regarding the nature of sexuality to the difficult moral questions surrounding birth and death – which reflect in turn the meaning of life itself.

An alternative way of illustrating the nature of vicarious religion is to consider the place of religion and the continuing role of religious institutions in European societies when they face the unexpected or the tragic. The reactions provoked by the death of Princess Diana in August 1997 offer an iconic illustration that had echoes all over Europe (and indeed the world). What happened in the week following the car accident in Paris cannot by any stretch of the imagination be described as either rational or secular, but nor was it conventionally religious. So, what was it? One point is clear: a great deal of the improvised and markedly heterogeneous rituals that emerged among ordinary people at that time took place in the vicinity of centrally placed churches. It was these churches, moreover, that housed books of condolence and facilities for lighting candles – ordinary people queued for hours to make use of these resources – and it was the established church (the Church of England) that took responsibility for her funeral. Even more important, however, is the fact that the reactions to Princess Diana's death (or any number of more recent equivalents) are simply 'writ-large' versions of what goes on the everyday lives of individuals and communities all the time. People die, sometimes

[7] The problem is nicely exemplified by the furore that greeted the Archbishop of Canterbury, following a much-misinterpreted remark concerning sharia law that preceded the foundation lecture in the Temple Festival series at the Royal Courts of Justice in London, February 2008. Available at http://rowanwilliams.archbishopofcanterbury.org/articles.php/1137/archbishops-lecture-civil-and-religious-law-in-england-a-religious-perspective and associated sites (accessed 20 January 2018).

unexpectedly, and communities suffer, sometimes with little apparent justification. What is to be done on these occasions and who is to do it?

This, of course, is not the whole story. Alternative agencies are emerging all over Europe to respond to such situations, including social workers, professional counsellors, and an increasing number of secular officiants trained to undertake the ceremonies that mark the turning points of life. It is equally clear that vicarious religion resonates more strongly in some generations than others. Specifically, the idea as it is understood here is widespread among Europeans who reached adulthood before the 1960s; it is much less present among younger people. Vicarious religion, moreover, is more easily evidenced in some parts of Europe than in others. A good example can be found in the Nordic countries and in Germany where church tax, or its equivalent, remains the norm.[8] Paradoxically, on a wide range of other indicators, these are some of the most secular parts of the continent. Further south and east, the elision between national and confessional identities plays a similar role. To be Italian or Polish, for example, means to be Catholic; to be Greek or Romanian means to be Orthodox, in the sense that active members of minority faiths are less easily absorbed than non-practising or even unbelieving adherents of the respective majority churches.

A short footnote concludes this section. I have introduced the idea of vicarious religion in a wide variety of places in Europe. It is rare that it does not provoke a response, followed very often by a string of illustrations that capture its essence in the society in question. The underlying resonance is clear even when an interpreter has struggled to find a translation for an unfamiliar term. Conversely, to talk of vicarious religion in the US is much more difficult. Here an entirely different history, not least the absence of a dominant or state church, has produced a markedly different religious culture in which an idea prevalent in Europe is conspicuous by its absence. Vicarious religion may be fading in Europe as secularisation takes its toll; it remains nonetheless a revealing indicator of Europe's shared religious inheritance.

From Obligation to Consumption

Vicarious religion is but one factor among others that constitute the complexity of Europe's religion in the late twentieth and early twenty-first centuries. Equally important is a gradual but increasingly observable mutation, best summarised as a shift from a culture of obligation or duty to a culture of consumption or choice. What was once simply imposed on Europeans (with all the negative connotations of this word) or inherited (which has a rather more positive echo), becomes instead a matter of personal choice. Religiously active

[8] That is a system in which contributions to the church in question are collected through the secular tax system. All members of the population make such a contribution unless they contract out. The point to grasp is that relatively few choose the latter option, though the numbers are growing, notably in Germany and Sweden.

Europeans now go to their historic churches or to an increasingly wide range of alternatives because they choose to, sometimes for a short period or sometimes for longer, sometimes regularly and sometimes occasionally, but – quite clearly – they feel no *obligation* either to attend that church in the first place or to continue if they no longer want to.

As such, this pattern is entirely compatible with vicariousness: the historic churches need to be there in order that Europeans may attend them if they so choose. Their nature, however, gradually alters – a shift that is discernible in both practice and belief, not to mention the connections between them. There is, for example, an easily documentable change in the patterns of baptism in some, if not all, parts of Europe. The Church of England offers an excellent illustration of this shift. In England, the overall number of baptisms has dropped dramatically in the post-war period, clear evidence of institutional decline and of advancing secularisation. At the same time the rite as such is evolving: no longer seen as a ritual associated with Englishness, it has become instead a sign of membership in a chosen voluntary community – a model that is likely to increase. The process is uneven but, in some countries, 'voluntarism' is beginning to establish itself *de facto,* regardless of the constitutional legacies of state churches or the denomination in question.

A second point follows from this. If choice rather than obligation is becoming the ascendant mode of religious belonging, what are the most popular choices of modern Europeans when it comes to religious attendance? The following paragraphs relate in particular to northern Europe, but their content is doubly interesting in the sense that it reveals not only the strengths and weaknesses of the present situation but also that the predictions of an earlier generation (both scholars and church people) were largely incorrect. Specifically, in the current period northern Europeans are disproportionately drawn to two kinds of religious organisation: charismatic evangelical churches on the one hand and cathedrals or city-centre churches on the other. The former epitomises firm commitments, strong fellowship and conservative teaching, offset by the warmth of the charismatic experience. The latter allows a much more individualistic (even anonymous) expression of religious commitment. Moreover, in 'cathedral-type' churches the appeal is often associated with the beauty of the building, the quality of the music, the traditional nature of the liturgy and the excellence of the preaching. The important point to grasp is that in both cases there is a noticeable *experiential* element, albeit very differently expressed.

In the mid post-war decades, something rather different was envisaged. Conservative teaching was firmly out of fashion and cathedrals were often classed as 'dinosaurs' – in the sense that they were less and less relevant to the modern world and very expensive to maintain. They are still expensive to maintain, but the data indicates that they are increasingly attractive to late modern populations, whether they come as regular worshippers, less regular worshippers, tourists or pilgrims – noting that the lines between these categories are distinctly porous.[9] Conversely, rather more liberal forms of Protestantism, often associated with the ecumenical movement and noticeably fashionable in the 1960s, have not fulfilled their earlier promise. There are, of course, important exceptions to this rule but by and large the purely cerebral has less appeal in the twenty-first century than many people thought would be the case.

Three interrelated points link this section to the one that follows. The first indicates a shift in organisational forms right across Europe. This is best captured by an economic analogy in the sense that there is a discernible if gradual shift away from what might be called a public utility model of religious provision (i.e. one that is available at the point of need to those who live in a designated place) towards a mode of operation that looks more like a market. In some parts of Europe, this shift has barely begun; in others it is well-developed – those, moreover, where secularisation is more advanced. This interrelationship between secularisation and the market constitutes the second point: as the public utility weakens there is more room for the market to grow. The third introduces the following section: incipient markets are urban rather than rural and are noticeably expanded where in-migration is significant.

New Arrivals

No observer of the religious scene in post-war Europe can ignore the influence of new arrivals in this part of the world, noting there are four stages in this continuing process. The first was closely linked to the urgent need for labour in the expanding economies of post-war Europe – especially in Britain, France, West Germany and the Netherlands. Each of these countries looked outwards to enhance their supply of workers – Britain, France and the Netherlands to their former colonies, and West Germany to Yugoslavia and Turkey. The second wave of immigration took place in the 1990s and included, in addition to the places listed above, the Nordic countries, Ireland and the countries of Mediterranean Europe (Greece, Italy, Spain and Portugal) – keeping in mind that many of these had until well into the twentieth century been countries of emigration rather than immigration. Indeed, the turn from one to the other was extraordinarily rapid. A third stage occurred rather later and took a different form: this was the movement of people from the east to the west of Europe prompted by the enlargements of the European Union in 2004 and 2007, which permitted the free (or freer) movement of labour from the countries formerly under Communist domination to the more developed west.

The economic crisis of 2007-08 did not halt, but seriously diminished, migration into Europe. That said, a new phase began in 2015, provoking widespread debate. This was the flight of many different groups of people from the Middle East, especially from Syria, as the violence and destruction brought

---

[9] In parenthesis, it is important to note that pilgrimage is an increasingly popular activity all over Europe, as it is elsewhere. The phenomenon merits a study in its own right.

about by civil war escalated. It is difficult to discern the long-term consequences of this protracted and damaging destabilisation, which has put significant pressure on the European Union as a whole and on certain countries (notably Greece and Italy) in particular.

In the first three of these phases, it is safe to say that the motivations for migration were economic rather than religious; the fourth is more complex. But either way the implications for the religious life of Europe are immense. For a start, new arrivals brought new life into the Christian churches: from sub-Saharan Africa (into Britain, France and the Netherlands); from Latin America (into Spain and Portugal); and from Asia and the Pacific Rim to many different places, good examples being the Filipino community in Italy and the widespread proliferation of Chinese churches. In each case, the traditional flows have reversed. No longer are Europeans seen as the 'suppliers'; they are rather on the receiving end as innovative expressions of Christianity establish themselves in the larger cities of the continent. The 'story', however, is ambiguous. Those arriving in the mid post-war decades from sub-Saharan Africa or the Caribbean – often from churches founded by European missionaries – were not always made welcome by their host communities, who found both the incomers themselves and their more exuberant styles of worship discomfiting. The latter reacted by setting up their own congregations, which have become some of the most vibrant in modern Europe. They are a recognised and increasingly well-studied phenomenon.[10]

The in-migration of Christians in the late twentieth century is a crucial variable in understanding Christianity in modern Europe and its relative vibrancy in *urban* areas. Even more significant is the arrival of other faith populations: specifically, significant numbers of Muslims (and in Britain, of Sikhs and Hindus as well). The reason is clear: here are sizeable communities of people whose cultural heritage is very different from the majority and whose religious lives do not fit easily into the 'categories' developed to deal with these issues in post-Enlightenment Europe – notably the notion that faith should be a private matter proscribed from public life (i.e. from the state and its various services). Those who have been socialised elsewhere have markedly different convictions and offer – simply by their presence – a challenge to the European way of doing things.

It is equally important to remember that the impact of these encounters varies from place to place and depends as much on the host society as on the

---

[10] See, for example, the chapters by Hugh Osgood, Richard Burgess and Amy Duffuor in David Goodhew (ed.),*Church Growth in Britain: 1980 to the Present* (Farnham: Ashgate, 2012) and Gerrie ter Haar's classic text: *Halfway to Paradise: African Christians in Europe* (Cardiff: Cardiff Academic Press, 1998). In London, it is worth noting that there are more ethnic minority individuals than white ones on Sundays in the Christian churches taken as a whole. See Peter Brierley, *Capital Growth: The London Church Census* (Tonbridge: Brierley Consultancy, 2013); for more information see http://www.brierleyconsultancy.com/capitalgrowth (accessed 20 January 2018).

new arrivals themselves. Britain and France offer an instructive comparison in this respect. In Britain immigration has been much more diverse than in France, both in terms of provenance and in terms of faith communities. Britain is also a country where ethnicity and religion criss-cross each other in a bewildering variety of ways (only Sikhs and Jews claim ethno-religious identities). Third, until very recently, Britain has been more ready than many of her European neighbours to embrace diversity – a tradition that stretches back to a colonial past where rule through local elite was the norm. The situation in France is other: here immigration has been largely from the Maghreb, as a result of which France has one of the largest Muslim communities in Europe – an almost entirely Arab population. Rightly or wrongly, Arab and Muslim have become interchangeable terms in popular parlance in France. France, moreover, firmly rejects the notion of *communautarisme*, in the sense that French citizens are welcomed as such but their primary identity is to France, not to an intermediate group, be it religious or another. Once again, the resonance with colonial policy is clear: French rule in the colonies meant direct rule from Paris.

Beneath these differences lies a common factor: the growing presence of other faith communities in general and of the Muslim population in particular, is challenging some deeply held European assumptions. The point can be exemplified in a whole series of episodes, which have brought the question of religion to the forefront of debate in Europe. A by no means exhaustive list would include the Rushdie controversy in Britain, which erupted in 1989; the *affaire du foulard* in France, which began at much the same time; the murders of Pim Fortuyn (2002) and Theo van Gogh (2004) in the Netherlands (together with the subsequent defection of Hirsi Ali to the US); the furore over the Danish cartoons of Mohammed in 2005; the bombings in the transport systems of both Madrid and London in 2004 and 2005 respectively; the challenge to the legality of minarets in a Swiss referendum (2009); and in some parts of Europe the total ban on wearing the niqab (or face veil) in public (in 2011 in both France and Belgium). Some issues, moreover, erupt in more than one place. The debate about representations of Mohammed spread to Sweden (from 2007 on), and in 2015 it reignited violently in both France and Denmark with dramatic consequences.

The above list spans 25 years and is likely to continue, evidence in itself of the intractability of the underlying questions. It is these, moreover, that lie beneath the paradox outlined at the outset of this chapter: that is the rising profile of religion in public debate in many parts of Europe alongside the falling indicators of religious activity.

Secular Reactions

More immediately it is important to note the reactions of Europe's more vociferous secularists to such events and the questions that lie beneath them. Secular voices have existed in Europe since the Enlightenment; they have, however, become not only more numerous but also more insistent in recent decades, paralleling the greater visibility of religion in public life. Visible religion brings with it visible secularism. That said, secular constituencies – just like their religious counterparts – vary markedly from place to place. Key in this respect is an appreciation of the secularisation process – specifically, an awareness that this has taken place differently in different European countries.[11] For example, what in Britain, and indeed in most of northern Europe, occurred gradually (starting with a de-clericalisation of the churches from within at the time of the Reformation), became in France a delayed and much more ideological clash between a hegemonic, heavily clerical church and a much more militant secular state. The result was 'la guerre des deux Frances' (Catholic and *laïque*), which dominated French political life well into the twentieth century. The legacies still remain in the form of a self-consciously secular elite, and a lingering suspicion concerning religion of all kinds – the more so when this threatens the public sphere. The fact that these threats are no longer Catholic, but Muslim does not alter the underlying reaction.

Norway offers a rather different illustration. Proportionally speaking Norway houses a surprisingly large number of secularists. Many of these are members of the Norwegian Humanist Association, which has campaigned for the separation of church and state and the full equality of all religions and life stances in Norway. The Association actively encourages secular ceremonies for rites of passage, similar to those provided by the churches. Particular attention is paid to schools (including the place of religious education in the curriculum) and to young people, for which reason a separate youth organisation was established in 2007. The Association becomes in fact a parallel institution to the majority church and is, in many ways, similar to this. It is, for example, partly financed by the equivalent of 'church' tax (there is also an annual membership fee).[12] Above all, the tone of the debate, despite some sharp differences in opinion, is distinctively Norwegian – it is very different from the French case. Both, however, should be considered in the same context: as articulate statements of the secular prompted by the renewed attention to religion in the public sphere.

Is Europe an Exceptional Case?

The final factor introduces a rather different perspective. Indeed, it reverses the essential question: instead of asking what Europe is in terms of its religious existence, it asks what Europe is not. It is not (yet) a vibrant religious market such as that found in the US; it is not a part of the world where Christianity is growing exponentially, very often in Pentecostal forms, as is the case in the global south; it is not a part of the world dominated by faiths other than

---

[11] David Martin, *A General Theory of Secularization* (Oxford: Blackwell, 1978).

[12] More detail on the Norwegian Humanist Association is available at https://human.no/om-oss/english/ (accessed 20 January 2018).

Christian, but is increasingly penetrated by these; and it is not for the most part subject to the violence often associated with religion and religious difference in other parts of the globe – the more so if religion becomes entangled in political conflict. Hence the inevitable, if at times disturbing (for some) conclusion: that the patterns of religion in modern Europe, notably its relative secularity, might be an exceptional case in global terms.

This point is all the more crucial if we remember that the paradigms of social science emerge from the European case and are very largely premised on the notion that modern societies are likely to be secular societies. It follows that the traditional, European-based understandings of social science may be markedly less suitable for the study of religion in other parts of the world. Indeed, they are not always helpful in Europe itself given the complexities of religious life in the early years of the twenty-first century.

Conclusion: A Persistent Paradox

Each of these factors contributes to the overall picture that – as already indicated – is best seen as a paradox. At one and the same time, Europe is becoming both more secular and more religiously diverse. This is a difficult combination to handle in so far as the former leads necessarily to a reduction in religious knowledge and a diminishing capacity to talk well about religious issues, while the latter ensures that religion is more rather than less present in public discussion. All too often the result is an ill-informed and ill-mannered debate about issues of extreme importance to a modern democracy. Those responsible for mission should see themselves as part of this conversation – as much to ensure its courtesy as its content.

The implications for missionary activity as such can only be introduced in outline at this point. It is important to note the following – Europe is hardly a blank slate; it is permeated by two millennia of Christian history that have influenced very profoundly patterns of human living in this part of the world. There exists, moreover, a network of historic churches, some of which are significantly eroded, whereas others retain considerable power – political as well as religious. The growing gaps in this network are correctly interpreted as evidence of secularisation.

That, however, is not the whole story as new forms of religious life begin to find their place in an expanding religious market, a process accelerated by immigration. The latter merits the closest possible attention for several reasons: the renewal of the Christian churches especially in urban areas; the increase in religious diversity; and the consequences of the latter for public debate. Religion is more talked about now than it was in the immediate post-war decades when secularisation was largely assumed. One reaction to the re-emergence of religion in public life has been new and diverse forms of secularism – these vary in their readiness to accommodate correspondingly diverse expressions of religion, for which reason, attention to detail is essential. This is not a case of one size fits all.

The final factor in this analysis points to developments taking place outside rather than inside Europe. Crucial in this respect is the awareness that the relative secularity of Europe should not be seen as a global prototype; it is rather an exceptional case.[13] Put differently, an approach that explains the present state of religion in Europe in terms of its Europeanness – i.e. as the result of a distinctive and identifiable history – is more helpful than an approach that talks simply in terms of modernity. In almost every other global region, rising indices of modernisation have not – or not yet – brought about corresponding increases in secularisation.[14]

Bibliography

Brierley, Peter, *Capital Growth: The London Church Census*. Tonbridge: Brierley Consultancy, 2013. For more information see http://www.brierleyconsultancy. com/capitalgrowth.

Byrnes, Timothy and Peter Katzenstein (eds.), *Religion in an Expanding Europe*. Cambridge: Cambridge University Press, 2006.

Danopoulos, Constantine, 'Religion, Civil Society, and Democracy in Orthodox Greece.' *Journal of Southern Europe and the Balkans* 6:1 (2004).

Davie, Grace, *Religion in Britain since 1945: Believing Without Belonging*. Oxford: Blackwell, 1994.

Davie, Grace, *Religion in Modern Europe*. Oxford: Oxford University Press, 2000.

Davie, Grace, *Europe: the Exceptional Case. Parameters of Faith in the Modern World*. London: Darton, Longman and Todd, 2002.

Davie, Grace, 'Religion in Europe in the 21st Century: The Factors to take into Account.' *European Journal of Sociology* 47:2 (2006).

Davie, Grace, 'Vicarious Religion: A Methodological Challenge'. In *Everyday Religion: Observing Modern Religious Lives*. Ed Nancy Ammerman. New York: Oxford University Press, 2007.

Davie, Grace, 'Vicarious Religion: A Response.' *Journal of Contemporary Religion* 25:2 (2013).

Davie, Grace, *Religion in Britain: A Persistent Paradox*. Oxford: Wiley-Blackwell, 2015.

Fokas, Effie, 'Religion: Towards a Post-secular Europe?' In *Sage Handbook of European Studies*. Ed. Chris Rumford. London: Sage, 2009.

---

13 Grace Davie, *Europe: The Exceptional Case* (London: Darton, Longman and Todd, 2002).

14 See Pew Forum on *Religion and Public Life, The Global Religious Landscape*, available at http://www.pewforum.org/2012/12/18/global-religious-landscape-exec/ (accessed 20 January 2018).

Foret, François (ed.), *L'espace public européen à l'épreuve du religieux*. Bruxelles: Editions de L'Université de Bruxelles, 2007.

Jenkins, Philip, *God's Continent: Christianity, Islam, and Europe's Religious Crisis*. Oxford: Oxford University Press, 2007.

Goodhew, David (ed.), *Church Growth in Britain: 1980 to the Present*. Ashgate: Farnham, 2012.

Martin, David, *A General Theory of Secularization*. Oxford: Blackwell, 1978.

Pew Forum on Religion and Public Life, *The Global Religious Landscape*, available at http://www.pewforum.org/2012/12/18/global-religious-landscape-exec/ (accessed 20 January 2018).

Pollack, Detlaf, Olaf Müller Gert Pickel (eds.), *The Social Significance of Religion in the Enlarged Europe: Secularization, Individualization and Pluralization*. London: Routledge, 2012.

Schjørring, Jens Holger and Norman A. Hjelm. (eds.), *History of Global Christianity, Vol.III: History of Christianity in the 20th Century*. Leiden: Brill (forthcoming).

Ter Haar, Gerrie, *Halfway to Paradise: African Christians in Europe*. Cardiff: Cardiff Academic Press, 1998.

Triandafyllidou, Anna and Ruby Gropas, 'Constructing Difference: The Mosque Debates in Greece.' *Journal of Ethnic and Migration Studies*, 35:6 (2009).

Vilaça, Helena, Enzo Pace and Inger Furseth (eds.), *The Changing Soul of Europe*. Farnham: Ashgate, 2014.

Willaime, Jean-Paul, *Europe et religions: Les enjeux du XXIe siècle*. Paris: Fayard, 2004.

Willaime, Jean-Paul, *Le retour du religieux dans la sphère publique*. Paris: Olivétan, 2008.

Secretes of the Secular: On the Conditions and Possibilities of Faith in and Beyond the Secular Age

Raag Rolfsen

It seems to me that the religious instinct is indeed in the process of growing powerfully – but the theistic satisfaction it refuses with deep suspicion.

Nietzsche, Beyond Good and Evil, Aphorism 53

I wonder how many gonna be surprised, when they look straight up and see Him coming through the skies.

Larry Norman

Introduction

What are the conditions of religious faith in our time? Is faith in God meaningful in an age that is enclosed in an ever-expanding secularity? Can science, which constitutes a core of secular reason, replace God, or should we rather return to faith in an omnipresent God belonging to an age when "there was no 'secular'"?[1] Alternatively, should we be content with a God that can guarantee the natural and moral order, which modern reason, in its turn, can decode?

The question of religion today is clouded in ambiguity. Machine technology and, later, digital coding translate secular, scientific reason into tools that can calculate and control an increasing part of existence. Human beings, too, are put under the scrutinising look of science. Never before have we, through genetics, biology, brain chemistry, psychology, data technology and sociology, been able to understand, predict, and control human behaviour to such an extent as today.

On the other hand, the need for an agency that can provide answers to existential and ethical questions that a descriptive, secular reason in principle cannot give, is growing urgent. We can thus describe the ambiguity that clouds

---

[1] John Milbank, in *Theology and Social Theory: Beyond Secular Reason*. Malden: Blackwell Publishing, 2006, 9.

religious questions as an unsolvable conflict inherent in secularity itself. "Our age is," in Charles Taylor's words, "deeply cross pressured."[2]

Disenchantment is an intrinsic element in secularisation. This entails that secular reason needs to exclude the magical dimension of reality, in order to prepare it for a purely rational approach. When it succeeds in its goals, however, secular reason finds that it can neither explain nor extinguish dimensions that belong inextricably to human existence. These are meaning-seeking features that motivated the secular project in the first place, as I will claim below.

These juxtaposed and interrelated successes and failures already mark a stage beyond a purely secular age. Unlike earlier transitions from one era to another, the new configuration is not simply a replacement of the previous one. Secular reason will continue to dominate in the foreseeable future, not least because of its conversion to the digital format. The calculating approach to reality will persist as automation, robotics and artificial intelligence. "Automation" names the inner nature of this continued rule of technical reason. It will be self-animating, self-thinking and self-moving. However, it will fail to be relevant to basic questions of human existence.

My aim is to show that the best way to describe our times is neither as secular nor as 'post-secular'. It is more fruitful to describe them as juxta-secular, signifying that the secular cannot sustain its proclaimed closed worldview. Juxtaposed with secularity, the secrete[3] that seeps through its closed fist is deposited as that which cannot be contained by secular reason. In this way, secularity holds secrets; secrets that once motivated it as a human endeavour, but that it will not or cannot admit or accept openly today.

There is a 'beyond' the secular. This beyond is neither 'pre-' or 'post'-secular, but something else. In order to identify it, I will trace how the experience of God, reality and the human has changed in the Western mind. I will refer to Charles Taylor, Gilles Deleuze, Max Weber and Martin Heidegger. I will pay special attention to a totalising tendency that arguably belongs to the core of modern and secular reason.

My argument contains a warning to some strategies of popular apologetics (i.e. defenders of traditional Christian faith), when it borrows the argumentative weapons from its opponents, the 'new atheists'. I will also detect a fundamental inconsistency belonging to a secular self-understanding when it opposes faith to knowledge. This inconsistency eventually leads to the failure described here, namely its inability to communicate meaningfully with questions of an existential character. This, I will conclude, leaves a space open for Christian faith.

---

[2] Charles Taylor, *A Secular Age*. Cambridge, Massachusetts and London, England: 2007, 727.

[3] Here I use the word "secrete" also as a noun, meaning "that which is secreted", i.e. "secretion".

First Transition: From the Pre-modern to Modernity

The timeline from an early medieval conception of truth to a modern one is complex. New patterns of thought led to new perceptions of reality. Geographic, demographic and power-related factors, however, postponed and displaced this change. We can nonetheless observe the long-term effects of the transition. They are observable in how we experience God, human beings and the world.

In Charles Taylor's terminology, we go from a reality where God intervenes to a reality that God has structured once and for all. Taylor states: "[T]here is a drift away from orthodox Christian conceptions of God as an agent interacting with humans and intervening in human history; and towards God as architect of a universe operating by unchanging laws, which humans have to conform to."[4] Taylor names this doctrine of God as architect "Providential Deism". This doctrine is a decisive stage towards the completion of a secular stance, namely "exclusive humanism" or atheism.[5]

Parallel to, and interdependent of, this change, there occurs an anthropological shift. In Taylor's coinage, a *porous* self, which is open to the all-permeating divine forces, is replaced by a *buffered* self that enables itself to stay disengaged from external reality and thus to relate to it rationally.[6] In a similar vein, but from a Foucauldian approach, Gilles Deleuze describes a transition from a "classical historical formation" to the "historical formation of the nineteenth century". The form of the human, according to Deleuze, arrives because of an interaction of the forces of the human – the force to imagine, remember, conceive, wish and so on – and the external forces of the historical formation. He labels the human form in these two historical formations as the "God-form" and the "Man-form", respectively.

The historical formation that creates the God-form is a reality where everything "in a force, 'equals' perfection, and so can be raised to infinity (the infinitely perfect), the rest being a limitation and nothing but a limitation".[7] Thus all phenomena in existence point beyond themselves to something perfect and without limit – to God.

It takes an intellectual effort to conceive this, because this historical formation represents the opposite of our modern historical formation. We, living in a post-Kantian civilisation, connect *reality* indissolubly to experience.

---

[4] Taylor: *A Secular Age*, 270.

[5] See, Taylor, "Providential Deism", in *A Secular Age*, 221-269.

[6] See, Taylor, *A Secular Age,* 37ff.

[7] Gilles Deleuze, *Foucault.* Translated by Seán Hand. Minneapolis and London: University of Minnesota Press, 2006, 124.

The real is what stands before us. Even when what stands before us is a chimera, we connect its reality as chimera inextricably to its appearance.[8]

The classical and pre-Kantian formation raises the very reality of phenomena to infinity. In this formation, therefore, perfect reality is beyond the phenomenon. Reality as it appears thus constitutes a lack or a limitation of reality. Everything that humans encounter is what it is *as limitation*. Knowledge is another example. In the classical age, knowledge, according to Deleuze, is only a limitation of a perfect knowledge.[9]

Despite the difference in terminology, Deleuze's presentation aligns closely with Taylor. Human beings in the pre-modern age are porous selves. Deleuze claims: "[M]an is limited and cannot himself account for this more perfect power that passes through him."[10] Divine forces flow through these permeable selves. The universe they lived in was a truly magical one. The world is "hyper-referential". Everything is what it is through being limited and is as such pointing to something higher and beyond itself. The world, according to Deleuze, is an endless continuum that is impossible to overview and control.

We can picture the modern world, in the ambition of its most fundamental project, in categories opposite to the medieval world. Here we find a buffered self, or subject, disengaged from the objects of the world. The objects, on their side, are clearly separated entities belonging to their own distinguished areas of reality. What happens, according to Deleuze, is a thoroughgoing interruption of the infinite reference of all things: "[S]omething breaks the series and fractures the continuums, which … can no longer be developed."[11] This is what Deleuze, with Foucault, calls the "Fold".

Both the subject and the objects fold in upon themselves and make them available as separate entities. This thoroughgoing curvature of everything puts in place the premises upon which the idea of an inherently ordered universe can succeed. It neutralises reality through the assumption that everything – subjects, objects, history and the cosmos itself – folds back on themselves. Accordingly, they do not point to a reality beyond this world age. The separate entities within this immanent universe no longer relate to one another, and beyond, in a mysterious continuum. Natural laws regulate their relation. These laws serve as fixed notions of motion. In this way, natural laws transform what previously appeared as a constant flow of change, into something that reason can control.

Importantly, when focusing on the secular, we can only encounter these entities as such inside a folded, immanent reality. Framing the modern project

---

[8] An interesting parallel to this argument is found in Ludwig Wittgenstein, "A Lecture on Ethics," in *The Philosophical Review*, 74 (1965): 3-12. Reprinted in J. H. Gill (ed.), *Philosophy Today*, No. 1. New York: Macmillan, 1968: 4-14.

[9] Deleuze, *Foucault*, 124-125.

[10] Deleuze, *Foucault*, 125.

[11] Deleuze, *Foucault*, 127.

and belonging essentially to it, there is the great folding of the continuous line that previously pointed to the infinite perfection of God. Secularisation constitutes the process that follows from the underlying perception of reality as confined within the time and space that this fold establishes. The curving of the modern formation does not allow any beyond. There is then no other space for God than to become an entity among entities inside or on the fringe of this immanent frame. This is the providential deity of Taylor. God thus becomes the being that guarantees transparent and controllable immanent reality. In the next step, when modern science experiences that it can do without this explanatory device, it rejects this form of the metaphysical God as an unnecessary hypothesis.

Second Transition: From Modernity to Post-modernity

Although the forces that raise everything to infinite perfection dominated the pre-modern period, it is the forces of finitude that now govern the modern formation. This not only leads to a change in how we perceive God and the world but also it alters how we understand the human and how humans understand themselves. Deleuze says: "All this means that when the forces within man enter into relation with forces of finitude … then and only then does the set of forces compose the Man-form (and not the God-form). *Incipit Homo.*"[12] What we today recognise as the human as such, Deleuze therefore claims, emerges when the forces at work in the human interact with a particular historical formation.

The significance of this contention is that the human form is not a stable configuration. This claim contests the modern self-confident and totalising approach that projects the present form of the human to the whole era of human history, from its beginning to its end. According to Deleuze, however, and implicitly also to Taylor, this form did not exist before the modern formation. This also implies that the human will be configured differently when a new formation replaces the modern one. Deleuze professes:

> We can already foresee that the forces within man do not necessarily contribute to the composition of the Man-form but may be otherwise invested in another compound or form: even over a short period of time Man has not always existed and will not exist forever.[13]

After the God-form and the Man-form, Deleuze prophesises, we will have the "superman". The influence of Foucault and Nietzsche is obvious in this prophecy. There are numerous signs; however, that what these thinkers predicted, is beginning to come through. Currently, we find terms like

[12] Deleuze, *Foucault*, 127.
[13] Deleuze, *Foucault*, 124.

"posthuman", "transhuman", "antihuman" and "metahuman", denoting different but related positions.[14] They all point to new configurations of the human, though. The prospect of these new forms of the human, and beyond the human, invokes hope for some and horror for others. More significant here, they indicate that the modern formation in our days is threatened. We are, in Taylor's words, living at the "unquiet frontiers of Modernity".[15]

A notion that is important to understand modernity, not only as a field of research but also to apprehend how the modern project bites its own tail, is "reflexive modernisation". The idea, closely associated with the sociological work of Ulrich Beck and Anthony Giddens, captures a complex feature of modernisation.[16] This trait, coming increasingly to the fore as modernity matures, consists in the fact that the challenges that the modern project has to face are results of the same project.

Modernity, in this understanding, is more and more left to fix problems that stem from its own undertaking, and in doing so, stands in danger of creating new ones. A new kind of hyper-referentiality thus occurs. This time the phenomena do not refer to the infinitely perfect, but back to modernity itself. Instead of, as in the first phase of modernity, relating to reality as something external and given, modernisation relates to its own consequences and constructs.

The outcome of modernity, in reflexive modernisation, is that the disengagement and the ensuing division of reality into subjects and objects, so fundamental to the modern project, is undermined. Reality no longer stands over against (cf. the German *Gegenstand*) the modern subject. The spheres of the object and the subject flow into each other. In this way, the division of the world into subjects and objects blurs and dissolves. This development compromises a major tenet of the modern project. We thus approach a new epistemological and ontological situation; a new historical formation, in Deleuze's terms.

In the context of this work, where we are endeavouring to understand the meaning of the secular, it is significant to see that this development relates to

---

[14] See, Francesca Ferrando, "Posthumanism, Transhumanism, Antihumanism, Metahumanism, and New Materialisms. Differences and Relations", in *Existenz – An International Journal in Philosophy, Religion, Politics and the Arts*, Volume 8, No 2, Fall 2013, 26-32, and Yuval Noah Harari: *Homo Deus. A Brief History of Tomorrow*. London: Vintage, 2017.

[15] See, Taylor, *A Secular Age*, 711 ff.

[16] See, Ulrich Beck, *Risk Society, Towards a New Modernity*. Translated by Mark Ritter. London: Sage Publications, 1992; Anthony Giddens, *The Consequences of Modernity*. Stanford, California: Stanford University Press, 1990; Anthony Giddens, *Modernity and Self-Identity. Self and Society in the Late Modern Age*. Stanford, California: Stanford University Press, 1991; Ulrich Beck, Anthony Giddens and Scott Lash, *Reflexive Modernization. Politics, Tradition and Aesthetics in the Modern Social Order*. Malden: Polity Press, 1994.

the death of the providential and metaphysical God. This providential God plays a transitional role in the shift from pre-modernity to modernity. The ultimate being, the *causa sui,* or first mover is initially placed on the very horizon of an immanent world to guarantee a pre-given order of reality.

For Heidegger, this ultimate being does not cease to exist as soon as the explicit belief in this God fades. Modern science and life-views, mostly implicitly, believe in this ultimate source. This God, or rather, in Heideggerian terms, this "onto-theo-logy", remains the hidden presupposition of modernity.[17] It appears on the stage in new disguises, as world spirit, progress or freedom. It operates in the spaces left empty by a purely technical reason as suppositions of an inherently orderliness of the universe, the truth of scientific knowledge, and that there must be a meaning to it all. When this implicit belief starts to wane, a vacuum appears.

The new human form seeks to fill this void. In order to do that, it takes over the attributes of the dying God. These qualities are independence, creativity, freedom, wisdom and power. It soon becomes clear, however, that the new being is infected by the same disease as its predecessor. When reality turns away from its eternal source to face the human to ask for its source and meaning, this becomes an unbearable task. Without the support from a providential deity, the burden of providing sense to reality becomes too onerous to carry.

Deleuze says that we should not recognise Nietzsche as the thinker of the death of God. Ludwig Feuerbach, he claims, was the last thinker to think through this. He continues: "[F]or Nietzsche this is an old story … What interests him is the death of man … When the Man-form appears, it does so only by already incorporating the death of man." He formulates the reason for this in a rhetorical question: "[W]here can man find a guarantee of identity in the absence of God?"[18] In the end, there is no way to explain how the human being can be sustained as subject, both disengaged from and supporting the meaning of this world, without anchoring this unity in some (quasi-) transcendent source.

Guarding Modernity: New Atheists and Defenders of Faith

During the history of modernity, the anchoring of the ordered structure of the world in something that is not part of that structure weakens. This threatens the structure with a possible collapse. What are the conditions and possibilities of faith in God in this situation?

The phase of reflexive modernisation makes this question more intrusive. Our own time is a period characterised by frenetic activity to save our very

[17] See, Martin Heidegger, *Identity and Difference*, transl. Joan Stambaugh, New York: Harper & Row, Publishers, Incorporated, 1969.
[18] Deleuze, *Foucault*, 130.

ground. Modernisation is transformed by its own inner logic into an accelerating effort to save modernity from threats and risks following from its own activity. Reflexive modernisation constitutes a sign of a possible breakdown of modernity. This threat constitutes the very framework for how both the defenders and the deniers approach the question of faith in God.

Both ardent secularists and militant new atheists, on the one hand, and the apologists defending a traditional religious stand, on the other, are reactive forces defending modernity against its possible breakdown. They represent two parties in a domestic argument, where both sides are trying to preserve the order of the house of modernity. They only disagree on what we should consider the guarantor of this order. One party points to science as the only solid and objective reference, while viewing religion as a step back to superstition, thus threatening the modern rational order. The other party claims that this order is both incomprehensive and unsustainable without anchoring it in an ultimate being.[19]

The unfortunate move of the apologists of faith, in my view, is to defend the providential deity that science has done away with already. Werner Keller's book *The Bible as History* represents an innocent but telling example of the reductionism involved in the effort to preserve this anaemic god in the order of our world.[20] The goal of the book is to use scientific evidence to show that biblical events are likely to have taken place.

Keller might succeed in making some of the biblical stories more credible. More serious for the possibility of religious faith, however, he just confirms that everything that happens ultimately are natural phenomena in a closed and immanent universe. He thus supports the belief that scientific thought can decode, explain and control everything. Instead of questioning the violence that attempts to force all of existence into an explanatory framework and to deprive everything that does not fit in there of the status as real, Keller reduces religious truths to something that can fit into the scientific picture.

The weakness of this apologetic approach has two sides. First, it accepts the method and the weapons of the battle from its opponents. The danger, when encountering an enemy more resourceful in this combat, is that the apologist easily can stumble and fall on his own sword. The second weakness is that the divine being that the apologists try to prove, carries little resemblance to the personal God in whom Christians seek comfort when crises befall. This is, in short, a God for the head and not for the heart.

We can observe a similar limitation in the debate after the publication of Richard Dawkins' work *The God Delusion*.[21] Creston Davis, in the introduction to *The Monstrosity of Christ*, claims that this is a debate only in appearance.

---

[19] The Lausanne Movement: *The Cape Town Commitment. A Confession on Faith and a Call to Action.* Lausanne: 2011, 26.

[20] Werner Keller, *The Bible as History*. New York: Bantam Books, 1983.

[21] Richard Dawkins, *The God Delusion*. London: Bantam Press, 2006.

The participants share the same premises. Concerning the God that Dawkins' opponent Alister McGrath defends, he says: "[T]he theistic 'God' of McGrath et al. is not so much a being as a dematerialised logic that never touches, much less changes, the world."[22] Davis claims that the debaters are on the same side, since they share the underlying assumption, namely secular reason.[23]

A Secular Faith

There is an inconsistency haunting secular reason. In its innermost understanding of itself, the secular approach builds on knowledge and not on faith. This knowledge, although categorised in the spectrum of probability, is meaningful only as a contrast to faith.[24] Secular reason understands itself historically as an emergence from darkness to light, from superstition to science, and from faith to knowledge. That which haunts the modern secular project is that it is a human undertaking. It is an effort to make sense of it all, fuelled by a strong conviction that it is possible through scientific reason. This drive to create meaning belongs essentially to the human. It is a basic "human force", to borrow Deleuze's term.

This dimension is decisive when we try to understand secularity. The modern, secular project is itself motivated by a basic human effort to create meaning. It is itself faith-based, even in its distinction between faith and knowledge. The disclosure constitutes a step towards revealing the conditions and possibilities of faith in our time.

One of the first scholars to define the development of secularisation was Max Weber. He called it "disenchantment" (Ger. *Entzauberung*, literally meaning "to remove the magic"). In "Science as a Vocation", he identifies the "knowledge" that the modern enterprise opposes to faith, as "conviction". In an English translation, he says:

> The increasing intellectualisation and rationalisation do not, therefore, indicate an increased and general knowledge [Kenntnis] of the conditions under which one lives. It means something else, namely, the knowledge or belief that [das Wissen davon oder den Glauben daran] if one but wished [nur wollte] one could learn it at any time.[25]

---

[22] Creston Davis, "Introduction: Holy Saturday or Resurrection Sunday? Staging an Unlikely Debate," in Slavoj Žižek and John Milbank, Creston Davis (red.), *The Monstrosity of Christ. Paradox or Dialectic?* Cambridge, Massachusetts: MIT Press, 2009:2-23, 10.

[23] See, ibid., 8.

[24] See, Dawkins, *The God Delusion,* 50. The title of Dawkins' book *The God Delusion* points to this prominence of knowledge. The antonym of "delusion" is "truth".

[25] Max Weber, "Science as a Vocation", in H.H. Gerth and C. Wright Mills (translated and edited), *From Max Weber: Essays in Sociology*. New York: Oxford University Press, 1946: 129-156, 139.

Although the most common translation of *Wissen* is "knowledge", it is clear that it is here a mistranslation. The correct translation is "conviction". This becomes obvious firstly because this second "knowledge" is opposed to the first occurrence of the word in the translation, which translates the German *Kenntnis*, meaning "actual knowledge". Second, the conditional clause makes clear that it is not knowledge that is in question, but the conviction that knowledge is possible. Third, the word-pair *Glauben und Wissen* is the German technical term for "Faith and Knowledge". In Weber's phrase, *Glauben* should not be understood as an alternative to *Wissen*, but as an explanation of what kind of knowledge is at stake here. A possible translation could then also be "the knowledge, or rather faith ..."

Fourth, and most decisively, "knowledge" means "conviction" because the conviction or faith-character of modern reason is the very theme of the whole paragraph. Weber insists that disenchantment realises itself in and through the strong conviction that it is possible to realise – "in principle" – as he repeats: "Hence, it means that principally there are no mysterious incalculable forces that come into play, but rather that one can, in principle, master all things by calculation. This means that the world is disenchanted."[26]

What Weber argues, therefore, is that the secular conviction implies a strong conviction, which can best be described as faith. This should not surprise anyone, since it is a human undertaking, searching the meaning of existence. It shares this conviction-character with all faiths and world views. Inconsistency haunts the secular project, however, because it fails or refuses to identify this dimension. It achieves this suppression through mixing the meaning of "knowledge" and "conviction". The very blurring of this distinction belongs to the very nature and function of secular reason. The exposure of it, however, opens a general space for faith in our time.

Science and the Appearance of the Incalculable

In "The Age of the World Picture", Heidegger sets out to reflect on the metaphysical basis of modernity.[27] Modern science constitutes his point of departure. In the same manner as Deleuze, he finds the implicit background of the emergence of modern science in the previous interconnectedness of everything. Modern science accomplishes breaking into this hyper-referential reality through mapping and isolating different fields of research for the specialised sciences. The rigour of the sciences is to stick to their respective ground plans. Only that which can find a meaningful place in that ground plan counts as real.

---

[26] Weber, "Science as a Vocation", 139.

[27] Martin Heidegger, "The Age of the World Picture", i, *Off the Beaten Track*, edited and translated by Julian Young and Kenneth Haynes. Cambridge et al: Cambridge University Press, 2002: 57-85.

Natural laws are essential to the procedure that keeps the changeable objects of the research field in place: "Procedure must … represent the changeable in its changing; it must bring it to stand and yet allow the motion to remain motion."[28] Science achieves this through procedural rule and natural law, which is the sole way to determine the facticity of facts: "Only from the perspective of rule and law do facts become clear as what they are."[29]

Heidegger underlines that it belongs to the essence of science not to be a *fait accompli*. "The approach [of science] aims to an increasing degree at the possibilities that its own activity opens up."[30] Results, therefore, do not constitute the goals of modern science. They rather work as stepping-stones on the way to a final goal. Modern science, therefore, is less a comprehensive body of actual knowledge and wisdom than an aspiration. The fundamental drive of scientific activity is a strong conviction that the global success of the ambitions inherent to it is possible.

The faith-character of secular reason again becomes apparent. Science, however, does not experience this trait as a weakness. It rather represents its strength. Science needs to be convinced that everything could be calculated and mastered, in principle, to refer back to Weber. It can even perceive its failures as possibilities of progress. In addition, one science can take the failure of another science as a stepping-stone for its own further advancement. Heidegger likens this trade in deficits to the industrious activity of the business community.

Heidegger calls this dimension of science *Betrieb*. The translators render it "constant activity" and it denotes science as an ever-expanding busy-ness that is gradually becoming a frenetic and self-referential bustle (*Betriebsamkeit*). It continues, however, to aim at a constantly withdrawing goal. Heidegger says of this goal: "[B]ecause the essence of research is constant activity, the industrious activity of mere busy-ness … creates the appearance of a higher reality behind which the excavations of research work are accomplished."[31] This retracting goal is the possibility to calculate and control everything. Heidegger's contribution is to point out that the faith-character of modern science stays in close relation to its totalitarian tendency.

The title of Heidegger's essay reveals his main concern. It is not "The World Picture of the Modern Age". It is "The Age of the World Picture". The configuration of the world as picture fundamentally characterises the modern age. We would therefore continue to exert the violence of our secular age if we presume that people of all ages and cultures have had world pictures. Persons in the medieval era, for example, and in the way maintained here, did not live

[28] Heidegger, "The Age of the World Picture", 60-60.
[29] Heidegger, "The Age of the World Picture", 61.
[30] Martin Heidegger, "Die Zeit des Weltbildes", in *Holzwege*. Frankfurt am Main: Vittorio Klostermann, 2003, 84. My translation.
[31] Heidegger, "The Age of the World Picture", 73-74.

in a configuration where they could keep the world at arm's length. There was a floating boundary between what was within the human self and what was outside.[32]

The possibility of both the subject and the objects to fold back upon themselves, and thus to place the world as objective reality within the frames of a picture, belongs to the modern age. This is the way to disengage and to reach a position from where calculation and control is possible. Heidegger claims that it requires a tremendous effort to maintain this distance. Humans must "fight for the position in which he can be that being who gives to every being the measure and draws up the guidelines."[33]

In addition, different positions struggle against one another: "The decisive unfolding of the modern relationship to beings becomes a confrontation of world views." This fight puts everything at stake: "For the sake of this battle of world views, and according to its meaning, humanity sets in motion, with respect to everything, the unlimited process of calculation, planning, and breeding."[34]

This all-involving battle carries a deep rift at its core. The human being is both inside and outside the picture. In order to encompass everything, secular reason also has to understand the human. Thus, it places the human inside the frame of the picture. In order to sustain the picture as picture, however, the human who understands needs to disengage from the picture. This hyper-reflexive dynamic threatens to dissolve the essential distance between the picture and the one who observes it. When the modern self upholds this distance, it is continuously torn apart.

Heidegger concludes that the only quality that remains in the picture is the measurable. The only valid quality is quantity. This defines the essence of the violence of secular science. It excludes everything that it is unable to calculate. The incalculable, however, does not go away. It acquires "its own special quality". Heidegger continues: "This incalculability becomes the invisible shadow cast over all things … Through this shadow the modern world withdraws into a space beyond representation and so lends to the incalculable its own determinateness and historical uniqueness."[35] It is as if everything in existence that secular reason cannot measure, calculate and control, evaporates. Today, these spoils from the secular factory are acquiring their own quality and determinateness as something real outside the ongoing secular project.

---

32 See, Taylor, *A Secular Age*, 71.
33 Heidegger, "The Age of the World Picture", 71.
34 Heidegger, "The Age of the World Picture", 71.
35 Heidegger, "The Age of the World Picture", 71.

Secretes of the Secular

I have here asked the question of the conditions and possibilities of religious faith in our time. From this perspective, basic ambiguities that belong to the secular age have become apparent. The modern, secular age has proved a powerful replacement of the classical configuration. The forces of the infinite, raising all phenomena to perfection, to God, had to give way to the forces of finitude. These new forces fold everything back on itself, objects, the subject and the cosmos. The universe and everything in it are prepared for the calculation and control of the secular gaze.

Looking ahead, the dominance of secular reason seems uncontested. Through its translation into machine technology and the digital format, secular calculation and control appear unstoppable in the ambition to encompass ever-greater parts of existence. The secular project is growing automatic, that is, self-animating and self-going.

I have identified, however, signs that the secular project as such is both inconsistent and potentially self-destructive. Its inconsistency consists of its failure to admit to the basic faith-character that motivates it. Secular faith believes that if one "just want to, one can, in principle, master all things by calculation". In addition, this faith feeds on its failures. The continued dominance of the secular, and this comes to the fore in the late, reflexive phase of modernity, consists of a trade in deficits and use of the failures caused by itself as stepping-stones in order to reach an ever-withdrawing goal of total dominance. The inability to communicate with questions of existential meaning becomes increasingly evident.

Charles Taylor sums up this situation when he says, "The whole culture experiences cross pressures between the draw of the narratives of closed immanence on one side, and the sense of their inadequacy on the other."[36] Control and calculation give hope of prediction and security. The comfortable place to be is in the picture. The compulsion to seek meaning, belonging essentially to the human, cannot be satisfied with observing human existence from afar.

How, then, are the conditions and possibilities of faith in God in this situation? Given the insistence of the secular, the prospects for religious faith do not seem good. The hope of a return to a time when there was no "secular", proposed by the advocates of Radical Orthodoxy, seem unlikely. The hope of reinstalling a life-world permeated by the omnipresent participation in God is not much more than nostalgia.[37] For other reasons, the defence of a providential deity guaranteeing the world order does nothing but accepting secular reason. Moreover, this God is nothing more than a dematerialised logic, not touching upon basic human needs.

---

[36] Taylor, *A Secular Age*, 595.

[37] See, Simon Oliver, *Radical Orthodoxy. An Introduction*. London: Routledge, 2007.

The prospects of a continued dominance of scientific and secular reason also make it hard to conceive that a space will be allowed for a divine being in the future, at least not at the core of the dominating rationality. A chronological approach, therefore, looking back or looking ahead, does not seem promising regarding the prospects of religious faith. If we look to the side, however, the situation changes. At the borders of the dominating dynamics, we see life as it is lived and experiences, not as science observes and calculates it in view of control. It is more fitting, therefore, to visualise the "beyond" of the secular, not in terms of time, but of space.

In this approach, the outside of the secular age establishes itself as in parallel to the ongoing dominance of the modern configuration. I therefore prefer the preposition "iuxta", meaning "at the side of", rather than prepositions that denote an overcoming of the secular ("post", "trans", "meta" or "supra"). The beyond of the secular is the "juxta-secular" or the "juxta-modern".

The limits of the secular closure consist in that it cannot attain to the totalising grip of reality to which it aspires. The incalculable refuses to go away. It evaporates and establishes itself as a field in human existence. In the very execution of the totalitarian ambition of the secular, namely to grasp everything, that which it cannot contain seeps through the fingers of its clenched fist. This is the secrete of the secular.

The domain that establishes itself as a deposit of the waste that secular reason cannot contain is a truly human field, where phenomena acquire qualities beyond the calculable. In this field, water is more than H2O. Water quenches my thirst after a walk on a hot summer day. It cleanses and wakes me in the morning. In this domain, grief is not primarily something to be explained by brain chemistry, sociology or psychology. It is the experienced love of someone who is no longer there and who will not return, and whose radical absence makes us feel an intense presence. Love, here, is infinitely more than a biological drive for procreation.

The space that thus establishes itself is an open space. It is open because it is secreted and thus freed from the closed confines of the secular. Therefore, the language that tries to deal with it must be open-ended. It cannot lean on calculation and control.

In the course of European history, Christian faith and churches have found themselves at the core of a system that has secured and strengthened the current power relations. This position has benefitted the church through easy access to power and resources. In the secular age, the church was politely referred to a more modest place, but its role was still to secure the system. Now it is time for Christian faith to move out from a closed secular system and into the juxta-modern space that opens. In that space, it has two tasks.

The first task is to validate the reality that the secular closure secretes. The dominance of secular reason gives a subordinate status to everything it cannot contain. It arrives in the newly opened space as waste from a machine, often labelled in negative terms, such as weakness, vulnerability, unpredictability or poverty. In many cases, it will be the role of Christian faith to confirm or rename that which the system marks with nothingness – the secrete – as the very mystery, the secret of existence.

The church is the guardian of an ancient language and of rites and ethics. It is part of its task to renew these resources. The church can address the search for meaning that goes on in the border zone of the secular. Walking side by side with people, it can help transform what is secreted into elements of an existence that, even if it is uncontrollable and incalculable, is still experiences as abundant.

The second task is to prepare and patiently wait for the coming of God. When Heidegger, in the *Spiegel* interview, sums up his thinking, he returns to the question of the possibility to surpass the secular. He concludes that we are caught up inside the present formation. This, however, does not exclude the possibility of an intrusion from the outside. What we can do in this situation is to get ready for what might meet us:

> Philosophy will not be able to effect an immediate transformation of the present condition of the world. This is true not only of philosophy, but of all merely human thought and endeavor. Only a god can save us. The sole possibility that is left for us is to prepare a sort of readiness, through thinking and poetizing, for the appearance (*Erscheinung*) of the god … in the time of foundering (*Untergang*).[38]

We should not confuse this task with the revival of the God of the classical or modern age. Heidegger explicitly warns against this strategy, "The flight into tradition … achieves in itself nothing, [it is] merely a closing the eyes and a blindness towards the historical moment."[39] Turning back is a turning away from the challenges we are facing in our own age. In addition, it is not only an impossible task but it also involves restoring the historical formations of which the earlier conceptions of God were an inextricable part.

At the beginning of the nineteenth century, Hegel celebrated the enthronement of the immanent God. At the same time, he celebrated, as a decisive moment in history, the death of God seen as a transcendent and thus void entity. He there refers explicitly to the historic death of Christ on Good Friday. He acclaims the enthronement of the World Spirit as the very principle of a closed and immanent reality. In the final paragraph of *Phenomenology of Spirit*, Hegel claims that this moment "forms alike the inwardizing and the Calvary of absolute Spirit … and the certainty of his throne".[40]

---

[38] Augstein and Wolff, "Only a god can save us" [the *Spiegel* interview], in Richard Wolin (ed.), *The Heidegger Controversy*. Translated by Maria P. Alter and John D. Caputo. Cambridge, Massachusetts and London, England: MIT Press, 1993, 91-116, 107.

[39] Heidegger, "The Age of the World Picture", 72.

[40] Hegel, *Phenomenology of Spirit*, 493.

Today, we can identify this enthronement as the exact moment when the providential and immanent deity was set in place as the guarantee of the secular order and age. Two hundred years later, the certainty is gone, and the throne is empty. The notion of the spiritual has trickled down into the interstices of modern reality. Today, spiritual life only exists at the margins of the secular structure, as its waste. We can therefore imagine the secular age until its closure in our own days, as the time separating the crucifixion and the resurrection. When God turns to us anew, we will be just as surprised as the disciples were. Instead of struggling to revive a dead metaphysical God, therefore, the church should rather prepare for that encounter.

Part 2

Perspectives on the Secular Formation of Culture

The Search for Identity in Secularised Contexts

Hielke Wolters

An interesting phenomenon in today's societies are the selfies. Many young people have a strong urge to portrait themselves and to share the (self-) images with friends or even a wider circle of followers on social media. Teenagers, especially girls, like to share images of themselves as aspirant models preferably in front of a yacht or another symbol of the rich and wealthy. Tourists, not only from Europe, portrait themselves in places of interest: I was here! Why are so many people keen to focus on themselves and to share their images with others?

One could say that taking selfies is an expression of the central place that individuality has in our societies. Every person is considered unique, or even better, is the unique result of one's efforts to shape and mould one's life in comparison with and different from others. Having the right education, a successful career and an interesting social life are the crucial ingredients of each individual life project. The formation and presentation of personal identity is an essential part of this project. In this chapter, it will become clear that developing a personal identity is not an easy affair in a society that has lost its traditional social, moral and religious communal guidelines. One can easily feel being lost in the wilderness of the endless possibilities. Perhaps the search for individual identity has become one of the major quests or even obsessions in many societies in Western Europe. Taking a selfie is probably the most straightforward way of confirmation: this is me!

In the context of this book, the question must be raised whether the search for individual identity has become more complex in secular societies. The "I am…" question has lost an important dimension when religion has become irrelevant as a social marker. One can easily say: I am Dutch; I am an engineer, a theologian; I am a mother, a father; I am young, old. However, what used to be probably the most important identifier in Western European societies was "I am a Christian". What happens to the search for identity in secular contexts in which the expression of faith has become irrelevant, odd or even suspect?

Reflecting on this question, it is clear that the meaning and impact of secularisation needs to be explored in relation to the overall transition from traditional towards modern or even post-modern forms of social and individual life. Secularisation can hardly be understood apart from reflecting on developments in education, changes in family life, the weakening of rural and urban communities, the increasing role of the internet and (social) media, changing labour relations, and a strong dominance of national and global economic factors. The series of 'isms' so frequently used in missionary literature, such as liberalism, individualism, materialism, rationalism and relativism, to explain the reason for secularisation is not helpful. Such lists of 'modern sins' do not help us to understand the inner dynamics of the social and individual life in current secular contexts. Moreover, they implicitly claim that secularisation can be avoided by a faithful, traditional moral life and hinder a deeper investigation into its nature and reflection on the question how faith can be relevant in secular contexts.

Therefore, this chapter aims to explore the different aspects of secular individual and social life and their influence on the search for personal identity. This will be done by first analysing how secularisation is a process inherent to the development of the Christian traditions, in particular Protestantism, in Europe. A deeper understanding of this process will help us to see how language, ways of learning and communication played and still play a crucial role in secularisation and the search for identity. This exploration will open the way for an assessment of the blessings and challenges of secular social and individual identity in Western Europe today. Finally, some observations will hopefully help to develop a relevant missionary approach.[1]

Secularisation Processes in Western Europe

One can raise the question whether the secularisation processes in Western Europe are unique compared to similar processes in other parts of the world. The general secularisation thesis is that progress of science, the introduction of modern technology and the globalisation of economic development entail a loss of interest in religious traditions and convictions. However, this generalised understanding of secularisation processes has become less and less convincing now recent developments show a resurgence of religion almost throughout the world. Data collected by the Pew Research Center show that "as a share of all people in the world, religious 'nones' are projected to decline from 16% of the total population in 2015 to 13% in 2060."[2] Besides, new forms of fundamentalism and radicalism appear in almost all major religions. These developments show that it is possible for individual persons as well as for entire societies to combine traditional religious convictions with modern scientific insights and highly advanced technological skills. The assumption

[1] Parts of this chapter have been published earlier in my article "The Search for Identity and Self-understanding in a Secularised Society" in *The Ecumenical Review*, 68.2-3, November 2016, 224-233.

[2] http://www.pewforum.org/2017/04/05/the-changing-global-religious-landscape/. "Nones" include "people who identify as atheist or agnostic as well as those who have no religion".

that scientific and technological progress will eventually result in religious decline seems to be less convincing than it has been for decades. Secularisation processes are not the same throughout the world. They have a distinctive contextual colour resulting in a diversity of new combinations of religious beliefs and rational insights depending on particular cultural settings and religious traditions.

What is the specific nature of the secularisation processes that have taken place in Western Europe? There is a need to make a distinction between these processes in the different parts of Europe. The Eastern Orthodox traditions in Eastern and Central Europe on the one hand and the Roman Catholic and Protestant traditions in Western Europe on the other, have gone through divergent historical processes, resulting in rather different social roles and positions of religion. This is confirmed by, for instance, Charles Taylor, who studied the secularisation processes in what he called Latin Christendom.[3] He states that secularisation in Western Europe is closely related to the inner dynamics within Latin Christendom because of its strong distinction or even separation between the 'secular' and the 'spiritual' world, between the immanent and the transcendent realities. He is convinced that this clear separation is one of the inventions of Latin Christendom. Also, other cultures and religious traditions distinguish between secular and spiritual realms. However, the clear separation between the two, eventually leading to the independence of the former, is specific for the Latin Christendom in Western Europe.[4]

Taylor shows that this secularisation process in Latin Christendom has gone through a number of stages before full independence of the secular order was reached. In the early stage, widespread in the eighteenth century, the claim of independence was only limited and partly. God was still seen as the creator of the universe, and the natural order and beauty stand as proof of his existence. The moral and spiritual leadership of the church was therefore still acceptable and by many seen as useful for maintaining good social order. In the next phase the relation between the secular and the religious became more tense and competitive, especially in the time of the French Revolution. The moral and spiritual leadership of the church in the social, economic and especially the political realms was challenged and eventually rejected. Finally, the sidelining of religion from the state resulted in a loss of its relevance in public life. Of

---

[3] Charles Taylor, *A Secular Age* (Cambridge, Massachusetts, London: The Belknap Press of the Harvard University Press, 2007). See also Charles Taylor, "Western Secularity" in Craig Calhoun, Mark Juergensmeyer, Jonathan Van Antwerpen (eds.) *Rethinking Secularism* (Oxford University Press, 2011).

[4] An important question is whether this clear separation between the 'secular' and the 'spiritual' realms, developed in Western European Latin Christendom, has influenced the theology in churches in other parts of the world established by migrants (North America) and missionaries (Africa, Asia, Pacific) to the extent that the inherent secularisation processes will determine their future as well.

course, these different phases in the Western European secularisation process cannot be distinguished so clearly. They form aspects of a rather complex process in which also the disenchantment of nature (resulting from scientific and technological progress), and the uneasy relation or even rivalry between reason and faith play significant roles.

One can argue that the Reformation has fuelled the secularisation process by focusing on God's Word and the personal faith of the individual: *sola scriptura*, *sola fide*, *sola gratia*. The removal of statues and religious paintings from churches and the critical attitude towards the religious symbols and rituals of the Roman Catholic Church have strengthened the process of rationalising and personalising faith to the extent that it finally became a private affair. Of course, the Reformation and the rise of Protestantism are not the only factors that have contributed to a growing individualism. Yet, it cannot be denied that they have played a significant role in the shift from religion as a communal affair towards individual faith commitment.

These processes of separation between the religious and the secular realms ending in loss of relevance of the former, the disenchantment of nature and the focus on individual rather than communal life have resulted in a culture in which faith is felt irrelevant, odd or even suspect. This secular culture is the environment in which young people grow up and try to understand who they are and what they want to do with their life.

The Secular Me

The questions 'who am I?' and 'who do I want to be?' have become urgent in a secular culture that denies that life and identity is given by God. However, the search for identity has become even more important as modern culture proclaims perfectibility as the highest 'article of faith'. This doctrine of perfectibility, advanced by Rousseau and others, means that people are capable of achieving perfection through natural means, without the grace of God. It implies a high level of individual freedom. It also means that those who are not able to make a success story of their life will be labelled a failure, a loser. What does this doctrine of perfectibility mean for the search of personal identity?[5]

The debates around identity usually focus on the question of nature versus nurture: either the personal identity is formed by the environment in which one grew up or the identity is genealogically determined. This dilemma has become prominent again in the discussions on results of neurological research. However, there seems to be a general agreement that personal identity is informed by both, nature as well as nurture. The influence of the social

[5] An interesting study of the effects of the doctrine of perfectibility on the formation and deformation of identity is presented by the psychologist Paul Verhaeghe, *What About Me? The Struggle for Identity in a Market-Based Society* (London: Scribe Publications Pty Ltd, 2014).

environment on the formation of identity is strong through a constant process of mirroring. Identity is never a once and for all given quality, but far more an ongoing reflexive process in which one responds to events and signals in the social environment. As Anthony Giddens, whose ideas on reflexive modernity will be studied later in this chapter, says: "Self-identity is not a distinctive trait, or even a collection of traits, possessed by the individual". On the contrary, identity "is *the self as reflexively understood by the person in terms of her or his biography*".[6] The accumulation of responses to events and signals and the reflexion on them by the individual show their identity.

If personal identity is so much influenced by the social environment, it cannot be denied that the secular nature of today's society and culture provokes a specific response. A person will either adopt the secularised mode of life or will try to reject it by becoming even more religious. The phrase 'try to reject' is used here intentionally as it will become clear that, despite the promises of full freedom of choice, a secularised society constantly challenges the relevance of religious beliefs.[7] This inherent pressure is felt through, for instance, education and media and their specific use of language and modes of learning. As language and learning are important for the formation of identity, there is a need for further study of their function in a secular society.

Language and Learning in Modern, Secularised Societies

The German sociologist Niklas Luhmann has extensively reflected on the role of language and learning in what he calls social systems.[8] For him, a social system consists of actions based on a meaningful communication. His focus on communication has long-reaching implications for how we need to understand social differentiation that is so typical for a modern society. Other scholars have studied social differentiation as result of the increasing division of labour and the growth of functional subsystems. For Luhmann, the fundamental change from traditional to modern societies is the shift from a dominance of *stratified* differentiation to a dominance of *functional* differentiation.

In a society marked by stratified differentiation, the different subsystems have a more or less hierarchical relationship. It cannot be denied that also in medieval societies the nobility, the priests, the soldiers, the craftsmen, the labourers did have a functional division of labour. However, this functional division was dominated by a stratified hierarchy in power and influence. Communication between the different layers in pre-modern societies had a normative nature. The highest layers had the authority to dominate and to direct

---

6 Anthony Giddens, *Modernity and Self-Identity* (Cambridge/Oxford: Polity Press (1991) 1997), 53 (italics by Giddens).

7 Verhaeghe, *What About Me?,* chapter 6 "Identity: Powerless Perfectibility".

8 See, for instance, Peter Beyer, *Religion and Globalisation* (London: SAGE Publications (1994), 2000), 33-41.

lower levels whether or not they had the required technical and functional expertise.

The fundamental change is, as Luhmann sees it, that the relation between the different social layers has lost this normative nature. The functional differentiation in a modern society is based on shared language, inherent modes of learning, and lines and sources of authority developed and accepted *within* the different subsystems. The modern society has gone through a process of re-ordering in which each functional subsystem has developed its own ways and means of communication. For instance, the financial subsystem communicates through the language of numbers, losses and gains, financial prospects and risks. The political subsystem communicates through power and influence. The subsystem of science uses theories, models and proven evidence to communicate progress in learning. These new functional subsystems have contributed tremendously to globalisation as they facilitate communication that goes beyond the boundaries of local languages and hierarchical social structures.

An important aspect in this fundamental shift is the mode of learning. In hierarchical social structures, learning has primarily been a normative nature dominated by the higher layers in society. The shift towards functional differentiation has given prevalence to cognitive modes of learning within the subsystems. Learning itself has become important as a way to deal with expectations and complexities. Cognitive modes of learning allow for more open ways of communication, actions and changes in expectations than in a normative approach. Modern societies are composed of self-learning subsystems. This way of learning is an essential precondition for further progress, economically and politically as well as socially and culturally.

This change in the ways of learning has long-reaching implications for the position of churches and religion in general. Knowledge is not acquired anymore through the pre-modern hierarchical stratification in which religion had a natural status of authority. Religion has lost that position as each of the functional subsystems has its own way of learning. Theology is not any more the queen of science. Therefore, this shift from stratified, hierarchical differentiation towards functional differentiation had a great impact on the secularisation process. Through processes of modernisation and globalisation, societies have been re-ordered in such a way that religion has become just another functional subsystem with its own ways of communications, modes of learning and sources of authority. It has lost its influence on other subsystems.[9]

One of the problems in Luhmann's understanding of functional differentiation is the question of the human identity. How can the human

[9] Luhmann has reflected on the place of religion in this fundamental shift. His reflections on religion have been published after his death in *Die Religion der Gesellschaft*, edited by André Kaiserling. Niklas Luhmann, *Die Religion der Gesellschaft* (Frankfurt: Suhrkamp, 2002).

person's engagement in so many subsystems lead to a convincing integrated personal identity? Does the engagement in, for instance, a technical profession, the involvement in political life, being a member of a family, being confronted with the requirements of medical systems, etc. not lead to the disintegration or even the fragmentation of life, at the individual as well as at the social level? As each of the subsystems has its own language and modes of learning, the search for an integrated identity has become extremely complex. And religion, being one of the subsystems, has lost its authority and normativity to give direction to this search.

To address this fundamental question, there is a need to listen to another sociologist, Anthony Giddens, as he approaches the reality of the subsystems from the perspective of the search for personal identity in what he calls reflexive modernity.

The Search for Identity: Reflexive Modernity and Risk Management

This British sociologist Giddens highlighted a few aspects that are important for our understanding of the search for identity in a modern, secular society. Addressing the question of social fragmentation, he prefers not to speak of post-modernism, but as a new phase in modernisation itself. Giddens frequently uses phrases like 'late modernity', 'high modernity', or closer to his own vocabulary, 'reflexive modernity'.

The reason for his frequent use of the term 'reflexive modernity' is that, as he sees it, social and individual life is very much a human life-project. Self-awareness and reflexivity are at the core of this project. In that sense he comes close to Luhmann's understanding of functional subsystems, although Giddens prefers to use the phrase 'abstract systems'. The economic, the financial, the political, the medical systems are abstract systems in which the human person is involved. Reflexivity is not only a fundamental aspect of these abstract systems. The human individual him/herself is engaged in a reflexive life project.

This reflexive life project, and the need to constantly jump from one subsystem to another (family, work, sports, politics, etc.), involves existential anxiety as success is not self-evident. The study of Paul Verhaeghe, referred to earlier, shows that involvement in the modern society with its promise of perfectibility and risks of failures leads to a considerable number of 'modern' diseases and disorders.[10] One of the ways of coping with this existential anxiety is the introduction of risk assessment and risk management as part of the life planning in modernity. Risk calculations have become a fundamental part of abstract systems. Each of the systems, the medical, the economic, the political, etc., have their own experts in assessing risks and making them part of the

---

[10] Paul Verhaeghe, *What About Me?*, chapter 7.

planning processes. "The reflexive monitoring of risk is intrinsic to institutionalised risk systems," Giddens writes.[11]

Giddens explains that individuals apply to a large extent similar patterns of risk assessment and risk mitigation, especially in fateful, decisive moments in their life. For instance, when applying for a job, when deciding to marry or to have children or in moments of serious illness, individual persons almost automatically make risk assessments. He therefore concludes that "the intrusion of abstract systems into day-to-day life, coupled with the dynamic nature of knowledge, means that awareness of risk seeps into actions of almost everyone".[12]

Giddens explains that day-to-day life in modern times is not riskier than in pre-modern eras. The change is that we are more thinking in terms of risks. Risk assessment has become more or less an ever-present exercise. It has become an integral part of individual and collective life planning. "Individuals seek to colonise the future for themselves as an intrinsic part of their life-planning," Giddens writes. "All individuals establish a portfolio of risk assessment, which may be more or less clearly articulated, well informed and 'open'; or alternatively may be largely inevitable and most people will be conscious also of the risks of refusing to think in this way, even if they may choose to ignore those risks."[13]

Deskilling Effects

The fact that people are so familiar with risk management has made life in many ways less vulnerable. Especially when we look at the achievements in, for instance, medical sciences, but also in how today food is produced, houses are built and traffic is controlled. However, the downside is that increasingly we have difficulties with the unexpected and uncontrollable aspects of life. Giddens explains that "living in the circumstances of modern social institutions, in which risk is recognised as risk, creates certain difficulties for the generalised vesting of trust in 'discounted possibilities' – possibilities that are bracketed out as irrelevant to the individual's self-identity and pursuits. The psychological security that conceptions of fate can offer is largely foreclosed, as is the personalising of natural events in the shape of spirits, demons or other beings".[14] He rightly points at the phenomenon that in a society in which almost everything can be planned and controlled, we find it difficult to deal with the uncontrollable aspects of life, misfortune, illness and death. "Yet notions of fate refuse to disappear altogether and are found in uneasy

---

11 Giddens, *Modernity and Self-Identity*, 119.
12 Giddens, *Modernity and Self-Identity*, 112.
13 Giddens, *Modernity and Self-Identity*, 125f.
14 Giddens, *Modernity and Self-Identity*, 129.

combination with an outlook of the secular risk type and with attitudes of fatalism," he concludes.[15]

With this observation he points at a contradiction at the heart of modernity itself: "There is greater security in many aspects of day-to-day life – yet there is also a serious price to pay for these advances. Abstract systems depend on trust, yet they provide none of the moral rewards which can be obtained from personalised trust or were often available in traditional settings from moral frameworks within which everyday life was undertaken."[16]

This is not only a theoretical or philosophical problem that can be solved by further study and reflection. People experience this inherent contradiction in modernity in their day-to-day life. We ought to trust the abstract systems of which we are very much part. At the same time, we know that they will not be able to solve the most fundamental questions and dilemmas in our life. Moreover, being to a large extent determined by the risk-calculating abstract systems of which we are part, we have lost our capacity and skills to deal with the unexpected events in our lives. Giddens observes that modern abstract systems disempower and deskill individuals to cope with the uncontrollable aspects of life. He writes: "Abstract systems deskill – not only in the workplace, but in all the sectors of social life that they touch. The deskilling of day-to-day life is an alienating and fragmenting phenomenon so far as the self is concerned. Alienating, because the intrusion of abstract systems, especially expert systems, into all aspects of day-to-day life undermines pre-existing forms of local control."[17]

How do individual persons deal with this in modern life? Giddens sees more or less three ways in which individuals might be re-skilled and empowered. The *first* is the tendency to withdraw from the abstract systems as much as possible. Although it is almost impossible to withdraw fully, one can minimise, for instance, the involvement in the political system, dependency on modern medical sciences and dependency on financial systems. The *second* possible response is to again rely on traditional authorities for important personal lifestyle decisions. Giddens sees that "more attenuated forms of religious belief, however, may clearly also offer significant support in shaping significant life decisions".[18] A *third* way forward might be to seek solutions in the abstract systems themselves, especially in fateful moments: "Hence it is not surprising that at fateful moments individuals are today likely to encounter expert systems which precisely focus on the reconstruction of self-identities: counselling or therapy."[19] Counselling and therapy have become important for life in reflexive modernity.

---

[15] Giddens, *Modernity and Self-Identity*, 130.
[16] Giddens, *Modernity and Self-Identity*, 136.
[17] Giddens, *Modernity and Self-Identity*, 137.
[18] Giddens, *Modernity and Self-Identity*, 142.
[19] Giddens, *Modernity and Self-Identity*, 143.

Although these three, what I would call *modi vivendi,* may provide us with ways of coping with the uncontrollable, fatal events in modern life, they do not help us with final solutions. Giddens is aware of that and continues his analysis of modernity at a deeper level. He sees that modernity actually wants to sequestrate, seclude, isolate or set apart personal life experience. Modern abstract systems have difficulties with human experience, especially in fatal moments. Giddens gives a number of examples of how experience is secluded in modern life: madness, criminality, sickness and death, sexuality and nature in general. This sequestration of experience is needed in modern abstract systems to establish large tracts of relative security in day-to-day modern life. However, as Giddens sees it, "its effect, which as we have seen should be regarded largely as an unintended consequence of the development of modern institutions, is to repress a cluster of basic moral and existential components of human life that are, as it were, squeezed to the sidelines".[20]

Moral and Existential Dilemmas

Such a repression of basic moral and existential components of human life has its costs, at the social as well as at the individual level. It confronts the individual with a number of dilemmas that are not easy to solve. Giddens highlights four such dilemmas:

- Unification versus fragmentation.
- Powerlessness versus appropriation.
- Authority versus uncertainty.
- Personalised versus commodified experience.

As he sees it, these dilemmas have an underlying dynamic with a serious threat of meaninglessness: "It follows that the project of the self has to be reflexively achieved in a technically competent but morally arid social environment. Underlying the most thoroughgoing processes of life-planning – and each of the various dilemmas mentioned above – is the looming threat of personal meaninglessness."[21]

The individual and collective struggles with the dilemmas in modernity, and the inherent threat of personal meaninglessness, will most probably lead to "a return of the repressed at the very heart of modern institutions", as Giddens sees it.[22] This means that the project of reflexive modernity itself is at risk if it continues to seclude or sequestrate basic human experience. Giddens sees in modern societies a number of ways of what he calls "the return of the repressed", the personal anxiety with the unplanned and unexpected tragedies leading to moral dilemmas and challenging the meaning of life. One of them is the reconstruction of tradition, including religious traditions. This can include

[20] Giddens, *Modernity and Self-Identity*, 167.
[21] Giddens, *Modernity and Self-Identity*, 201.
[22] Giddens, *Modernity and Self-Identity*, 202.

the resurgence of traditional religious beliefs and convictions, for instance, in the form of religious fundamentalism. Examples of this return to fundamentalism can be found in the current developments in the Islam, but also in other religions including Christianity. But this is not the only possible response. New forms of religion and spirituality may provide a response to the moral dilemmas and sense of meaninglessness. As Giddens writes: "New forms of religion and spirituality represent in a most basic sense a return of the repressed, since they directly address issues of the moral meaning of existence which modern institutions so thoroughly tend to dissolve."[23]

Faith Responses to the Search of Identity

Giddens' reflections point at some pertinent questions, which are crucial in the search for personal identity in secular contexts. There are no easy answers and there is no way back into a traditional communal life that provides individual identity to its members. The search for identity must take into account the observation that individual and social life is in many ways a reflexive but also a risky project, full of unsolved dilemmas and false promises. The phenomenon of almost constantly taking selfies, to which I referred in the beginning of this chapter, not only appears to be a self-confident confirmation: 'This is me!'. It is at the same time an expression of deeply felt uncertainty: 'Is this me?' The search for identity seems to be at the heart of the individual life project in which each of us is engaged and taking selfies has become an intrinsic monitoring tool of how far I have come on this risky path. A pastoral, but also missionary, approach starts with affirming such life projects and accepting their vulnerabilities. By developing a positive approach, churches may be relevant partners in addressing some of the fundamental questions raised by Giddens.

These questions, related to the individual and social life projects in reflexive modernity, manifest themselves at least at three levels: (1) the *unsolved moral and existential dilemmas*, resulting from the repression of experience in abstract systems, and leading to (2) the *threat of meaninglessness*; and finally (3) the contribution to the *public debates on life politics* that can give guidance to moral and existential choices in individual and social life.

First, the ongoing reflection and debates about the unsolved moral and existential dilemmas in modernity require dialogue with and within the abstract systems on the question of how to overcome the seclusion or sequestration of life experience. For instance, how can the financial and economic systems more intentionally include the experiences of vulnerability of human beings and of nature in general? Similarly, how can science and technology develop methodologies and tools that include the fragility of natural environments leading to, for instance, climate change? Reflection, research and debates on more holistic approaches are not new and increasingly receive attention within

[23] Giddens, *Modernity and Self-Identity*, 207.

the abstract systems themselves. Can churches and theologians engage themselves in a meaningful way in these technical debates among experts and contribute to finding more sustainable and inclusive approaches in future developments?

With the inclusion of human and natural experience in the abstract technical systems, progress can be made in overcoming the dilemmas inherent to reflexive modernity. The four dilemmas highlighted by Giddens – unification versus fragmentation; powerlessness versus appropriation; authority versus uncertainty; personalised versus commodified experience – are so much determining the lives of people and their search for identity that churches and theologians need to engage themselves in finding ways forward. It is not too difficult to see that the Gospel speaks to these dilemmas and that the wisdom built up in the Christian traditions can relevantly contribute to the reflection and debates on them. The proper way forward seems to be not to deny or ignore reflexive modernity, but rather to intensify reflexivity by including moral and spiritual dimensions related to the day-to-day experiences of joy and vulnerability.

Second, the search for ways of inclusion of experience in abstract systems and the reflection on the dilemmas inherent to modernity, address the more fundamental concern of meaninglessness. The core of the Christian faith is to give meaning to life in the face of its vulnerability and finiteness. It is therefore urgent that we develop and nurture forms of spirituality that give guidance and support to people living in times of late, high or reflexive modernity.

Third, Giddens calls for the development of life politics that can give guidance to the public and political debates on the fundamental questions of life and death and the technical and medical opportunities available, now and in the future. Churches have always seen the importance of giving moral guidance to public debates on issues such as birth control, abortion, euthanasia, etc. However, too often the contribution of churches was formulated from a pre-modern, normative perspective, rather than being fully engaged in the reflection on inherent dilemmas. This way of dealing with the fundamental life issues has strengthened the public image of the church as being conservative and not relevant in the current debates.

In Conclusion

This chapter started with the phenomenon of taking selfies as an expression of the ardent search for identity in a secularised culture that denies the God-given nature of life. As language and learning is determined by almost autonomous social subsystems, churches have lost their moral and spiritual authority to give guidance to the search for identity. At the same time, secularised, modern life shows its inherent contradictions by promising perfectibility in social and individual life projects on the one hand and deskilling people in coping with the unexpected, tragic events on the other. The unsolved moral and existential dilemmas lead to strong feelings of personal meaningless. A missionary approach requires genuine attempts to understand the dilemmas in modern, secular life and to provide informed accompaniment to individuals (and societies) in their search for identity, accepting that traditional ecclesial expressions of moral and spiritual leadership will be very critically assessed in secular contexts.

Believing in a Secular Way: A West-German Perspective

Michael Biehl

A German novelist recently said in an interview that poetical writings like his own should be seen as opening the eyes for the "marvellous" (Wunderbare) in life. That prompted the interviewer to ask the question whether the author considers himself religious. The author: "What does that mean, religious? I am a Roman Catholic and sometimes I think back to that club with a sentimental feeling of devotedness. But I never attend a service. In my childhood in a mineworkers' village which was so grimy black, the church was a place of consolation, also aesthetically, with the lush bunch of flowers, the gold and glitter of the costumes with incense fragrance. I was a passionate ministrant then. But all of this had gone when I had been done with puberty."[1]

This is a rather typical example of the intricate relationship many have with church and with faith or what they think religion is about today in Germany. The question of religion is triggered by the author's statement that he wishes poetical writings not to explain reality but to offer something that is beyond reality ("das über aller Realität ist"), the marvellous. His reply seems to indicate that with that wish he had not been thinking of religion but art and that he is unsure what to be religious could mean. To him, religion and faith are not linked to his search of what is beyond reality, but to a past period in his life, a childhood experience that did not make it across the threshold into adulthood. And yet, it lingers on in his life as a memory, and may be looked upon as overcome but not as something to be opposed. Obviously, he has not being doing fully away with it, at least that is what comes to mind seeing that he opens his comment with the statement that – even today – he "is" a Roman Catholic.

How to interpret to "be" a Roman Catholic or more generally a Christian in the line of that argument and then in the light of that encounter? Both the way the question on religion popped up in that conversation, and the answer in its complexity indicate that the equation of secularisation with the waning away of

---

[1] "Unsere Wurzeln liegen in der Luft". Interview mit dem Schriftsteller Ralf Rothmann in *Der Spiegel, Nr.18, 28.4.2018*, 118-121, here: 120. "Was heißt schon religiös? Ich bin katholisch und denke manchmal noch mit so einer sentimentalen Anhänglichkeit an den Verein. Aber ich gehe in keinen Gottesdienst. In meiner Kindheit in der verrußten Bergarbeitersiedlung war die Kirche allerdings ein Trost, auch in ästhetischer Hinsicht: Diese üppigen Blumensträuße, das Gold und der Kostümflitter im Weihrauchduft. Ich war schon leidenschaftlich gerne Ministrant. Aber das hat sich mit der Pubertät erledigt." (my translation).

religion is too simple. The author, his interviewer and the public they are both writing for are part of a context, which is rightly labelled secular, but one in which faith and religion continue to exist in an intricate constellation.

This paper discusses mission and evangelism in such a context where, that is the thesis, people do not believe against the secular but in a secular way. My reading of the religious situation in Europe and more especially in Western Germany[2] is informed by the understanding that the people's consciousness and perceptions are formed by being part of a nation with a history in which religion is entangled in the collective memory and by living in a society in which religion and politics are separate realms. Religion is embedded in that cultural formation in various ways. Such an approach should help to see more clearly that being secular in Northwestern European societies is not well understood if it is taken as the opposite of religion or in this case of church.[3] It also could assist in establishing a better understanding that the majority of those who choose to still be members of a church don't opt for faith or religion in opposition to the rest of the society. This paper hence focuses on the believers, and its contention is that in the perspective of mission and evangelism being secular is best approached as a cultural and social formation in which people who continue to be members of the churches are immersed and by which they are formed.

The Secular City

The title is taken from an influential book Harvey Cox wrote in 1965. In his introduction to its re-edition (2013) he repeats his argument that becoming secular has been in a way inherent in the biblical faith according to which humans meet God in this world and in history, e.g. not only in the sacred but also in the secular realm.[4] Cox had attempted to formulate on that basis a theology for his time that would discern God's presence outside the church in all of life, including the political and cultural dimensions, and he had claimed that in the secular city people of all faith will meet. Fifty years later he

---

[2] For the difference to Eastern Germany see Martin Reppenhagen in this volume and Michael Herbst, 'Plural Mission and Missionary Plural in a Post-Socialist Context: Using the Example of a Post-"Volkskirche", East German Region', in Rolv Olson (ed.), *Mission and Postmodernities* (Regnum Edinburgh 2010 Series, Oxford: Regnum Publs. 2011), 39-57.

[3] See for further elaboration of that aspect Christoph Anders, Michael Biehl, Gerrit Noort, 'Called to Transforming Discipleship in North-Western Europe. Some Reflections on Witnessing in Secularised Contexts', in *Resource Book. Conference on World Mission and Evangelism, "Moving in the Spirit – Called to transforming Discipleship"*, 8-13 March 2018, Arusha, Tanzania, ed. by Jooseop Keum (Geneva: WCC, 2018), 84-101.

[4] Harvey Cox, *The Secular City.* With a new introduction by the author (Princeton: Princeton University Press, 2013), XII.

comments that with the resurgence of religious movements worldwide matters have become more complicated.

If one considers the secular especially linked to the urban area like Cox proposed, one could recall that unlike in 1965, today already more than half of the world population is living in such areas and that these form the space where more than 60% of the world's Christians dwell, which has remarkable effects on the face of world Christianity.[5] If one approaches the city of Hamburg in Northern Germany from the South, six towers mark the skyline. The tower of St Michael's has been a landmark for Hamburg and for a long time its height of 132 m was the benchmark for how tall buildings in this area of the city were allowed to be. Today it threatens to be replaced in that function by the silhouette of the recently constructed Elbphilharmonie.

The tower of the nearby St Peter's Church is approximately 200 m from the entrance of the City Hall with its own bold tower, both of which overshadow the surrounding buildings. The city hall is the seat of parliament of this federal state of Germany. The two towers facing each other can be interpreted as a sign of secularisation in the sense of symbolising a specific constellation of civil and religious powers: separated but in defined coalition. That is at least part of the self-understanding of the Protestant Church. The church tower can be said to represent the perception of the regional Lutheran mainline church, being a visible part of civil society and being a counterpart to the political power. All the

Hauptkirchen (major church buildings) in the inner-city area to which the mentioned towers belong – St Michael, St Peter, St Catherine, St Jacob, St Nicolai – offer themselves as churches in the city and their building and congregation as spaces for political, cultural and societal debates beyond being places of worship. The tower of St Peter can thus stand for the remaining approximately 38% membership of the two mainline churches, the regional Lutheran and the Roman Catholic Church, whose archdiocese resides at the nearby dome, St Mary. The church tower is not just a mere memory of the hold the churches once had on society. It is still tall and indicating that the church of today understands the secular city as a space in which its members and visitors live and into which it wishes to reach out with its offers, also to politicians.

The city hall tower in turn can be associated with the 1.8 million inhabitants of Hamburg. However, the 38% church members are also citizens, and such buildings that are easily identifiable as religious places in the city, represent today only part of those places that the people living in Hamburg use for religious assemblies. Some temples and mosques can be identified in town. In this sense the buildings could be interpreted as a symbol for another development, the growing presence of other religions, especially of Muslims, which some populist voices in Germany consider a threat to the Christian

[5] See Johnson, Todd M. and Kenneth R. Ross (ed.), *Atlas of Global Christianity 1910-2010* (Edinburgh: University Press, 2009), 241-255.

Occident. Because of the decline in numbers, the regional Lutheran church decided to close several of its church buildings. This provoked discussions, especially after one church building was bought by a Muslim congregation and was subsequently turned into a mosque.[6]

Along with the decline of the mainline churches, other Christian traditions have become more visible in the city area by taking over such buildings. There is Grace church (Gnaden-Kirche), which is used by the "Russian-Orthodox Church of the Saint John of Kronstadt" for its services. The former Simeon-Church in Hamburg-Hamm is used by a Greek Orthodox Church, a church building in Hamburg-Borgfelde and the Nathaniel-Church in Hamburg-Hamm are used by African congregations.[7]

However, walking through the city, one can easily find in the shadow of these representative religious buildings signs that indicate that here in an office building is a Spanish-speaking congregation or there in another building an African congregation is meeting, not to mention the Chinese, the Korean, the Indonesian and other fellowships and churches residing in the city.[8] This is a reminder that the well-known figures reflect only partially the religious situation in that city because beyond them numbers are blurred and uncertain. There are only estimates about how many people in the city consider themselves beyond the mainline traditions a member in a Christian congregation whose rooms one easily overlooks because they are less visible. Neither are there more than estimates of how many people in that city are considering themselves regular participants of another religious tradition such as Islam[9] or Jewish faith or Sikhs or Hindus or Buddhists. Nor are there established figures of how many people in the city are still considering themselves religious or spiritual, and less, which concepts they hold.

The decline in membership of the mainline churches is an indicator that a considerable portion of people chose to leave the church behind as an institution, and that has already changed the mainline churches.[10] Giving up

---

[6] This is taken from Michael Biehl, 'Die Christenheit spricht in vielen Dialekten. Zur Vielfalt christlicher Kirchen und Gemeinschaften in Hamburg', *Una Sancta* 71(1) (2016), 55-65.

[7] See, for instance, the list of the 35 members of the "Arbeitsgemeinschaft Christlicher Kirchen" [Christian Council] http://www.ack-hamburg.de/mitgliedskirchen.html (17.02.2018) and the list of 149 "Mitmacher" of the Evangelical alliance in Hamburg, dazu http://www.gemeinsam-fuer-hamburg.de (12.02.2018). See Biehl, 'Die Christenheit spricht in vielen Dialekten', 58-59.

[8] See Wolfgang Grünberg, Dennis L.Slabaugh, Ralf Meister-Karanikas (eds.) *Lexikon der Hamburger Religionsgemeinschaften. Religionsvielfalt in der Stadt von A bis Z* (Hamburg: Dölling & Galitz, ²1995).

[9] See more recently Marion Koch and Joachim Reinig (eds.), *Moscheen und Gebetsräume in Hamburg. Untersuchung der räumlichen Situation* (Hamburg 2013).

[10] See especially the result of the last membership study of EKD, which is done every ten years. Heinrich Bedford-Strohm and Volker Jung (eds.), *Vernetzte Vielfalt. Kirche*

membership is often the last step in a long process of alienation from the church or an attempt to save money by not paying the membership fee.[11] But one should not overlook that this decline is not all that can be said about Christian communities and even less about religion in Hamburg.

Secularisation in this paper is approached from the angle of being a consequence of the separation of Christian(!) institutions from political power. Even if the decline of the membership numbers of the large mainline churches is taken as a strong indicator for a turning away from the Christian religion, the many places and communities that have their own spaces and own assemblies and congregations in the city of Hamburg are a serious hint that these two movements do not lead to a waning away of religion! The unknown number hints at a considerable pluralisation of forms of believing and belonging in a city like Hamburg, to which the various religious communities present in Hamburg add. All are affected by the cultural and religious formation that is a result of the intricate processes lumped under secularisation, but neither the people nor their communities share necessarily the same understanding of what secularisation is or should look like. The following observation should serve as one example of that complex situation: according to the survey Religions monitor (2013), 54%of the interviewed persons in the Western regions of Germany say that they believe in God, gods or higher beings – but only 12% of the same group would call themselves really religious and 13% that they are really spiritual.[12]

One other striking aspect of the cultural formation is that, unlike in other regions, there is not (yet) much movement between religious communities. Of those who have left the mainline churches behind, only a small minority has joined other churches or religious communities. It also can be said that what one could call the fragmentation and multiplication of faith dialects result in relativising discourses that understand themselves to a certain extent as absolute.

---

angesichts von Individualisierung und Säkularisierung. Die 5. EKD-Erhebung über Kirchenmitgliedschaft (Gütersloh: Gütersloher Verlagshaus, 2015).

[11] In 1991 a new "solidarity tax" was introduced for those in the Western regions of Germany with which the reconstruction of the eastern part of the country after the unification should be financed. This tax was approximately the same amount that many paid as a church membership fee, which was being deducted like a tax from income. A great number of people took this as the final impulse to give up their membership in the mainline churches and thus save the money that they were asked to pay for the solidarity tax.

[12] Detlef Pollak and Olaf Müller (eds.), *Religionsmonitor. Verstehen was verbindet. Religiosität und Zusammenhalt in Deutschland* (Gütersloh: Bertelsmann, 2013), 12.

Believing in a Secular Context

Since the numbers have been a point of reference, it should be mentioned that in 1948/1950, 96% of the population in the Western regions of Germany and 84% in the Eastern regions were members of the Protestant mainline churches or of the Roman Catholic Church[13] (the other church traditions – Baptists, Methodists, etc. – did numerically not play a comparable role). Today, one can see a clear threefold partition in the population: a bit more than a quarter of the population of 82 million are members of the Roman Catholic Church, another a bit smaller quarter are members of the mainline Protestant churches, and approximately one third "without a confession" is so called because that part is made up by people who once had been church members. The other religious communities such as Muslims (estimated around 4-5%) and churches (Orthodox, Baptist, Methodist, etc.) form approximately 7% of the population.[14] These are numbers for the Western federal states of Germany. In the Eastern area, after 40 years of a socialist system and anti-church politics, one has in some areas less than 10% and not more than 20% of the population as members of the mainline churches.[15]

This substantial decline in number has effected a change in quality. In the 1950s or early 1960s people evaluated their relationship to Christian faith and church based on their approval or distance to the faith claims and confessional texts of the mainline churches. Nowadays the main aspect is not whether people agree with the faith statements and confessions of the churches, but whether they are willing to include religious convictions or perceptions of the world and of life as part of their attempts to orient themselves in society and in time and space. On that basis they define their relationship with the churches.

The German sociologist of religion Armin Nassehi describes that changed attitude based on the data of the survey Religions monitor (2008): "It is less the living out of a given form of religious practices by the individual, no, the forms themselves have been individualised. It is evident that as well for the highly religious as for the religious interlocutors the reference for the plausibility of the sentences which can be uttered is the own life praxis."[16]

---

[13] Numbers taken from Michael Bergunder, "Säkularisierung und religiöser Pluralismus in Deutschland aus Sicht der Religionssoziologie", in Daniel Cyranka and Helmut Obst (eds.), *"…mitten in der Stadt". Halle zwischen Säkularisierung und religiöser Vielfalt* (Halle: Franckesche Stiftungen zu Halle, 2001), 213-252, here 213.

[14] Volkhard Krech, 'Kleine Religionsgemeinschaften in Deutschland. Eine religionssoziologische Bestandsaufnahme', in Hartmut Lehmann (ed.), *Religiöser Pluralismus im vereinten Europa. Freikirchen und Sekten* (Bausteine zu einer europäischen Religionsgeschichte im Zeitalter der Säkularisierung, 6, Göttingen: Wallstein Verlag, 2005), 116-144, here 123.

[15] See Bergunder, 'Säkularisierung und religiöser Pluralismus', 213, and Martin Reppenhagen in this volume. #.

[16] Armin Nassehi, 'Erstaunliche religiöse Kompetenz. Qualitative Ergebnisse des Religionsmonitor', in *Religionsmonitor 2008* (Gütersloh: Gütersloher Verlagshaus,

His conclusion is that the more intensively the interviewees experience their faith life, the more they move away from the official church practices and faith statements without fully renouncing them. It follows that especially highly religious people struggle with the demands of consistency of the confessional tradition of their churches. Nassehi observes that these individuals solve that conflict by embedding it in and relating it to an attempt of an authentic presentation of their life and by striving for consistency in it, not for consistency with church traditions. For them, the own life practice and being able to present it as authentic becomes the decisive point of reference and hence the solution to the conflict.[17] This authentic presentation, according to Nassehi, is striving at creating a vision of one's own life as unified, against the challenges of experiencing social differentiation, inconsistencies and incomprehensible moments, which tend to make life meaningless. In attempting to create such a holistic understanding the interviewed individuals lend to life a transcendent dimension. In this way these attempts remain in line with more traditional understandings of religion as connecting with transcendence – but not in its form as authentic presentation. Nassehi: Matters look really religious only if one can emphasise that they are originating in the person and its uniqueness, not in church tradition.[18]

The last survey of the Evangelical Church in Germany (EKD) of its members comes to a surprising insight that supports these observations. Forms of religiosity that exist outside the churches and faith statements foreign to their confession texts are highly likely to be accepted by members of the church. Half of the interviewed people of the EKD survey say that they integrate aspects of various religious traditions in their individual household of religion. Matthias Pöhlmann comments that it seems more likely to find a plurality of beliefs and the acceptance of religious concepts and ideas that are foreign to the tradition of the mainline churches in persons inside these churches. This

---

2009), 118. "Es geht nicht nur um das individuellere Erleben einer gewissermaßen feststehenden religiösen Praxisform, sondern es sind die Formen selbst, die individualisiert werden. Sowohl bei den hoch religiösen auch bei den religiösen Gesprächspartnern wird sehr deutlich, wie die Plausibilität der sagbaren Sätze sich der eigenen Lebenspraxis verdankt." (Translation M.B.)

[17] Nassehi, 'Erstaunliche religiöse Kompetenz', 120: "an denen sich die Religiosität gerade von Hoch-Religiösen abarbeitet, sondern die authentische Präsentierbarkeit des eigenen Lebens, das sich den Konsistenzzumutungen konfessioneller Praxis unmerklich, aber deutlich entzieht. Man kann es aufgrund unseres Materials geradezu auf eine Formel bringen: je intensiver unsere Interviewpartner ihr eigenes Glaubensleben erleben, desto mehr geraten sie in eine innere Distanz zur kirchlichen Praxis, ohne diese freilich generell abzulehnen. Inkonsistent ist dann nicht mehr das Problem – sondern die Lösung für authentische, unverwechselbare Präsentierbarkeit."

[18] Nassehi, 'Erstaunliche religiöse Kompetenz', 120, 122, 128. An interesting Danish parallel to that is analysed by Ina Rosen, *I'm a believer – but I'll be damned if I'm religious. Belief and religion in the Greater Copenhagen Area. A focus Group study* (Lund Studies in Sociology of Religion, 8; Lund: Lund University, 2009).

undermines an assumption according to which there is Christian faith within the churches and free-floating or patchwork religion outside the church: "The own internal religious plurality is grouped around the church in a strange way." That would, for instance, also reconfigure the understanding of the inner relation of believing without belonging.[19]

One of the consequences of these observations is that most people obviously do not follow what the churches teach and offer – they use their agency to construct their authentic presentation of life in faith – if they still see some meaning in church. Another consequence is that the forms these persons use are in a way the individual reflection of the plurality and fragmented image of religion in the broader secular context where everyone is free to choose and cannot be forced to comply with official religious dogmatic.

One could well imagine such persons to walk the city of Hamburg while attempting to live authentically their own faith in that secular city, facing at the same time the fragmentation of the Christian faith community, the multiplicity of religions and the secular expressions of giving meaning to life. Today the virtual space definitely would need to be added to the physical space of the city because social media, websites, forums, etc. have become decisive focal points for information and discussions of religious and less religious walks of life – an aspect that cannot be developed here. But it should caution against a too individualistic reading of the mentioned agency of people when it is exercised in a communication community.

Believing in a secular way should then indicate that the religious situation as it is exemplified in a city like Hamburg is far beyond the seemingly clear distinction between secular and religious. What makes it more complicated is that the same individuals read what is secular and what is religious quite differently and deal differently with these realms. As Nassehi points out, their way of handling the distinction is closely related to their need and ability to experience and interpret their life practice as coherent and consistent with their own understanding of faith and religion. The discourses on religion in society, on tolerance and freedom of religion are forming a broader framework in which people try to make their own life understanding meaningful and practical, also in a religious perspective.

One aspect of this cultural formation is that the role of the mainline churches in Germany is still defined by their access to social and political institutions. The church offering professional services and contributing to public life still has a high reputation. There are voices against the churches – but in many cases these voices question the privileges of the churches and maybe their political influence, not their faith. Surveys on the beliefs and thoughts of the

---

[19] Matthias Pöhlmann, 'Länderberichte. Deutschland', in Reinhard Hempelmann, Martin Hochholzer, and Johannes Sinabell (eds.), *Heute glauben in Europa. Zwischen Religionsdistanz und Religionsfanatismus* (EZW Texte, 247, Berlin: EZW, 2017), 44-55, here: 42.

members continuously done over 40 years by the mainline churches demonstrate quite convincingly that already in the 1990s a significant percentage saw their membership as participating in a meaningful institution because it is doing good for others. They did not expect much for themselves from that membership and their "religion" was a mixture of not knowing much about the Christian tradition and being proud of individual religious constructions, which included elements of beliefs that were not part of the official teachings.[20]

Secularisation and the Multiplication of Religious Convictions

The indicated cultural formation is the framework for interesting debates on religion in the public. One example is taken from such a debate around Christmas 2015. The "Spiegel", an influential weekly magazine in Germany, published a dialogue between the English astrophysicist Ben Moore and the Lutheran theologian Jan-Hinrich Claussen, the then newly installed representative for cultural affairs of the EKD.[21] The astrophysicist says that he feels awe when he looks into the cosmos and tries to decipher the origins of the universe, but nowhere did he look for God. He does not say that he did not find God, but he does not look for him, neither as part of the explanation of how the universe came into existence nor as a dimension of his personal life. When the theologian counters that everyone has questions about the end of life and the thereafter, indicating that no one can evade the dimension of mortality and finality, Moore denies. About that attitude he is not alone, as research shows that has been done recently in East Germany. The question there was whether one could detect a religious dimension in the worldview of people who claim to not believe in anything. The research could only underline that people who do not believe in God do not miss anything. They, according to an assumption based on this research, may not have questions about the afterlife and even seem to live more peacefully than those troubled by thoughts about the hereafter.[22]

---

[20] See especially Klaus Engelhardt, Hermann v. Loewenich, Peter Steinacker (eds.), *Fremde Heimat Kirche. Die dritte EKD-Erhebung über Kirchenmitgliedschaft* (Gütersloh: Gütersloher Verlagshaus, 1997).

[21] '"Wir wollen unsterblich sein". Spiegel-Streitgespräch. Der Hamburger Pastor Johann Hinrich Claussen und der britische Astrophysiker Ben Moore über den Sinn des Glaubens und die Abgründe der Religion', in *Der Spiegel Nr 53, v. 24.1.2105,* 12-21.

[22] See Petra-Angela Ahrens, *Die Konfessionslosen im Kirchenkreis Lichtenberg-Oberspree: Ergebnisse einer Repräsentativbefragung* (Hannover: Sozialwissenschaftliches Institut der EKD, 2015), 3-4. 75, 7% of the interviewees in an area in Eastern Germany said they are not religious or that they are atheists. They denied believing in a supernatural power and 78.7% percent of them feel they have a good life.

Now, what is surprising is that the agnostic scientist still has a clear idea about what religion should be. Moore challenges the theologian: The Bible is the book you have to believe in. Either you follow the book or not. But to interpret it in each and every age in a new way like his theological counterpart proposes – that does not work for Moore! The theologian responds that the Bible is not true in the literal sense and does not try to explain the world like sciences do. The story of creation is interpreted by him as an attempt to lend meaning and a goal to the world – a telos – not as a story of an origin people have to believe in in order to know where they should be heading to!

Here, tables have been turned around. The intellectual despiser of religion has an almost fundamentalist understanding of the Bible. The theologian proclaims a theology that is imbued by a culture of secularism in which the mainline churches do not fight science or society. Instead they accept science and interpret the tradition they communicate as an offer to the society and believers and non-believers alike. So, a part of the mission of the church is to offer this kind of "secularised" and enlightened theology to a public in which opponents like Moore still claim to know better what "religion" is about and why they have reasons to be against the church.

What is highlighted here is that in that secular formation the theology of the (mainline) churches is definitely not what some opponents still believe: opposing modernity, science and rationality and a striving to control the consciousness of people. But it is at the same time a signature of the cultural secular formation that non-religious groups or persons claim to know what religion is about. Like Moore, without knowing what these churches actually teach and preach, some of them have only one place for religion in their worldview: it is the origin of conflicts and warfare. Hence, the only expectation they have towards religious people and communities is to end their bloody fights and allow for peace.

Conclusion

From this limited study on secularism and secularisation in Germany one can conclude that secularisation is a convenient label for manifold and multifaceted realities and for diverse discourses that are, however, not easily brought into one single theory. Instead of having finished off with religion, one observes in the secular society in Germany a multiplication of its forms in which individuals and groups claim in various ways the authority to interpret religion and faith instead of allocating it to churches. If, as shown, the marker for something to be religious is the authenticity of the appropriation of faith and beliefs, the tradition and the confessional expression of faith residing in the churches are devalued. That aspect could be understood as a critical echo of the periods when churches were attacked for attempting to monopolise the minds of their members. Such a constellation is one of the challenges for mission in a secular context.

Believing in secular ways is thus understood as realising how even within the churches and among their membership individualised forms of believing exist that are formed by and immersed in the secular way of life. Secularisation can thus not be equated with what is outside of the churches,[23] instead churches in Germany have to and do reinterpret their faith and their role in, not against, a secular society, and that affects their witness and practice.

In a multi-cultural city like Hamburg one of the burning questions is whether Christians will be willing to recognise the many Christians from other countries in Europe but even more those with an African or Asian background as citizens of the local Christian life. Too often they are identified by their assumed place of origin, which implies in turn that they have nothing to contribute to the Christian life in the secular city, especially not if they are under suspicious to bring in powers and principalities.[24] If they will not be reduced to their (assumed) origins but will be recognised as a valid expression of the multiplicity of the body of Christ, the Christian life in Hamburg will be learning to speak in many tongues.

Religious pluralisation has certainly added to the presence of religions – statistically there is not much evidence that someone who has lost interest in the Christian tradition is looking elsewhere for religious inspirations. But one insight from that should be that mission definitely should welcome pluralisation[25] and is called to cooperate with people of other faiths for the common good as the document "Christian Witness in a multi-religious world" challenges churches and mission bodies: "Christians should continue to build relationships of respect and trust with people of different religions so as to facilitate deeper mutual understanding, reconciliation and cooperation for the common good."[26] The document links freedom of religion to the freedom for mission. This has been picked up by a study paper on "Discipleship in secularised contexts" from a Northwestern European perspective prepared for the World Mission Conference in Arusha: "As Christians we are free to evangelise and to call to discipleship, as long as we keep in mind that the other always has the freedom to decide not to accept the invitation. People are free to choose and have the right not to be coerced or dominated by religious convictions. It includes, as stated in the document, that the freedom to do

[23] A point Martin Laube highlights, see his '2.1 Religion als Praxis. Zur Fortschreibung des christentumssoziologischen Rahmens der EKD-Mitgliedschaftsstudien', in Heinrich Bedford-Strohm and Volker Jung (eds.), *Vernetzte Vielfalt,* 35-49.

[24] See Michael Biehl, 'Zur Zukunft des Christentums und der Ökumene in missionswissenschaftlicher Perspektive', in Thomas Bremer and Maria Wernsmann (eds.), *Ökumene – überdacht. Reflexionen und Realitäten im Umbruch* (Quaestiones disputatae, 259, Freiburg/Br.: Herder-Verlag, 2014), 276-300, hier: 289-291.

[25] See also Herbst, 'Plural Mission and Missionary Plural in a Post-Socialist Context'.

[26] https://www.oikoumene.org/en/resources/documents/wcc-programmes/interreligious-dialogue-and-cooperation/christian-identity-in-pluralistic-societies/christian-witness-in-a-multi-religious-world, 5 (accessed 24 January 2018).

mission is a freedom for all, not only for Christians. In our secular contexts Christian mission cannot have any legitimacy if it doesn't include upholding the right of people of other religions to invite as well to embrace their faith."[27]

These diverse challenges lead to the assumption that proclaiming the good news in such a secular and cultural formation is basically a challenge to translate Christian beliefs and faith into a language and practices that people immersed in that formation can relate to. In the light of discussions on "Gospel and Culture" and the respective passage in the mission document "Together towards Life", there is a need to discern the Spirit in the secular culture, which includes in some cases a judgement on cultural aspects.[28]

Paradoxically, religion gained new importance in secular society through the politicisation of religion and the religionisation of politics on a global scale, as Johnson Mbilla (PROCMURA) has put it repeatedly. The sociologist of religion Grace Davie (UK) finished a paper given at a conference, "Mission in Secularised Contexts", by formulating a tension she was observing in Western European societies. On the one hand there is what she called a ruthless secularisation that leads in some realms of societies to a threatening religious analphabetism. On the other hand, there is the mentioned growing presence and worldwide impact of religions, as well in the public as in the private sphere. This tension is a big challenge in those societies, which do not know how to cope with it because they have lost knowledge of religion and religious communities or banned it from the public sphere. This tension challenges Christians, religiously indifferent people as well as atheists alike, because the attitude of none of these groups to Christian faith, to churches or to religions implies by itself competences to understand and judge the role of religions or their actors. In that sense beyond theology, a bundle of competences is necessary to deal with religion in the secular society of today: intercultural, inter-confessional and interfaith competences as well as knowing what people believe or don't. So, one dimension of mission in a secular society is to develop such competences and for churches to offer assistance to members and non-members alike. That would pick up the demand of the document "Christian witness" that Christians should not be giving false witness on other faiths. What exactly can be considered and is acceptable as an adequate witness on other faiths in a secular context, is a current challenge for mission in the multi-religious and secular city.

---

[27] See Anders, Biehl, Noort, 'Called to Transforming Discipleship in North-Western Europe', 89.

[28] See Christopher Duraisingh (ed.), *Called to one Hope. The Gospel in Diverse Cultures* (Geneva: WCC, 1998). https://www.oikoumene.org/en/resources/documents/commissions/mission-and-evangelism/together-towards-life-mission-and-evangelism-in-changing-landscapes (accessed 24 January 2018).

Secularisation in Eastern Germany

Martin Reppenhagen and Thomas Schlegel

Introduction

Different studies suggest that Eastern Germany is the most secularised context in the world (Smith 2012, Tomka 2003) – or at least unique in religious matters (Pollack/Rosta 2015, Pickel 2011).[1] It is not our intention to discuss these results[2] or to compete with other regions described in this volume. All the contributions demonstrate in their own way the uniqueness of their respective

---

[1] Tom W. Smith analysed the material of the International Social Survey Program from 1991, 1998 and 2008 (*Beliefs about God across Time and Countries, Report for ISSP and GESIS*, Chicago 2012). The evaluation clearly revealed East German atheism – particularly in an international comparison with 29 other countries. Eastern Germany is in almost every category at the top of the list. 59.4% of the population say, "I don't believe in God and I never have" (Czech Republic and Sweden follow with 51.2% and 32% [Table 2, page 8]) and only 13.2% agree with the statement, "I believe in God now and I always have" (Czech Republic and Japan follow with 19.7% and 25% [Table 2, page 8]). Only 8.2% have a conception of a "personal God" (Czech Republic and France follow with 16.2% and 18.7% [Table 3, page 9]) and in relation to the question concerning "a strong faith in God", the former GDR is in bottom place (2.5% – Japan and Czech Republic have 3.3% and 5.8% [Table 4, page 10]). Smith concludes that "Eastern Germany [is] of course anchoring the secular pole" (6). Miklós Tomka had already reached similar conclusions in 2003 as a result of his studies. In his broad European survey he found that atheism here is "more common, compact and intense" than in "comparable Protestant countries in western, eastern or northern Europe. When people in eastern Germany call themselves atheists they mean a total lack of any religious affiliation". (*Religion in den neuen Bundesländern. Im internationalen Vergleich*, in Karl Gabriel et al. [ed.], *Religion und Kirchen in Ost(Mittel)Europa. Deutschland-Ost* [Ostfildern: Schwabenverlag, 2003], 343–370. All quotations from page 350f.). Other scholars (e.g. Gert Pickel or Detlef Pollack) underline the religious uniqueness of East Germany and try to explain it – historically and in comparison with other countries (Gert Pickel, *Ostdeutschland im europäischen Vergleich – Immer noch ein Sonderfall oder ein Sonderweg?* in Gerd Pickel/Kornelia Sammet (ed.) *Religion und Religiosität im vereinigten Deutschland, Zwanzig Jahre nach dem Umbruch* [Wiesbaden: VS Verlag, 2011], 165-190 and Detlef Pollack/Gergely Rosta, *Religion in der Moderne. Ein internationaler Vergleich* [Frankfurt/New York: Campus Verlag, 2015], 274-288.

[2] Doing so we would have to discuss different concepts of religion and secularisation as well – which would transcend the limited space here.

contexts as the background to mission. However, we found that at international meetings church leaders and pastors tend to measure their commitment to mission in terms of the absolute numbers of believers and non-believers in their societies. The percentage of those who are still members of the church or believe in a supernatural being are the currency they use in these competitions. It is something akin to a "disease of numberitis".[3]

Nonetheless the mentioned studies and the statistics speak for themselves. In the first part of this article we want to highlight some of these studies and portray the religious context of the church in Eastern Germany, particularly as seen by sociologists of religion. To do so, we will first retrace some historical developments. In the second section we highlight the reaction of the churches to this setting over the past years – from reform agendas to different practical ideas as to how to reach the people in the former heart of the historical Reformation region. Some missiological considerations will form the third part – and finally we will summarise our thoughts and give some recommendations for the future.

The Specific Situation in Eastern Germany

There is a story going around conferences and church meetings whenever Christians talk about the religious situation in Eastern Germany. In 1999 a student interviewed people passing by the entrance to Leipzig railway station. He asked them about their fears concerning the Millennium and also whether "their thinking was more Christian or atheistic". A group of young guys – obviously not prepared for the situation – answered, almost collectively: "Neither nor, just normal."[4]

This laconic response probably reflects the feeling of the entire younger generation. They no longer see the need to adopt positions in terms of religion, as the whole topic has become irrelevant. This attitude is reinforced by the old GDR Communist ideology that their parents were brought up on: "Religion is like an artificial addition to the natural human being, a feature that is acquired through education."[5]

Since then almost 20 years have passed. In the meantime religious indifference has spread all over Eastern Germany and has become quite normal – today, even church members can be included in this group.[6]

---

[3] Siga Arles, *World Religion Database: Realities and Concerns*, IBMR 34.1/2010, 20-21, 20.

[4] Monika Wohlrab-Sahr, *Religionslosigkeit als Thema der Religionssoziologie*, in PTh 90 (2001), 152-167, 152.

[5] Axel Noack, *Wo ist aus Sicht der Kirche "außen"?* in Hartmut Bärend (ed.), *Die so genannten Konfessionslosen und die Mission der Kirche. Festgabe für Hartmut Bärend* (Neukirchen: Neukirchener Verlag, 2007), 127–139.

[6] *Engagement und Indifferenz. Kirchenmitgliedschaft als soziale Praxis* (Kirchenamt der EKD [ed.], Hannover 2014).

To explain the situation some sociologists go back to the fact that the Lutheran reformation had its origin and centre in the eastern part of Germany.[7] There is some evidence that since the sixteenth century the church organised by the sovereigns – "cuius regio, eius religio" – was not rooted among the ordinary people – as it was in many Roman Catholic regions. In the nineteenth and twentieth centuries, labour movements were strong here and Protestantism always had its problems in reaching out to the working classes. Having said this, the hardline policy concerning the church and Christians in the German Democratic Republic is the most obvious reason for the atheistic or indifferent situation we have now. After the Second World War a majority of more than 90% of the population were still church members, but in 1989 this figure had dropped to around 25%.

Surprisingly, widely accepted atheism has shown its lasting strength even in post-socialist times. Thus, secularisation may be seen as the "most successful project"[8] of the government of the GDR. Even more than 20 years after reunification Germany remains split into two halves in this respect. Despite shrinking church membership numbers we still have a high percentage of church members in the western part of Germany compared to other European nations. On the other hand, the percentage of people unaffiliated to any church or religion in the eastern part of Germany is the highest in Europe.[9]

"These different percentages have an impact on the attitudes of church members and non-church members alike. There is a difference between living in accordance with or in opposition to the tacit 'norms' of a given context."[10] The "gravity of normality"[11] has an impact on the thinking and acting of individuals, which should not be underestimated. In Western Germany leaving the church is still a deviation from the "volkskirchliche" tradition of the

---

[7] The reasons are discussed in Gert Pickel, *Ostdeutschland im europäischen Vergleich – Immer noch ein Sonderfall oder ein Sonderweg?* (see footnote 1).

[8] Monika Wohlrab-Sahr/Uta Karstein/Thomas Schmidt-Lux, *Forcierte Säkularität. Religiöser Wandel und Generationendynamik im Osten Deutschlands* (Frankfurt a.M.: Campus Verlag, 2009), 14.

[9] Gert Pickel, *Konfessionslose in Ost- und Westdeutschland – ähnlich oder anders?,* in Detlef Pollack/Gert Pickel (eds.), *Religiöser und kirchlicher Wandel in Ostdeutschland 1989-1999* (Opladen: Leske + Budrich Verlag, 2000), 206-235, 210.

[10] Wolfgang Pittkowski, *Konfessionslose in Deutschland,* in *Huber, Wolfgang/Steinacker, Peter/Friedrich, Johannes (Hg.), Kirche in der Vielfalt der Lebensbezüge. Die vierte EKD-Erhebung über Kirchenmitgliedschaft* (Gütersloh: Gütersloher Verlagshaus, 2006), 89–110, hier 89.

[11] "The gravity of normality demonstrates its influence when it comes to the transmission of believes to the next generation. 53% of children of catholic parents will carry on being catholic – and 40% of the protestant. But almost all children of atheist parents will continue to be atheist (98%)." Hans-Werner Eichelberger et al., *Die Kirchen in der DDR vor und nach der Wende*, in Gabriel, *Religion und Kirchen*, 320 (see footnote 1).

parents,[12] whereas in Eastern Germany baptism is a conscious choice, as atheism is the norm.

People in East Germany rarely have problems with a particular denomination or official representatives of the church. It is not the church but religion per se that is suspect and alien.[13] An emerging culture of atheism ("atheisierende Kultur")[14] has developed. Those who are not church members in general do not believe in God or have any religious beliefs.[15]

In the long term the detachment from church and religion has not only reinforced atheism but also has made the entire subject irrelevant and has led to widespread religious indifference. Many people find unbelief a matter of no importance and moreover do not realise that they are non-believers. If the question of the existence of God is of no personal relevance, so is atheism.[16] The whole concept of world views or religions is ignored or rejected. Thus, areligious people don't see themselves as being areligious as long as they are not confronted with the negation, just as non-swimmers only see themselves as such when they go to a swimming pool.[17]

How Did the Churches React? Or: Mission in East Germany

"Although the term 'mission' had been largely suspect in German academic theological literature in general – even in the field of practical theology – the subject of mission has been an accepted concept in eastern German theology and in the church in eastern Germany since the 1960s."[18] One can find different reasons for this. In the 1950s hundreds of thousands of members left the church in Eastern Germany – mainly because of political repression. In 1958 the government dismissed many church members who worked in schools,

---

[12] According to Wolfgang Pittkowski, *Konfessionslose in Deutschland*, 91 (see footnote 16).

[13] 81.6% of the religious non-affiliated agree strongly with the statement that religions as such will result in conflicts and war (see ALLBUS 2008 [n=376]).

[14] Paul M. Zulehner, *Aufbrechen oder untergehen. Wie können unsere Gemeinden zukunftsfähig werden?* in Michael Herbst/Jörg Ohlemacher/Johannes Zimmermann (eds.), *Missionarische Perspektiven für eine Kirche der Zukunft* (BEG 1), (Neukirchen: Neukirchener Verlag, 2005), 17-29, here 18.

[15] Pickel, *Konfessionslose*, 224.

[16] Herbert Schnädelbach, *Religion in der modernen Welt. Vorträge Abhandlungen Streitschriften*, 2. Aufl. (Frankfurt a.M.: S. Fischer Verlag, 2009), 55. This phenomenon can also be called post-atheism, cp. Matthias Clausen, *Evangelistisch predigen vor Post-Atheisten*, in Matthias Clausen/Michael Herbst/Thomas Schlegel (eds.), *Alles auf Anfang. Missionarische Impulse für Kirche in nachkirchlicher Zeit* (Neukirchen-Vluyn: Neukirchener Verlag, 2013), 69-85.

[17] Eberhard Tiefensee, *Religiöse Indifferenz als interdisziplinäre Herausforderung*, in Pickel/Sammet (eds.), *Religion*, 79–101, 85.

[18] Wolfgang Ratzmann, *Gab oder gibt es eine ostdeutsche Praktische Theologie*, in PTh 100 (2011), 278-294, esp. 290.

universities, the police force, etc. There was a battle between the traditional confirmation for young baptised people and the atheist substitute: a socialist ceremony called "Jugendweihe", which conferred adult social status on 14-year-olds. The church failed to win this battle and the regime succeeded in marginalising the church(es)[19] and Christians.

In the 1960s the development was so dramatic that Günter Jacob, general superintendent in Cottbus, announced the end of Christendom.[20] Werner Krusche, one of the most influential bishops during these times, concluded in 1973 that "the church of Christ will increasingly become a diaspora church. However the response of the church to this situation should not be simply to care for those remaining, but to embrace the task of mission with hope in the face of discouragement".[21] In Krusche's view, the situation as a minority is a challenge to become "a church for others" (*Kirche für andere*). This expression, which goes back to Bonhoeffer, reflects the other root of a mission-oriented church in Eastern Germany, namely the living heritage of the Confessing Church (Bekennende Kirche), as many of the church representatives in the GDR had been opponents of the Hitler regime. Finally, debates in the WCC between 1961 (New Delhi) and 1968 (Uppsala) had a considerable influence on the churches in East Germany. An East German working group participated in the process and worked on the "missional structure of the church". Werner Krusche chaired this group in which other East German church leaders were also involved. As a result, major insights into a missional church were common in the churches of the former GDR. They considered themselves a "community for witness and service" (Zeugnis – und Dienstgemeinschaft) and referred to the concept of missio Dei quite naturally.

However, debate and reflection on mission cannot be equated with being missional. Therefore, one can critically ask whether the East German church was in fact reaching outsiders who then became followers of Christ. This is a difficult question to answer as there were no specific evangelistic tools or activities being developed at the time in East Germany. One special form of reaching children was religious education in church (Christenlehre). However, this was seen less in the context of mission but rather as a substitute for religious education classes that had been banned from schools. For Wolfgang Ratzmann, a professor of practical theology in Leipzig, the strong reference to mission was largely theoretical. Neither the lives of individual congregations nor the ministries of the pastors could claim to be missional.[22]

---

[19] In Eastern Germany "church" means mainly the Protestant Church. There is a Roman Catholic Church, but it totals less than 5% of the population.

[20] Günter Jacob, *Die Zukunft der Kirche in der Welt des Jahres 1985*, in ZdZ 21 (1967), 441-451.

[21] Werner Krusche, *Die Gemeinde Jesu Christi auf dem Weg in die Diaspora*, in Werner Krusche, *Verheißung und Verantwortung. Orientierungen auf dem Weg der Kirche* (Berlin-Ost: Evangelische Verlagsanstalt, 1990), 94-113, 95.

[22] Ratzmann, *Ostdeutsche Praktische Theologie*, 291.

In the 1980s the numbers of those leaving the church decreased and the shrinking of the churches had almost stopped. The image of the church was a positive one – mainly because of the space it gave to those who opposed the Socialist Unity Party (SED) regime. They were able to gather in churches, speak freely and sing their songs. The church was a realm that was free of the virtually ubiquitous power of the state, which dominated almost everything. However, although the revolution of 1989 was prepared and rooted in the church, the new society from 1990 onwards no longer needed this secure space. The churches were once again empty and found themselves criticised by historians who publicly argued that many unofficial members of the GDR secret police (IMs) had been working within the church during socialist times and that the churches therefore had been indirectly "controlled by the SED".[23]

In addition, because of the church tax (membership fee levied like a tax from church members) introduced after reunification, many thousands of people left the church after 1989/90, although a few regional churches – particularly in Western Germany – expected that people would return as members. They genuinely thought that the folk church (Volkskirche) would rise again. This did not happen. In fact, the loss of members accelerated with the 1990s. In retrospect the crisis in the Protestant churches was obvious. The experience of the churches under communism was no longer relevant in the changed situation and former church practices during dictatorship failed to help. The new capitalist context was calling for fundamental structural changes while at the same time church membership continued to decline.

Therefore, the congregations, pastors and governing bodies of the church were preoccupied with themselves. They simply did not have the energy to reach out to people in these changing times – times in which more people would probably have been open to the message of a trustworthy God.[24]

One of the first attempts to find a new direction was the paper "Minority with a Future" (Minderheit mit Zukunft).[25] This strategic publication was the result of the findings of a working group, "The Church of Tomorrow" (Kirche von morgen), commissioned by the East German churches. Anyone expecting a missional statement will be disappointed. The authors tried to interpret what had happened in the GDR and described the structural and financial consequences for the churches. The second document from a similar group was

---

[23] "SED-gesteuert" and "Stasi-verseucht": see Axel Noack, *Die wiedervereinigte EKD wird 20 Jahre alt*, in PTh 100 (2011), 295-305, here: 297.

[24] According to Wolf Krötke, *Das Gesicht der evangelischen Kirche in Deutschland. 20 Jahre nach der "Wende" Wahrnehmungen aus östlicher Perspektive*, in Texte aus der VELKD 152/2010, 11-22.

[25] Arbeitskreis "Kirche von morgen": "*Minderheit mit Zukunft*". *Überlegungen und Vorschläge zu Auftrag und Gestalt der ostdeutschen Kirchen in der pluralistischen Gesellschaft*, epd-Dokumentation 3a/1995.

entitled "Church with Hope (Kirche mit Hoffnung)"[26] and was published in 1998. For the first time an official publication addressed the concept of mission in the new context. An entire chapter was entitled "Church is Mission". It attempted to lay the theological foundation for a missional church, but still argued very conventionally (maintain church buildings, focus on families, etc.) and failed to address the issue of religious indifference.

In 2018 there has been no perceptible change. Churches are mostly concerned with adapting their structures to rapidly falling membership rates (around 2% per year) and are trying to maintain the old system of the folk church – as a minority. But there are some who see very clearly that this will not be an option in the future. Ilse Junkermann, bishop of the Central church of Germany (EKM), founded in 2009, stated: "The old system has come to an end. All our efforts have so far been unable to halt the decline."[27] As a consequence of this insight, the synod of the EKM started the process of fresh expressions of church (Erprobungsräume) in 2014.[28] It widened the view of the church to include other forms and allowed religious entrepreneurs to plant new congregations with a different profile. Today there are 27 fresh expression congregations in Eastern Germany. Christians meet in a school, at a railway station, in urban suburbs, in a café and are trying to communicate the Gospel to those who had never come into contact with Christians and the message of a loving God. So, a great deal is happening parallel to official church initiatives.

About half of those who attend religious education classes in school are not baptised. In villages where the church infrastructure is very weak, atheists and Christians alike take care of the church building and in 2017 – the anniversary of the Reformation – many non-Christians were involved in preparing the celebrations in different places. So, we can assume that many people are being reached by the Gospel, albeit not through strategically planned activities.

However, only rarely are synods and other church gatherings addressing the phenomenon of religious indifference. This debate is only being conducted in universities or at occasional conferences. One institute that is a front runner in this whole issue is the "Research Institute for Evangelism and Church Development" with its director, Michael Herbst.[29] It was founded in April 2004 and is situated in the far northeast of Germany – at the University of Greifswald. It tries to examine how non-Christians are reached[30] and suggests how to develop the church in an atheist context.

---

[26] Eine ostdeutsche kirchliche Arbeitsgruppe: *"Kirche mit Hoffnung". Leitlinien künftiger kirchlicher Arbeit in Ostdeutschland,* epd-Dokumentation 17/1998.

[27] Ilse Junkermann, *Gemeinde neu finden – Vom Rückbau zum Umbau,* in VELKD-Informationen 145/2014, 2-6, 2.

[28] www.erprobungsraeume-ekm.de.

[29] https://ieeg.uni-greifswald.de/en/.

[30] For example, Johannes Zimmermann/Anna-Konstanze Schröder (eds.), *Wie finden Erwachsene zum Glauben? Einführung und Ergebnisse der Greifswalder Studie* (Neukirchen-Vluyn: Aussaat, 2011, 2nd ed.).

Another centre of competence for the question of atheism was the "Centre for Church in Dialogue" (Arbeitsstelle Kirche im Dialog) in Rostock. Between 2011 and 2016 three regional congregations tried to explore "how the Church in northern Germany can communicate with secular people".[31]

In Halle a research unit, "Religious Communication and Learning Processes" (Forschungsstelle Religiöse Kommunikations- und Lernprozesse),[32] was established in October 2011 in the theological faculty. This unit is researching religious learning processes and methods of communicating the Gospel in a secular society – particularly in schools and other educational contexts.

Missiological Reflections

Considering all the aforementioned statistics and processes relating to Eastern Germany it is hardly surprising that a few sociologists and theologians still adhere to modified versions of the secularisation theory. However, in contrast to Berger there seems to be little evidence that "modernity does not necessarily lead to a decline of religion. What it does lead to, more or less necessarily, is religious pluralism".[33] In such a context one might be tempted to speak of the "eclipse of God" (Martin Buber) with the umbra shadow ("Kernschatten") right here. The old understanding of the *homo naturaliter religiosus* is being seriously questioned and being replaced with the concept of *homo areligiosus.* "Eastern Germany is as areligious as Bavaria is Catholic."[34] Eastern Germany seems to be highly immune to religion and spiritual quests. The majority of the population lives in an "immanent frame", where "science has disproved God",[35] or in the words of Lesslie Newbigin, think within "a system of belief (…) which in principle denies the existence (…) of realities other than those which can be measured by methods of natural science".[36] As Charles Taylor stated, "the level of understanding of some of the great languages of transcendence" has almost completely disappeared and a "massive unlearning" has taken place.[37] However, this is not necessarily the result of a considered

---

[31] https://kircheimdialog.de/.

[32] http://www.theologie.uni-halle.de/pt_rp/rkl/.

[33] Peter L. Berger, *Pluralism, Protestantization, and the Voluntary Principle*, in Banchoff, Thomas (ed.), *Democracy and the New Religious Pluralism* (Oxford: Oxford University Press, 2007), 19-29, 21.

[34] Eberhard Tiefensee, *Chancen und Grenzen von "Mission" – im Hinblick auf die konfessionelle Situation in den neuen Bundesländern*, in Matthias Bartels/Martin Reppenhagen (eds.), *Gemeindepflanzung – ein Modell für die Kirche der Zukunft?* (Neukirchen-Vluyn: Neukirchener Verlag, 2006), 68-85, 69.

[35] Charles Taylor, *A Secular Age* (Cambridge: The Belknap Press, 2007), 548-556. 593.

[36] Lesslie *Newbigin, Honest Religion for Secular Man* (London: S.C.M. Press, 1966, 2nd ed.), 8.

[37] Taylor, *Secular*, 534f.,727.

process or reflection, but rather of indifference and running with the crowd. One could call it "amnesic".[38] East Germans by and large don't miss transcendence. They are "happily unchurched".[39]

All the terms used here to describe the East German context are used by religious people. The unchurched or areligious people would never use such terms to describe themselves. They are just normal people, as stated in the opening passage. Christians or other people with religious persuasions and atheists are in a minority situation, as the majority of the population considers the issue of transcendence irrelevant. A Pomeranian pastor once put it this way: "I tried to live according to 1 Pet. 3:15 – 'Always be prepared to give an answer to everyone who asks you to give the reason for the hope that you have.' (NIV) But no one ever asked."

In such a context it is not enough to speak of a post-Christendom situation; what we are seeing is a post-Christian culture where the Christian narrative has lost its impact on society and on individuals. The experience of the church in the GDR shows how Christian symbols and rituals can be replaced with state-backed secular symbols and rituals, just as the "Jugendweihe" (youth initiation ceremony) replaced Protestant confirmation for the majority of teenagers.

The Missiological Challenge

The challenge in such a context is how is it possible to communicate a religious message to people who are not asking religious questions. To quote Dietrich Bonhoeffer, the question is: "How can Christ become Lord of the religionless as well?"[40] Or in the words of Dutch missiologist Hendrik Kraemer: "There is the obligation to strive for the presentation of the Christian truth in terms and modes of expression that make its challenge intelligible and related to the peculiar quality of reality in which they live." And he continued that this should happen "against the background of the universal human problems of aspiration, frustration, misery and sin, because these men and women must be for us in the first place human beings, fellow-men, and not non-Christians".[41]

"Europe: Christendom Graveyard or Christian Laboratory" was the headline on the title page of the International Bulletin of Missionary Research in 2007.[42] When we consider Eastern Germany with its strong signs of collapse, it is

---

[38] Danièle Hervieu-Léger, *Secularization, Tradition and New Forms of Religiosity: Some Theoretical Proposals*, in Eileen Barker and Margit Warburg (eds.), *New Religions and New Religiosity* (Aarhus: Universitetsforlag, 1998), 28-44, 31, 38.

[39] Hans-Martin *Barth, Konfessionslos glücklich. Auf dem Weg zu einem religionstranszendenten Christsein* (Gütersloh: Gütersloher Verlag, 2013).

[40] Dietrich Bonhoeffer, *Letter 30 April 1944*, in Eberhard Bethge (ed.), *Dietrich Bonhoeffer: Letters and Papers from Prison* (London: SCM Press, 1981), 92.

[41] Hendrik Kraemer, *The Christian Message in a Non-Christian World* (Grand Rapids 1956, 3rd ed.), 303.

[42] IBMR 31/3 July 2007.

tempting to apply the graveyard verdict. Without ignoring the still ongoing process of church decline, as Andrew Walls pointed out, the "Christendom graveyard" could be the very best "laboratory for new forms of faith, new structures of organisation and interaction that can accommodate to a dominant secular environment".[43] According to Walls, the expansion of Christianity is a history of advance and recession. Former centres of Christianity may be marginalised while Christianities at the margins may become future centres. It is at the frontiers in particular that Christianity can be potentially strengthened, whereas in the centres of Christianity without such an interaction the Christian faith is weakened.[44] "That means, in one sentence, that faith is kept strong by living on the frontier. *It is the church which lives on the frontier that will be ready to advance in strength.*"[45]

Searching for Points of Contact

While searching for a point of contact, first, missiological humility is called for. What we are experiencing is not success and major breakthroughs but rather our own helplessness and uncertainty.[46] But there is a growing awareness of the fact that in a secular society there are no longer any non-religious reasons to adhere to religion and that the church may have to free itself from social control and divest itself of political power in order to strengthen its own witness in an areligious context.[47] Thus, the churches' witness may remain a "defective testimony. But it is not therefore ineffectual – quite the contrary".[48]

The question is: how is it possible to find a point of contact for a religious message in a society without religious awareness or religious curiosity?

Even the typical points of contact don't apply in the Eastern German context. There is no common knowledge of God. A common code of ethics, although basically Christian, is not related to the Christian faith or to the church. And even a personal crisis is usually confronted on an immanent level

---

[43] Philip Jenkins, *God's Continent: Christianity, Islam, and Europe's Religious Crisis* (Oxford: Oxford University Press, 2007), 19.

[44] Andrea F. Walls, *The Cross-Cultural Process in Christian History* (Maryknoll: Orbis Press, 2002), 30.

[45] Lesslie Newbigin, *The Pattern of Partnership*, in *Lectures, The East Asia Christian Conference 1959 and the John R. Mott Memorial, A Decisive Hour for the Christian Mission* (London: SCM Press, 1960), 34-45, 44f.

[46] Even the Free Evangelical Churches (Freie evangelische Gemeinden), which have expanded in Western Germany, have been unable to make breakthroughs after the fall of the Berlin Wall. *Schröder, Sabine, Konfessionslose erreichen. Gemeindegründungen von freikirchlichen Initiativen seit der Wende 1989 in Ostdeutschland* (Neukirchen-Vluyn: Neukirchener Verlag, 2007).

[47] Niklas Luhmann, *Die Religion der Gesellschaft* (Frankfurt am Main: Suhrkamp Verlag, 2000), 136. 145.

[48] Lesslie Newbigin, The Light has Come: An Exposition of the Fourth Gospel (Grand Rapids et. al.: William B Eerdman, 1982), 20.

without recourse to a transcendent being or God. There is neither a common longing for any transcendence nor an experience of a void that could be met by a god or a religious message.[49]

One might start by questioning the existence of a religious market and the rational choice theory. The basic assumption here is that all individuals have a god-shaped void that can only be filled by religion. All the religions are competing with one another on the religious market and seek to win followers and people make rational choices concerning religion.[50] This results in what could be called a religious-need-oriented exchange programme.[51] But could it be that simply focusing on human needs restricts the proactive power of the message of the cross? In doing so the Gospel becomes an affirmative but not challenging power that transforms lives and leads men and women to new horizons. It is the boundless dynamism of the Gospel and the Christian faith bringing answers to questions many people don't dare to ask.[52] Consequently it is a "breaking out into the broader field".[53]

On the basis of Ludwig Wittgenstein's assertion – "For an answer which cannot be expressed the question, too, cannot be expressed"[54] – any arbitrary quest for God cannot be answered by the Gospel. It is rather the case that divine revelation and the word of God prompt the quest for God. In a post-Christian context, talking about God or witnessing to the Gospel does not depend on arbitrary religious questions or some inkling of transcendence, but on the faithful remembrance of and witness to God's revelation as narrated in the Bible. Furthermore, in an areligious or even a context hostile to religion, the distinction between communication of the Gospel and religious communication is crucial, because the critique of religion is an essential part of the biblical

---

[49] Thomas Schlegel, *Mission im Osten Deutschlands und das Problem des Anknüpfungspunktes,* in Matthias Clausen, et al. (eds.), *Alles auf Anfang. Missionarische Impulse für Kirche in nachkirchlicher Zeit* (Neukirchen-Vluyn: Neukirchener Verlag, 2013), 116-134.

[50] Roger Finke and Rodney Stark, *The Churching of America 1776-2005: Winners and Losers in Our Religious Economy* (New Brunswick et al. 2005); Laurance R. Iannaccone, *Rational Choice: Framework for the Scientific Study of Religion*, in Lawrence A. Young (ed.), *Rational Choice Theory and Religion. Summary and Assessment* (London: Routledge, 1997), 24-44, 26f.

[51] For a deeper critical interaction see Stefan Paas, *Church Planting in the Secular West. Learning from the European Experience* (Grand Rapids: William B Eerdman, 2016), 127-146.

[52] Gerhard Wegner, *Religiöse Kommunikation und Kirchenbindung. Ende des liberalen Paradigmas?* (Leipzig: Evangelische Verlagsanstalt, 2014), 64f.

[53] Taylor, *Secular Age*, 769.

[54] Ludwig Wittgenstein, *Tractatus logico-philosophicus (es 12)* (Frankfurt am Main: Suhrkamp Verlag, 1977, 12. ed.), Nr. 6.5 (114).

tradition. Thus, witnessing to the Gospel and criticism of religion are intrinsically linked.[55]

Communicating the Gospel in Eastern Germany still means entering unchartered territory. But as a part of an incarnational mission, as a part of God's kenotic coming into the world, a missional approach seeks to encounter and interact with people and the context in which they live.

A Christian Faith Equipped for Diaspora Situations

The Christian church finds itself in Eastern Germany in a minority situation where the majority of people believe in other plausibilities.[56] In such a situation a Christian faith that is equipped for diaspora situations does not give in to the pressures to conform to majority views but has its own impact on the surrounding context. This is particularly important in contexts where the Christian faith is no longer a matter of course in society and individual lives. Where plausibility structures in society are lost, where it is no longer plausible to be a Christian, the church as a "cognitive minority" (Peter L. Berger) needs to find its own ones. The church becomes its own plausibility structure. The transition from a culture-based Christian faith to a personal faith lived in community has to be made. This needs to be grounded in a missional understanding of the church as to how to communicate the Gospel and assume responsibility for the context in which the church lives.

---

[55] Ulrich H.J. Körtner, *Resonanzen. Über die Reichweite der Kirche in der Gesellschaft*, in Detlef Pollack and Gerhard Wegner (eds.), *Die soziale Reichweite von Religion und Kirche. Beiträge zu einer Debatte in Theologie und Soziologie* (Würzburg: Ergon Verlag, 2017), 217-230, 228.

[56] The following thoughts are taken from Johannes Zimmermann, *Diasporafähiger Glaube: Eine Herausforderung für christliche Gemeinden in einer pluralen Gesellschaft*, in Martin Reppenhagen (ed.), *Kirche zwischen postmoderner Kultur und Evangelium* (Beiträge zu Evangelisation und Gemeindeentwicklung, 15) (Neukirchen-Vluyn: Neukircher Verlag, 2010), 39-62.

Mission in Secularised Contexts of Europe: An Orthodox Perspective, with Special References to the Romanian Context

Daniel Buda

Introduction and Some Terminological Clarifications

In this article I try to present an Orthodox perspective on secularity, secularisation and secularism by formulating, in the first part, a few general principles on these issues that might be accepted by all Orthodox living in different contexts today. In the second part, I refer to Romania, my home country, as a secularised context in Europe, describing and analysing its specificities both in the communist period and in the post-communist time, mainly as I perceive it at a personal level. This self-imposed restriction is necessary because there is a large diversity of "secularised contexts" in the Orthodox world caused by different contexts, so they cannot be all properly presented here.

Everyone who is dealing with secularity, secularisation and secularism faces a terminological dilemma, as these terms are used with different understandings from context to context, language to language and even person to person. Therefore, I will explain here what I personally understand by using them (exceptions are, of course, the quotations). *Secularity* means "worldly", something that belongs to this world, i.e. to a specific context, generation and time. *Secularisation* is a process that leads to a certain type and level of "secularised context". *Secularism* means an extreme form of the process of secularisation, i.e. a certain context in which the "death of God" has been declared and where there is no or very little space for any form of religiosity in public or even in private space.[1]

I concur with the terminological proposal of the editors of this volume to speak about "secularised context(s)" as milieus where the process of secularisation has reached a certain level. Therefore, I will speak about Romania as "a secularised context" and describe in detail what that meant in

---

[1] Melvin Tinker, *Secularization: Myth or Menace? An Assessment of Modern 'Worldliness', Themelios,* 38:3 (2013), 403.

the communist time and what it means today, i.e. in the post-communist period (after December 1989).

Is there a Generally Accepted Orthodox Position Regarding Secularisation?

In the past decades, many Orthodox scholars researched the phenomenon of secularisation in their contexts and proposed solutions to limit or even overcome it, having as starting points the Orthodox tradition and its wisdom in dealing with the world and with increasingly different contexts in which different Orthodox churches and their believers have lived in the past decades. The interest of Orthodox for this phenomenon grows, as secularisation has for a long time been a reality also in countries where the Orthodox are a majority. In the past century, in many countries, especially in Central and Eastern Europe, communism and its ideology imposed upon Orthodox churches an aggressive and state-guided secularist ideology that was aimed, if not to immediately destroy religions and religiosities of any kind, at least to lead in the long term to such a result. In countries that did not face communism as a ruling ideology – such as Greece – the process of secularisation developed following in general the same parameters as in Western Europe or in North America. As Orthodoxy became in the past 200 years a more and more global confession, being present in all parts of the world and not only in its own traditional regions (Central-Eastern Europe and the Middle East), it was confronted with all sorts of secularised contexts. Starting from this present reality, I will try to present here briefly a few leading principles that the Orthodox use as guidelines while dealing with secularisation.

1. The first principle is that in the Orthodox tradition, *the created world* to whom human beings belong as image of God (cf. Gen. 1:27), *is perceived as God`s creation and is therefore good.* God himself defined it as such: "God saw everything that he has made, and indeed, it was very good" (Gen. 1:31). Exegeses of Eastern Church Fathers of Gen. 1:31 confirm and deepen this fundamental belief that the world is good because it was created by God and it remained good also after the fall of the human being into sin. Throughout centuries, the Eastern Church condemned the Gnostics and other heretic groups that considered that the created world has an evil nature because it was created by an ignorant and inferior demiurge and not by the true God.

The fact that the nature of the created world is good means that human beings must have interest for the world and everything related to it. "Let us give all attention to *saeculum*"[2] – this is how Ion Bria, a well-known Romanian-Orthodox missiologist summarises an important aspect of Dumitru Staniloae's theology, one of the most prominent Orthodox theologians of the

[2] Ion Bria, *Tratat de Teologie Dogmatică şi Ecumenică*, Bucharest, 1999, 53.

twentieth century. The Orthodox are interested in the world and in what is happening in the world, and also in phenomena like secularisation.

2. *The human being has a leading role and a God-given responsibility in and for the created world.* This responsibility was assigned by God: "God blessed them (i.e. the man and the woman), and God said to them, 'Be fruitful and multiply, and fill the earth and subdue it'" (Gen. 1:28).[3] Therefore, the human being cannot be indifferent to anything that happens in the world, including any form of society or political order the human being lives in. For centuries, the Orthodox Church condemned separatist-heretic groups that showed disregard for the world, for the society and for the state order by demanding their members not to pay taxes or not to bring children into the world. Genuine monastic life of any form does not contradict this principle. The monks might leave the world, but they do it "for the world". It means that they continuously pray for the world while they are not living in the world. Also, when the Church or a community was in extreme danger, the monks living in isolation left their places and came into cities to save them. There are many examples of this. The famous Anthony the Great († 356) left the Egyptian desert when he heard that his name was used by the Arians to propagate their teaching in the metropolis of Alexandria. He "descended from the mountain, and "having entered Alexandria, he denounced the Arians".[4] More recently, in the nineteenth century, Hesychast monks from Mount Athos descended into Greek cities when the very existence of the nation was endangered. Social and political engagement of Orthodox believers, even in state orders that are quite averse, is part of the Orthodox ethos.

3. A leading principle in Orthodox tradition for dealing with the state order and therefore with multiple forms of secularised contexts is the one formulated by our Lord Jesus Christ: "Give therefore to the emperor the things that are the emperor's, and to God the things that are God's" (Mt. 22: 21). The Orthodox are normally faithful to the state order they live in, meaning that they pay the taxes required and pray for the state leadership. *The Acts of Martyrs* – a collection of documents that witness the suffering and martyrdom of individual Christians or of groups of Christians in the pre-Constantinian Roman Empire – contain several statements of Christians who were facing court investigation in which they underline that they pay the taxes required by the Roman authorities and pray for the emperor and for the Roman state and authorities in which they live along with non-Christians; therefore their prosecution and penalty is without reason.

---

[3] All Biblical quotations are taken from NRSV, 2009.

[4] St Athanasius of Alexandria, *Life of Anthony (Vita Antoni)* in Athanasius: *Select Works and Letters*, Nicene and Post-Nicene Fathers vol. IV, Philip Schaff (ed.), NY, 1892, 444.

There are two fundamental attitudes regarding the world, worldly power and state order described in the New Testament: (1) *the Pauline one*, as expressed in Romans 13: 1-6:

> Let every person be subject to the governing authorities; for there is no authority except from God, and those authorities that exist have been instituted by God. Therefore, whoever resists authority resist what God has appointed, and those who resist will incur judgement. For rulers are not a terror to good conduct, but to bad. Do you wish to have no fear of the authority? Then do what is good, and you will receive its approval; for it is God`s servant for your good. But if you do what is wrong, you shall be afraid, for the authority does not bear the sword in vain! It is the servant of God to execute wrath on the wrongdoer. Therefore, one must be subject, not only because of conscience. For the same reason you also pay taxes, for the authorities are God`s servants, busy with this very thing.

(2) *the Revelation view*, as summarised in chapter 13 where "a beast" is described, which was followed by "the whole earth" (v. 3) and was "worshiped" by the "entire world" (v. 4). Exceptions are "the saints" and therefore the beast made war with them (v. 8).

It is certain that the Orthodox tradition was, during its bi-millenary history, closer to the Pauline approach from Rom. 13:1-6. Even the "beast" from Rev. 13 was not assimilated in Orthodoxy so much with a state order, but rather with the world that hates God and his saints.[5] This approach ensured Orthodoxy an uninterrupted existence, sometimes with growth and flourishing under worldly powers that considered Orthodoxy the official state religion (like the Byzantine Empire, medieval Russia or the medieval kings of Wallachia and Moldova) and even under worldly powers that did not persecute it, but were rather neutral to Orthodoxy; sometimes just surviving and struggling to maintain an already existing *status quo*, as was the case under the Ottoman Empire, which discriminated against its Christian citizens and sporadically persecuted them by not protecting them from certain forms and tendencies of what we call today fundamentalism.

4. *Authentic Orthodoxy always lived in a certain tension with the world and with the worldly authorities, spirit and way of being.* If this tension was not there, this was a sign that Orthodoxy stopped being prophetic and genuinely loyal to the Gospel. In other words, the world and any form of worldly authority contains a certain level of secularity, and a certain process of secularisation is going on. Also, for the Orthodox there is no context that is completely secularised. For the Orthodox, there is always a certain incompatibility and tension between the message of the Gospel and the spirit of this world. Orthodoxy felt always called to play a prophetic role by witnessing

---

[5] Adolf Martin Ritter, *Johannes Chrysostomus und das Römische Reich im Gespräch mit neuer Literatur, Studia Chrysostomica. Aufsätze zu Weg, Werl und Wirkung des Johannes Chrysostomus (ca. 349-407),* Tübingen, 2012, 142.

to the message of the Gospel in the world, also with the risk of sometimes angering the worldly power and its leading representatives, even if they were Orthodox Christians. The history of the Byzantine Empire and of medieval Russian, Wallachian, Moldavian, Bulgarian and Serbian kingdoms are full of cases in which emperors or kings broke the moral norms of the Gospel and eventually patriarchs, metropolitans or bishops refused to give them Eucharist and sometimes criticised them in public sermons for doings that were incompatible with Christian existence. There are countless examples when church leaders raised their voice for the marginalised and for the poor and against the rich who lived in greed and luxury, ignoring the sufferings of other fellow Christians. St John Chrysostom († 407) is probably the most famous example of a church leader who faced persecution, exile and martyrdom from a Christian emperor of the Byzantine Empire because he rejected luxury and a comfortable life for the sake of simplicity and humbleness, because he openly criticised the unchristian life of the Christian elite, including members of the imperial family, and because he asked clergy and monastics to genuinely live the Gospel and properly accomplish their ministries.

5. *Orthodoxy is very reluctant to any form of "political religion"; however, it would promote its values in any context, even in (extremely) secularised ones.* From an Orthodox perspective, theocracy is certainly not a solution for the world. Even the Byzantine Empire, the state that remained in human history as an Orthodox super-power, was not a theocracy.[6] Historical experience proved that imposed morality leads to grotesque forms of formalism and immorality. Orthodoxy is against any form of imposing Christian values with the support or with the means of a state or any other worldly authority. Patristic literature is full of motivational and moralistic sermons and treaties while its history does not know significant cases of coercion measures taken to impose an Orthodox way of life. Christian values have to be lived out and experienced based on and starting from an internal conviction.

In our times, Ion Bria excellently summarised all these ideas:

> The church becomes a place where people can have a new vision of history only if it is able to distinguish between the civil loyalty and the political ordination, by denying the messianic character of any social and political system. The loyalty of the Christians is an act of social transformation, not a force in maintaining the political stagnation. Instead the church should not impose a program of Christian social order as it does not have a comprehensive plan for humanity and it is not a secular power. Nevertheless, if the church does not continue to exercise its prophetic function and does not try to illuminate the organisation of the world, it

[6] See https://www.impantokratoros.gr/byzantine-stathe-theocracy.en.aspx.

hypocritically proclaims the Gospel and celebrates the Eucharist. Orthodoxy is very sensitive to any sign of confusion between theology and ideology.[7]

The lack of coercion measures for imposing Orthodox morality does not exclude the support of the Orthodox throughout history for having legislation that supports basic Christian-Orthodox values. The lack of their support, inclusive at a legislative level, is perceived as a form of secularisation. For example, some Orthodox churches living in a majority situation would campaign for having an anti-abortion law or a clear paragraph in the state constitution that defines marriage as a free union between a man and a woman. Also, the Orthodox would participate in pro-life manifestations, but genuine Orthodox would never condemn those mothers who choose to take abortion, or homosexuals, but rather morally support them, while the church would provide spiritual care and, where necessary, also material support. Also, when such a struggle is lost at the legislative level, Orthodox will continue to promote their values in societies they live in. There are Orthodox majority countries where abortion is legally allowed, and such a reality is certainly perceived as a sign of secularisation (or even of secularism). In such a context, the Orthodox will continue to promote (never to impose!) their basic moral values that life is a sacred gift of God and the human being is not allowed to interrupt it. Clergy would preach against abortion; pregnant mothers will be advised not to take an abortion because there is no reason for such an act. If material means for raising a child are not there, the church will provide them. I try to imagine what St John Chrysostom – one of the most famous Christian-moral preachers in history and my favourite – would say about a context in which Christians would do their best to avoid legalisation of abortion? I think he would say something like: "We did our best, and we did not succeed. Is this a reason for lamentation? Is this a reason for not promoting our values? No! As long as our mothers are not forced to abortion, there is no reason for us to sorrow! Does the state allow abortion? Convince our mothers to give birth to their children and in this way, we are the winners!"

6. I am personally convinced – and I hope that many Orthodox will agree with me – that *there are also positive aspects of secularity*. These positive aspects are not related only strictly with secularity understood as a certain age or time and the good reading of it (*kairos*), or with a certain context and the wise use of it, but also to what opportunities are offered to the church that is liberated from the protection (sometimes protectionism!) of a certain state order with all its uncertain or even negative consequences. I say this based on the experiences of several Orthodox churches in the recent past and nowadays in "religiously neutral" states or milieus. Many were thinking that in majority contexts Orthodoxy got so used to the protection of the states that inherited in

---

[7] Ion Bria, *Mission and Secularization in Europe,* International Review of Mission, 77:1 (1988), 122-124.

one way or another the byzantine tradition of supporting the church that it cannot survive or even develop in a "religiously neutral" context, like the US. The reality proved that Orthodoxy is able to grow and develop in such contexts, of course, as long as religious freedom is guaranteed. In the context of the New World, i.e. in a secularised context where state support, with all its positive and negative aspects, is not available, Orthodoxy seems to have the capacity of mobilising its values and missionary resources and eventually grow. I dare say that Orthodoxy would be able to grow in the same manner in any context that provides religious freedom, not only in North America or Australia where the church is growing nowadays.

Archbishop Anastasios of Tirana, one of the leading figures of Orthodoxy today, affirms that "secular features of modern life", which are for him the "rapid development of science and technology, international law, and international organisations whose programs are worldwide in scope", are "characterised as the secularised products of religion, and more specifically as the secularised products of Christian civilization". In his opinion, "we should not view such secular or (extra-religious) forces as rivals, but as collaborators in the struggle to realise our universal spiritual goals of world understanding and rapprochement."[8] Indeed, this is another good example of positive secularity with which the church could collaborate for the common good of all human beings.

7. *The church has to face courageously various processes of secularisation and stand for its values by bearing witness.* Genuine and deep discernment regarding secularity, secularisation and secularism is necessary. First, one needs to understand if what we use to label as secularisation or secularism is really regularisation or secularism. I often hear my colleagues, both professors of theology and clergy, saying: "Because of secularism…" this or that happens, usually negative. In a way, secularism became a kind of "scapegoat" for everything that is negative for the church. If secularism means the postulate of human beings free from religious rule and teaching, the Orthodox have a problem with such a statement. If secularism means the promotion of ethical choices that go against biblical principles and Christian ethical values, the Orthodox will refute it. For example, abortion and euthanasia have been and will be considered "great offences against divine order" for the reason that "the human being is the icon of God".[9] One needs courage and a prophetic voice for doing it. "In a divided world, the Church must be prepared to provide the truth of God."[10]

---

[8] Archbishop Anastasios (Yannoulatos), *Facing The World. Orthodox Christian Essays on Global Concerns*, translated by Pavlos Gottfried. WCC Publications: Geneva, 2003, 18-19.

[9] John Anthony McGuckin, *The Orthodox Church. An Introduction to its History, Doctrine, and Spiritual Culture,* Willey-Blackwell: 2011, p.416.

[10] Ion Bria, *Mission and Secularization*, 119.

The Orthodox are very worried of the way in which some churches of other traditions adapted in some more and more secularised contexts to "the spirit of this world" not only by accepting but also even promoting ethical values that for the Orthodox are unbiblical. In this way, some of the churches even became contributors to the process of secularisation and promoters of secularism.

The role of religion in general in relationship to secularisation and "secularism" (or "secular contexts") is both "prophetical and critical".[11] As we speak here about the prophetic and critical role of religion in its struggle with secularism, we affirm at the same time the need for cooperation, both at inter-confessional and, where possible and appropriate, at inter-faith level for successfully facing secularisation and secularism. And finally, one should not exclude from this cooperation "the people of good will" who might be non-believers but respect the choice of the majority of humanity since its existence to believe in a religious manner and accept proper religious manifestations, inclusive in the public sphere. It is maybe superfluous to add that people of faith should respect the right of anyone to be and even to become a non-believer, including appropriate manifestations that might result from it. Finally, none should forget that "secularisation remains a question of witness, not confrontation".[12] We do not need to confront secularisation, but to witness to the Gospel in secularised contexts, proposing in this way the Gospel as alternative.

Romania – A Specific Secularised Context in Recent History

Can we speak about a "Romanian form" of secularisation, or about Romania as an (East)-European "secularised context" in recent history, i.e. during communism and in the post-communist period? The answer is, in my opinion, certainly positive. I hope that my presentation that follows here will be convincing.

Much more than other political ideologies, communism claimed to possess the absolute and ideal solutions for all domains of public and private life. In this sense, communism claimed to be more a religion than an ideology, therefore it left little space for God and a religion aimed to worship Him. With the exception of Albania, which officially proclaimed itself in 1967 "the first atheistic state in the world",[13] in the rest of the communist countries freedom of religion was constitutionally guaranteed and the practice of religion was tolerated for those who were willing to continue embracing religious ignorance.

---

[11] Ciprian Iulian Toroczkai, *Secularization and Its Influence on the Work of Two Orthodox Scholars, The Ecumenical Review,* 68:2, 2016, 265.

[12] Ion Bria, *Mission and Secularization,* 124.

[13] Finnger Hiorth, Albania: An Atheistic State?, Occasional Papers on Religion in Eastern Europe, 10:5, 1990, 14.

Communist propaganda, however, made immense efforts to combat this "ignorance".

As there was a general hostile attitude of communist ideology regarding religion and religiosity, one may also agree that this ideology has been implemented in various specific ways in every country. For example, the situation in Albania or in the Soviet Union was much worse than in Romania. These differences emerged from: (1) the way communist ideology regarding religion and religiosity was understood by different communist leaders in different contexts; (2) the pre-communist history of every country and its religious specificities; (3) the general evolution and development in different communist countries in the communist period.

The Communist Period

The attitude of communists in Romania regarding religion was based on the experience of the communists in the Soviet Union with religion. After several years of brutal persecution of any form of religion in the Soviet Union, soviet communists realised that it is impossible to totally destroy religion. Therefore, in the first years after 1948, when communism was imposed in Romania with the support of the Red Army, the communists did not try to destroy any form of religiosity in Romania, but to drastically limit its dimension and especially its influence in the public sphere. Therefore, a lot of church properties were confiscated, many clergy, especially those who were part of right radical groups such as The Iron Guard or The Legion of Archangel Michael before the Second World War, were imprisoned and some of them condemned to death; monastic life was drastically restricted as many monasteries were closed down;[14] several theological schools were closed; social and diaconal networks of the church were destroyed. In other words, Romanian communists managed *to push religiosity out of the public sphere and to restrict it to church or worship buildings*. This policy was applied, more or less, to all churches and religious communities in Romania. The exception was the Greek-Catholic Church, which was outlawed, and its membership and property transferred to the Romanian Orthodox Church. As a majority church, the Romanian Orthodox Church was sometimes more exposed to restrictions and frictions; sometimes it was privileged and protected in comparison with other minority communities.

In the given situation, the Orthodox Church chose passive resistance. It reorganised its pastoral activities within the church buildings; it avoided having any statement or attitude regarding public life. The Orthodox Church continued to preach and eventually to passively oppose the communist ideology, the "science of salvation".[15]

---

[14] See Nicodim Nicolaescu, The Catastrophic Effects of Decree 410/1959 on Monasticism in Communist Romania, Teologia, 58:1 (2014), 9-26.

[15] Daniel Ciobotea, *Confessing the Truth in Love: Orthodox Perceptions of Life, Mission and Unity*, ed. Trinitas, Iasi, 2001, p.159.

A major change in Romanian communism took place in 1964: it turned to a nationalist form of communism after gaining ideological independency from the Soviet Union. This implied a major revision and reconsideration of Romanian history. By this revision, Romanian communists realised that the Orthodox Church was an inseparable part of Romanian history. They also realised that (1) The Orthodox Church *played a crucial role in the history of Romanian people*: the first schools, first translations into Romanian, first printed books, first hospitals, first orphanages; first pharmacies appeared and that the first Romanian scholars, first diplomats, etc. were clergy; and (2) The Orthodox Church *could not be accused of major sins related with the past*: Orthodoxy did not have Inquisition or other forms of oppression; it was not against progress and common national interest. On the contrary. For these reasons, after 1964 the communist regime has had a more tolerant attitude vis-à-vis religious life. However, religiosity was kept out of the public sphere. Mass media was not allowed to present any news about religious life. I remember that as a child I never heard a word on TV about Christmas or the birth of Jesus. Otherwise religious life was allowed to continue discretely. At least in small cities, like the one where I grew up, anyone could go to church in silence. Members of the Communist Party and those working in public service needed to be more discrete, therefore they went to monasteries for praying and for getting major sacraments like marriage or baptism of new family members. A large majority of children were baptised in communist Romania.

Romanian communists destroyed a lot, but what they did not destroy remained very well preserved. This affirmation based on Romanian realities applies also to religious life in Romania. Is it not a paradox that Romania is one of the most religious countries in Europe after 40 years of communism (1948-1989), and some of the West European countries have a high percentage of agnostics and atheists? This apparent paradox could be explained by two facts: (1) The communists radically diminished and marginalised religious life in Romania and did not try to destroy it, as was the case in Albania or the Soviet Union; (2) The Romanian communists isolated Romania from the rest of the world, even from other communist countries. In 1989, when communism collapsed, Romania was one of the most isolated countries in the world, comparable only with North Korea or Cuba. This prevented us from other multiple and more sophisticated forms of secularisation, and religious life remained somehow preserved. Isolationism also involved prohibition of any kind of proselytism made by any church or mission from inside, but especially from outside Romania. This prohibition was made by the communists not for the sake of protecting historical churches in Romania but as part of their paranoia that through external mission anti-communist ideas might penetrate the country.

Based on this brief description, one can conclude that in Romania, communism was a secularist ideology that was aggressively imposed by the state by all means available and in a systematic way. This implementation of communist secularist ideology combined with extreme isolation imposed by the communists upon Romania excluded other forms of secularisation. In the communist time, everyone knew who the enemy of the church on earth was and how to deal with him. The church learned also how to minimise the negative effects of communist policy on religious matters.

The Post-Communist Period

The surprising and unexpected but welcomed political changes from December 1989 put the church in a totally new situation for which Romanian churches and religious communities were not properly prepared. I will try to summarise the situation in post-communist Romania regarding secularisation:

- Romania was suddenly opened for the world. Multiple ideas, especially from the West, entered the country, including *multiple secularszing ideas* that were manifested very timidly in the first years after 1989 and more and more courageously in recent years. Because of the extreme isolation during the communist time, the Romanian population has had little or no discernment in separating what was genuine and valuable values of the West and what was sub-culture and fake values. The dominating perception was that everything coming from the West is good and everything local is obsolete and outmoded.
- Openness to the world also involved, especially in the 1990s, aggressive proselytist activities conducted by different groups coming especially from North America. They perceived Romania as *terra missionis* and came with the superficial idea that Romanians were totally de-Christianised by communism. Their proselytism was often associated with material support or promises made to a population that suffered because of the unfavourable economic situation that emerged after the fall of communism. Strangely enough, some clergy started regretting the protection (or protectionism!) of the communist regime, which did not allow such proselytism and responded with discourses like, "Do not sell your faith for a handful of lentils" or appealed to a nationalist discourse like, "To be Romanian means to be Orthodox." Only later more coherent pastoral strategies were developed for avoiding the consequences of such a proselytism whose level decreased constantly, perhaps because of not reaching the expected results.
- Religious education has been reintroduced in public schools. This process has been perceived as a reparation, as the communists abolished it. A large majority of students joined religious classes. In 2015 an initiative coming from humanist-atheist circles managed to change the legislation regarding religious education in public schools. While before those parents who wanted their children not to attend religious classes were asked to officially demand an exception, the new imposed legislation asked those parents who wanted their children to attend religious classes to apply for it. Mobilisation of churches and religious communities was very impressive. All campaigned for registering for

religious classes. Actors, singers, etc. were involved in this campaign. The result was that more than 90% of children were registered for religious classes.

- The church enjoyed high popularity, being perceived as one of the institutions that suffered the most under communism. For many years the church was the most popular institution in Romania. Especially in the first years after communism, but also today, any form of "secularisation is synonymous with oppression"[16] manifested in a new way.
- The principle of "laicité" presented by some atheist-humanist groups as a movement towards modernisation and imported from the French context makes little to no sense in the Romanian context and is associated rather with the communist past than with modernity.
- The imposed isolation in the communist time made the church make a lot of effort to be present in the public sphere. Impressive processions are organised for any occasions and mass media reports constantly about religious life. While in the first years of the post-communist period mass media reported positively about church and religious life, more recently more and more media reports are negative and critical regarding the church.
- Romanian churches are facing all forms of secularisation. Still, Romania is less secularised in comparison with West European churches. We have the great chance of learning from other churches how to face these forms of secularisation and to avoid some mistakes that they have made.
- Atheist-humanist groups have been formed. They are small but very vocal and try to implement without or with little discernment secularist and laicist approaches regarding manifestation of religious life in the public sphere. For example, an initiative coming from these circles tried to impose a law aimed at prohibiting the presence of religious symbols like the crucifix or icons in schools and in other public buildings. The argument that such religious symbols might disturb not only the atheists but also members of other religions who do not use images, such as Jews or Muslims, has seen official representatives of these religions in Romania officially speaking in favour of keeping religious symbols in public institutions. One can see that absurd and anti-religious initiatives of humanist-atheist organisations managed so far just to mobilise churches and religious communities and to increase their level of collaboration.
- "Secularisation is a challenge for everyone involved in mission."[17] This affirmation made in the communist time by Ion Bria has a new significance for the Romanian context today. Two major missionary shifts needed to be made in the Romanian Orthodox Church in terms of

---

[16] Ciprian Iulian Toroczkai, *Secularization and Its Influence,* 261.
[17] Ion Bria, *Mission and Secularization,* 118.

mission: (1) while in the communist time mission was allowed exclusively within the church buildings, in the post-communist period the church had to go out and carry out mission wherever this was possible, facing new forms of secularisation; (2) a significant number of Romanian Orthodox (a few millions) migrated to Western Europe and North America, living in different secularised contexts and facing new challenges. The Romanian Orthodox Church followed them and organised for them more than 1,000 parishes. This involved not only a major missionary effort but also carrying out mission in contexts about whom little knowledge was available. To be successful in this new missionary work, increasing collaboration with churches living in these secularised contexts is needed.

I would like to conclude by affirming that I am confident that my church will find appropriate ways to properly face multiple and various forms of secularisation that influence our fellow Christians. To properly witness to the Gospel to the world, we need committed clergy and lay people who understand both challenges and opportunities of their own contexts and genuinely live the Christian so that they can share them with the world.

Bibliography

Archbishop Anastasios (Yannoulatos), *Facing The World. Orthodox Christian Essays on Global Concerns*, translated by Pavlos Gottfried. WCC Publications: Geneva, 2003.

Ion Bria, *Mission and Secularization in Europe,* International Review of Mission 77:1 (1988), 117-130.

Daniel Ciobotea, *Confessing the Truth in Love: Orthodox Perceptions of Life, Mission and Unity*, ed. Trinitas, Iasi, 2001.

Emmanuel Clapsis (ed.), *The Orthodox Churches in a Pluralistic World. An Ecumenical Conversation*, Geneva/Brookline, 2004.

Melvin Tinker, *Secularization: Myth or Menace? An Assessment of Modern 'Worldliness', Themelios,* 38:3 (2013), 402-416.

Ciprian Iulian Toroczkai, *Secularization and Its Influence on the Work of Two Orthodox Scholars, The Ecumenical Review,* 68:2, 2016, 258-261.

Mission in Secularised Contexts of Europe: A Roman Catholic Perspective

Annemarie C. Mayer

The contention that Christianity is "the religion of the exit from religion"[1] sparked off a most controversial debate. As early as 1985, Marcel Gauchet claimed in his book *The Disenchantment of the World* that certain internal Christian developments play a particular role in those processes that led to a more and more secularised world. Although he rejects the concept of 'secularisation' and prefers to speak of "the exit from religion" (*la sortie de la religion*), he sees the decline of religion in modern society as both rooted in Christianity and a process against Christianity. This suggests that it ultimately would be a religion, Christianity itself, that causes its own abolition and fosters the elimination of religion as such. On the other hand, Peter Berger proposed in 1999 to speak of *The Desecularization of the World*.[2] Religion is on the rise again, although no longer in any established form like churches or organised religious institutions. Religiosity and religious sensibility are increasing again. This seems to suggest that the world would be witnessing simply a reversal of the previous process of secularisation, a return of religion or, if we adapt Gauchet's terminology, a re-entry into religion.

These two theories mark the opposite extremes of how to interpret the phenomena that one could observe during the past 30 to 40 years. Both theories claim to be applicable to *the world* in general, yet both seem to grasp but part of what was really going on in the West or, on a narrower scale, in Europe. Since then, different hypotheses about the end or the revival of religion have sprouted like mushrooms.

However, what likewise became evident during this period is that generalising theories that claim to apply globally prove more and more inadequate. The same is true even of the humbler ones that limit themselves to

---

[1] Marcel Gauchet, *The Disenchantment of the World* (trans. Oscar Burge; Princeton: Princeton University Press, 1999), 101–106, 109, 114–115; published as *Le Désenchantement du monde* in 1985. The word *désenchantement* directly refers to Max Weber's *Entzauberung*.

[2] Peter L. Berger (ed.), *The Desecularization of the World: Resurgent religion and world politics* (Washington, DC and Grand Rapids, Mich.: Ethics and Public Policy Center and Eerdmans, 1999), 9: "The world today is massively religious, is *anything but* the secularised world that had been predicted (whether joyfully or despondently) by so many analysts of modernity."

the Western world. In view of more recent developments, concepts such as that of 'multiple modernities',[3] or perhaps even multiple postmodernities, become increasingly plausible. If Jean-François Lyotard is right that one of the marks of postmodernity is the end of the grand narratives,[4] this end of grand narratives most likely also entails the end of grand theories,[5] at least in the sense that they would provide an overarching global explanation. Yet without all-comprising theories neither the world, nor the West, nor even Europe can be treated as one uniform entity. Consequently, it is no longer possible to speak about Europe as a single context.[6] This entails that the attempt to describe the diverging contexts within Europe from a variety of perspectives is the only viable approach to preparing the ground for a broader conversation about religion and church, or rather church*es*, in contemporary Europe.

This present contribution provides a Roman Catholic perspective on and an interpretation of the phenomena pertaining to religion in some of the secularised contexts of Europe. Mission from a Roman Catholic perspective has to begin with trying to understand 'the signs of the times'.[7] Increasing pluralism challenges traditional identities rooted in specific cultures and reflects the situation of a differentiated world that has no centre and no unity. The *universe* has become a *pluriverse*. Since anything termed Catholic is commonly equated with all-embracing or universal, it needs to be underlined that this can be only *a* Roman Catholic perspective, neither *the* Roman Catholic perspective nor a whole variety of Roman Catholic perspectiv*es*, although they undoubtedly exist and their diversity can have a quite important impact at times.

---

[3] Shmuel Eisenstadt, 'Multiple Modernities', *Daedalus* 129 (2000), 1-30; 1: "The notion of 'multiple modernities' denotes a certain view of the contemporary world – indeed of the history and characteristics of the modern era – that goes against the views prevalent in scholarly and general discourse. [...] They all assumed, even only implicitly, that the cultural program of modernity as it developed in modern Europe [...] would ultimately take over in all modernizing and modern societies; with the expansion of modernity, they would prevail throughout the world."

[4] Cf. Jean-François Lyotard, *The Postmodern Condition: A Report on Knowledge* (Theory and History of Literature vol. 10, trans. Geoff Bennington and Brian Massumi; Minneapolis: University of Minnesota Press, 1984), 37-41 and 60: "We no longer have recourse to the grand narratives – we can resort neither to the dialectic of Spirit nor even to the emancipation of humanity as a validation for postmodern scientific discourse. But as we have just seen, the little narrative [*petit récit*] remains the quintessential form of imaginative invention."

[5] I am aware that this is a theory that claims to be applicable to different contexts.

[6] The question remains whether this ever was justified at all.

[7] Pointing out that the church needs to attend more closely to the world, Vatican II's *Pastoral Constitution on the Church Gaudium et Spes* 4 states: "the Church has always had the duty of scrutinizing the signs of the times and of interpreting them in the light of the Gospel."

Mission needs to start with a cultural analysis. In this contribution I attempt such an analysis by sharing some of my practical experiences as a professor of Theology and Religious Studies at the Catholic University of Leuven. After having lived in Germany, the UK, Spain and Switzerland I can claim from experience that Belgium is both a thoroughly secularised country with a good deal of humanist influences (the Belgian terminology for anti-Catholic secularism), yet also a very multi-religious country with quite influential Muslim and Jewish communities.[8] As an international university town, Leuven itself knows a huge variety of cultural and religious strands. Its international student population comes not only from all the different European countries but also from all over the world. The Faculty of Theology and Religious Studies counts a considerable number of Muslim students who are enrolled in Religious Studies, since Islamic theology is not yet offered in Belgium. Its professors are in charge of teaching a very special course at all the faculties of the university, *European Perspectives on Religion and Meaning*. My experiences and observations when teaching this course to students of Law, Bioscience Engineering, Bioethics and Philosophy will help in assessing and interpreting some of the concepts related to the above-mentioned theories on secularisation. The question whether religion still has a place in Europe will lead us to exploring some of the consequences for and interrelations with mission.

European Perspectives on Religion and Meaning

The course *European Perspectives on Religion and Meaning* has existed in its Dutch version since 1942.[9] It was then introduced in all the faculties as an obligatory lecture to form the students' religious understanding in an academic way. It survived not only the Second World War but also the late 1990s, when the students vehemently questioned the '*K*' of *Katholieke Universiteit*.[10] It is not a conversion course, although its educational mission is also a mission and closely connected to what it means to study at a Catholic university: its aim is that everybody who holds a degree from Leuven should have spent some part of their time thinking about the place of religion in society and their own relation towards it. Thus, it is a measure taken against the potential religious illiteracy among the students, designed to enable them to make reason-based

[8] For example, in Antwerp or Brussels.

[9] It was then called *Vraagstukken uit de Godsdienstwetenschappen*; cf. Lieven Boeve, 'Religie, zingeving en levensbeschouwing: Resultaat van een universiteitsbreed en veelvormig leerproces', *Areopaag: tijdschrift van het theologisch forum* 4.2 (2004), 2-6; 2.

[10] Cf. Bart Eeckhout, 'Studenten bereid "K" van KUL te laten vallen', *Veto* 24.6 (1997) 1-2 (http://www.veto.be/pdf/jg24/veto2406.pdf). On the situation 20 years later cf. Nora Sleiderink and Nelis Jespers, 'Dossier K', *Veto* 44.3 (2017) 19-20 (http://www.veto.be/pdf/jg44/veto4403.pdf).

judgements not only *within* the realm of their own discipline but also *about* their discipline and *beyond* the boundaries of their studies in the framework of society in general. This comprises in most cases the search for identity in secularised contexts, which at the same time seem threatened by religion.

The course, as I teach it, offers a variety of perspectives on religion from different disciplines. The students first work with an article entitled *The Molenbeek Effect*, which deals with the integration of non-Christians in Belgium.[11] Then they look at religion in Europe from a sociological angle, while concepts such as 'believing without belonging' and 'vicarious religion' are discussed.[12] The important topic of fostering dialogue between religious and secular citizens is critically analysed from a socio-philosophical perspective,[13] which raises awareness for the dialectics between the religious and non-religious. As a necessary component, work on the theme of tolerance follows.[14] Finally, the topic of religious fundamentalism is discussed from a social-psychological point of view.[15] The readings provide the students with concepts for analysing and discussing the contemporary situation and situating themselves in it.

The target group of this course is wide and variegated. Yet the variety of backgrounds from which the students come proves to be an asset than a disadvantage. They learn from the different experiences of their fellow students. The course uses the internationality and the wide range of experiences for the learning process about religion. Looking back, the courses of *European Perspectives on Religion and Meaning* that I have taught so far always included three groups of students: the majority are students who describe themselves as *neutral* towards religion, by which they mean that they are not members of a particular religion or church and would never seriously consider this as an option for themselves. Yet they do not mind the fact that such religions or churches exist. A small minority are explicitly *areligious* students who either never have had any contact with religion (which frequently is the case when they come from China) or refer to themselves as atheists who at some stage in their lives took a free, well-informed decision against religion. The third group is the usually larger minority of students who describe themselves as *religious*

[11] Cf. Felice Dassetto, 'The Molenbeek Effect: The Facts Beyond the Myth', *Oasis* 24 (2016) 83-92.

[12] Cf. Grace Davie, 'Religion in Europe in the 21st Century: The Factors to Take into Account', *European Journal of Sociology* 47.2 (2006), 271-296.

[13] Cf. Jürgen Habermas, 'Religion in the Public Sphere', *European Journal of Philosophy* 14.1 (2006), 1-25.

[14] Cf. Johan De Tavernier, 'Tolerance, Pluralism and Truth', in Didier Pollefeyt (ed.), *Incredible Forgiveness: Christian ethics between fanaticism and reconciliation* (Leuven: Peeters, 2004) 103-120.

[15] Cf. Israela Silberman, E. Toray Higgins and Carol S. Dweck, 'Religion and World Change: Violence and Terrorism versus Peace', *Journal of Social Issues* 61.4 (2005), 761-784.

and are practising members of a religion. There hardly ever are any radical believers among them.

The values and convictions of the majority of *neutral* students are the most interesting to analyse in our context: There is a certain shyness to talk about religion, but also a vast deficit of knowledge concerning religion, both regarding different world religions and the Christian heritage of Western Europe. Their first task is that of learning to speak about religion. The value of dialogue is something that they acknowledge without questioning. They easily discuss and debate with one another. Yet this becomes more difficult if they are obliged to discuss with their religious fellow students. Here quite often the vocabulary and the understanding seem to lack. Especially for the two groups of neutral and areligious students, learning the art of tolerance can prove to be a challenge. Religious students have an advantage here, because in most cases their religious conviction already demands and inspires them to be tolerant.

Among the *neutral* students almost egalitarian approaches to religion seem to prevail, which challenge the uniqueness of the different religions and suppose that the effect they have (mostly seen as soothing the fear of the future) is more or less the same for all religions. Most of these students contend that to them the concept of believing without belonging[16] applies, since they believe in something supernatural in order to be able to anchor their value system somewhere.

Furthermore, their belonging to the present secular age is characterised, on the one hand, by religious illiteracy and, on the other, by religious fanaticism or, more precisely, the fear thereof. The key word here is *latent Islamophobia.* Whenever the role of religion in the public sphere is discussed or whenever it is stated that no religion is inherently violent, the question 'And what about Islam?' comes up. For a few participants it is a big surprise that they have Muslim fellow students taking this course together with them.

Does Religion Still Have a Place in Europe?

In this step I would like to correlate the observations on the Leuven students with the theories on secularisation and their concomitant concepts. Some of them clearly are corroborated, some challenged by the contemporary student-generation.

The students attest that there still is a certain difference between the radical *laïcité* of France and the relationship of church and state, for example, in Italy or Germany. In most European countries the traditional territorialisation of religion to which the principle of *cuius regio eius religio* had led seems to be on the wane. "[T]he corresponding confessionalisation of state, nation and peoples are the fundamental facts and formative principles of the Westphalian

[16] As explained by Davie, 'Religion in Europe', 274-277 and more elaborately, *Religion in Britain since 1945: Believing without Belonging* (Oxford: Blackwell, 1994).

system of sovereign territorial states which emerged in early modern Europe out of the so-called wars of religion."[17] The impact of these confessionalisations seems to be shrinking. Nevertheless, "[s]ecularisation in Europe takes primarily the form of 'unchurching' (*Entkirchlichung*), which should be understood as a form of liberation from the type of confessional religiosity which was the legacy of the Westphalian system."[18] The process of unchurching does not seem to vary greatly between countries with state churches and those without (with the exception of Poland perhaps). Secularity, understood as neutrality towards any form of religion, is the default attitude that the majority of students would want to see in society. In their personal convictions they endorse a differentiation between legitimate secularity and anti-religious secularism, which they mostly reject. The students' differentiation faintly recalls the description of secularism and secularity by Paul VI in *Evangelii Nuntiandi*.[19]

Furthermore, the students advocate an open attitude towards religion. Although they themselves choose not to be practising members of any religion, they do not want to deny anyone their right to be so. Moreover, the choice to practice and be religious does no longer have the stigma of being somewhat mentally backward. The post-Enlightenment attitude towards religion in many European countries had been marked by influences that ultimately reach back to the ideas of Comte and Tylor.[20] Comte's three stages[21] suggest a development that overcomes religion and does without it: from a theological stage in which all unknown phenomena are explained by referring to supernatural beings via a metaphysical stage where supernatural entities are gradually replaced by abstract philosophical concepts towards a positivistic

[17] José Casanova, *Secularisation, Religion and Multicultural Citizenship*, in Wolfram Weisse, Katajun Amirpur, Anna Körs, Dörthe Vieregge (eds.), *Religions and Dialogue. International Approaches* (Münster and New York: Waxmann, 2014) 21-32; 27.

[18] Casanova, *Secularisation, Religion and Multicultural Citizenship*, 27.

[19] Paul VI, 'Post-synodal Apostolic Exhortation *Evangelii Nuntiandi*' (8 December 1975). *Acta Apostolicae Sedis* 68 (1976) 5-76 (http://www.vatican.va/holy_father/paul_vi/apost_exhortations/documents/hf_p-vi_exh_19751208_evangelii-nuntiandi_en.html), 55: "We are not speaking of secularization, which is the effort, in itself just and legitimate and in no way incompatible with faith or religion, to discover in creation, in each thing or each happening in the universe, the laws which regulate them [...] Here we are thinking of a true secularism: a concept of the world according to which the latter is self-explanatory, without any need for recourse to God, who thus becomes superfluous and an encumbrance."

[20] Cf. Edward Burnett Tylor, *Primitive Culture, Researches into the Development of Mythology, Philosophy, Religion, Language, Art and Custom* (2 vols., Mineola, New York: Dover, 2016; reprint of the 2nd ed. 1873).

[21] Auguste Comte, *Course of Positive Philosophy* (1830), English text in Gertrud Lenzer (ed.), *Auguste Comte and Positivism: The Essential Writings* (New York: Harper, 1975), 71: "The law is this: that each of our leading conceptions – each branch of our knowledge – passes successively through three different theoretical conditions: the theological, or fictitious; the metaphysical, or abstract; and the scientific, or positive."

stage when the laws of nature are investigated without wondering why they exist and monotheism is about to disappear. Similarly, the evolutionist ideas of Tylor insinuate that an evolution from the primitive stage of personal causal factors (gods) to the more advanced stage of impersonal mechanic causal factors (laws and forces of nature) takes place. Since for Tylor science and religion are incompatible, religion will disappear. Influences like these were responsible for the modern 'stadial' mindset, which understood the overcoming of religion as a process of maturation and emancipation, as society's coming of age via scientific progress. Charles Taylor already pointed out that in this context, predominant in Western Europe, unbelief is neither simply the condition of absence of belief nor merely indifference. It is a historical condition that requires the perfect tense, "a condition of 'having overcome' the irrationality of belief."[22] For the neutral students of the present generation this is no longer the case. The choice for religion is not necessarily a less rational choice. They are aware of the fact that the secular also has its limits and that trusting in perennial scientific progress is not always the more enlightened option. Nevertheless, it is the more popular option. Yet there is no necessary devaluation attached to opting for a religious life. This corroborates the initial assumption that religion is gaining ground again despite the different secularised contexts it encounters in Europe; yet this does not mean a return to the *status quo ante* as if no secularisation processes had ever taken place.

In fact, faith is generally perceived as the unknown, the strange. This perception is further enhanced by the arrival of many migrants who carry with them religious traditions not commonly found in their new homelands. People with a neutral attitude towards religion are feeling increasingly challenged and at times even frightened by believers of other faiths. The fear of 'unknown' religions is increasing. They are perceived as an unfathomable threat to society. Certainly, political, societal and psychological factors also play a huge role in this perception, which among other expressions manifests itself in the unprecedented rise of populist parties all across the continent. Nevertheless, there is an undeniable religious proportion in it too. Admittedly, even Muslim students fear Islamism. Yet a diffuse fear of Islam in general is increasing, without even knowing anything about that religion or, at times, because one does not know enough about it.

Mission Revisited: A Catholic viewpoint

If the students' stance towards religion and church is in any way representative as the default situation for a wider group of Europeans, where is the place of mission in it and what could be its tasks and functions? I shall attempt an answer from a Roman Catholic perspective.

---

[22] Charles Taylor, *A Secular Age* (Cambridge, MA: Harvard University Press, 2007), 269.

Beyond regional differences or comparisons in development among populations of different European countries, it can be stated that within the past 50 years a huge learning process has been going on among Catholics in Europe. Before Vatican II, for most Catholics mission was something done far off, in foreign lands. It did not form part of their everyday lives but was a kind of adventure undertaken by courageous priests and audacious missionary congregations of women or men in the colonies and the distant missions beyond or at the margins of Western civilisation. Mission was not just territorial, it was done at the *other* end of the world. Yet ever since Vatican II, mission is perceived as the task of the whole church: "The pilgrim Church is missionary by her very nature" (AG 2). For God "works out the history of salvation by means of mission" (AG 9). Within the past 50 years, however, the contexts changed considerably so that this is no longer enough. Already in 1990 *Redemptoris Missio* widens the scope:[23] it distinguishes three situations of evangelisation. The first "is mission *ad gentes* in the proper sense of the term" (RM 33), proclaiming Christ to *non-Christians*. The second is pastoral care of *Christian communities*. And "[t]hirdly, there is an intermediate situation, particularly in countries with ancient Christian roots, and occasionally in the younger Churches as well, where entire groups of the baptised have lost a living sense of the faith, or even no longer consider themselves members of the Church, and live a life far removed from Christ and his Gospel. In this case what is needed is a 'new evangelisation' or a 're-evangelisation'" (RM 33). Already at that time 'new evangelisation' remained not without criticism.[24] Yet if mission is an outreach to persons and an outreach into foreign structures aiming at an evangelisation of the changing social and cultural realities of human life, the analysis of the self-understanding of the participants in *European Perspectives on Religion and Meaning* clearly shows that a new *areopagus*, to use *Redemptoris Missio*'s terminology, emerged that is even one step further away from or more basic than what is described there as 'new evangelisation'. It would be naïve to think that the major challenge of evangelising those who are neutrally distant towards faith would be to bring

---

[23] John Paul II, 'Encyclical *Redemptoris Missio*. On the Permanent Validity of the Church's Missionary Mandate (7 December 1990)'. *Acta Apostolicae Sedis* 83 (1991) 249-340 (http://w2.vatican.va/content/john-paul-ii/en/encyclicals/documents/hf_jp-ii_enc_07121990_redemptoris-missio.html).

[24] For example, Friedemann Walldorf, *Die Neu-Evangelisierung Europas*(Gießen: Brunnen Verlag, 2002), 46, who quotes Otmar Fuchs: "The term new evangelisation of Europe presupposes a relationship of Church on the one hand and society, culture and world on the other, that since Vatican II has to be rejected […] Talking about the new evangelisation of Europe suggests an evangelised Church that should lead the terribly secularised Europe back to the faith, with the Church possessing what Europe is lacking" [trans. Martin Üffing, 'Catholic Mission in Europe 1910-2010', in Steven Bevans SVD (ed.), *A Century of Catholic Mission* (Regnum Edinburgh Centenary Series 15; Oxford: Regnum Books, 2013), 34-43; 40].

them back to the church. Rather "they, wherever they are and most probably would remain, should be encouraged in their ability for hope".[25]

For this much more than just "vicarious religion"[26] is needed. The challenge for all the churches in Europe is how to find ways together that do not just stop a growing de-Christianisation, but rather foster a credible common Christian witness. In *Evangelii Gaudium* Pope Francis describes what he thinks is required for the Roman Catholic Church: "I dream of a 'missionary option', that is, a missionary impulse capable of transforming everything, so that the Church's customs, ways of doing things, times and schedules, language and structures can be suitably channeled for the evangelisation of today's world rather than for her self-preservation" (EG 27).[27] He appeals to the responsibility of the church to be approachable: "A Church which 'goes forth' is a Church whose doors are open" (EG 46). The *Francis effect* manifests that authentic witness is especially appealing to the younger generation.

Being approachable has also got to do with the ability to dialogue. "Mission has to take place in the mode of dialogue."[28] This statement should be interpreted in at least two different, though related, ways. The first one is substantiated by the famous Dutch-Reformed missiologist David Bosch, for whom dialogue "is not opting for agnosticism, but for humility. It is, however, a bold humility – or a humble boldness. We know only in part, but we do know. And we believe that the faith we profess is both true and just and should be proclaimed. We do this, however, not as judges or lawyers, but as witnesses [...]; not as high-pressure salespersons, but as ambassadors of the Servant Lord."[29] This is how mission in the mode of dialogue can succeed with encouraging hope in the religiously neutral.

The second way is more specifically Roman Catholic. It goes beyond Vatican II's idea that, despite the church having a unique meaning in mediating salvation, the possibility of salvation (in Christ through the Spirit) remains open to non-Christians.[30] On this basis *Redemptoris Missio* identifies inter-

[25] Walldorf, *Die Neu-Evangelisierung Europas*, 46.

[26] Cf. Davie, 'Religion in Europe', 277-280.

[27] Cf. also Pope Francis, 'Apostolic Exhortation *Evangelii Gaudium* on the Proclamation of the Gospel in Today's World (24 November, 2013)'. *Acta Apostolicae Sedis* 105 (2013) 1019-1137 (English version: http://w2.vatican.va/content/francesco/en/ apost_exhortations/documents/papa-francesco_esortazione-ap_20131124_evangelii-gaudium.html), 49: "I prefer a Church which is bruised, hurting and dirty because it has been out on the streets, rather than a Church which is unhealthy from being confined and from clinging to its own security."

[28] Üffing, 'Catholic Mission in Europe', 43.

[29] David Bosch, *Transforming Mission: Paradigm Shifts in Theology of Mission* (Maryknoll, N.Y.: Orbis Books, 1991) 489.

[30] Summing up this idea, *Lumen Gentium* 14-16 culminates in "Whatever good or truth is found amongst them [i.e. non-believers] is looked upon by the Church as a preparation for the Gospel (*praeparatio Evangelii*). She knows that it is given by Him who enlightens all men so that they may finally have life."

religious dialogue as a "method and means of mutual knowledge and enrichment" and refers to it for the first time as "part of the Church's evangelizing mission" (RM 55). To relate proclamation and dialogue is not a tactical move. Dialogue rather "is demanded by deep respect for everything that has been brought about in human beings by the Spirit" (RM 56). Yet "*dialogue does not dispense from evangelisation*" (RM 55). The 1991 document *Dialogue and Proclamation*[31] takes this point up and stresses "[p]roclamation and dialogue are thus both viewed, each in its own place, as component elements and authentic forms of the one evangelizing mission of the Church. They are both oriented towards the communication of salvific truth" (DP 2). In today's situation, mission in the mode of dialogue becomes tangible when a Christian missionary no longer pleads exclusively for their own church but draws a positive picture of religion in general and advocates other religions as well. Grasping what this means in practice, Pope Benedict XVI observed two directions of inter-religious dialogue: face-to-face and side-by-side: "As followers of different religious traditions working together for the good of the community at large, we attach great importance to this 'side by side' dimension of our cooperation, which complements the 'face to face' aspect of our continuing dialogue."[32] Today this side-by-side awareness among believers of different faiths needs to be enhanced.

To sum up, what is expected of Christians doing mission in the mode of dialogue is poignantly stated in *Lumen Gentium* 1, namely to be in our secularised contexts a "sign and instrument both of a very closely-knit union with God and of the unity of the whole human race".

Bibliography

Auguste Comte and Positivism: The Essential Writings, ed. Gertrud Lenzer. (New York: Harper, 1975).

Benedict XVI, Pope. *Address during Meeting with Clerical and Lay Representatives of Other Religions, London* (17 September 2010). (http://www.vatican.va/holy_father/benedict_xvi/speeches/2010/september/documents/hf_ben-xvi_spe_20100917_altre-religioni_en.html).

Berger, Peter L. (ed.). *The Desecularization of the World: Resurgent religion and world politics*. (Washington, DC and Grand Rapids, Mich.: Ethics and

[31] Pontifical Council for Inter-religious Dialogue. *Dialogue and Proclamation: Reflection and Orientations on Interreligious Dialogue and the Proclamation of the Gospel of Jesus Christ* (19 May 1991), *Acta Apostolicae Sedis* 84 (1992) 414-446 (http://www.vatican.va/roman_curia/pontifical_councils/interelg/documents/rc_pc_interelg_doc_19051991_dialogue-and-proclamatio_en.html).

[32] Benedict XVI, *Address during Meeting with Clerical and Lay Representatives of Other Religions* (17 September 2010). http://www.vatican.va/holy_father/benedict_xvi/speeches/2010/september/documents/hf_ben-xvi_spe_20100917_altre-religioni_en.html.

Public Policy Center and Eerdmans, 1999_.

Boeve, Lieven. 'Religie, zingeving en levensbeschouwing: Resultaat van een universiteitsbreed en veelvormig leerproces'. *Areopaag: tijdschrift van het theologisch forum* 4.2 (2004), 2-6.

Bosch, David. *Transforming Mission: Paradigm Shifts in Theology of Mission.* (Maryknoll, N.Y.: Orbis Books, 1991).

Casanova, José. *Secularisation, Religion and Multicultural Citizenship*, in *Religions and Dialogue: International Approaches*. ed. Wolfram Weisse, Katajun Amirpur, Anna Körs, Dörthe Vieregge. (Münster and New York: Waxmann, 2014), 21-32.

Dassetto, Felice. 'The Molenbeek Effect: The Facts Beyond the Myth'. *Oasis* 24 (2016) 83-92.

Davie, Grace. *Religion in Britain since 1945: Believing without Belonging.* (Oxford: Blackwell, 1994).

Davie, Grace. 'Religion in Europe in the 21st Century: The Factors to Take into Account'. *European Journal of Sociology* 47.2 (2006) 271-296.

De Tavernier, Johan. 'Tolerance, Pluralism and Truth', in *Incredible Forgiveness: Christian ethics between fanaticism and reconciliation.* ed. Didier Pollefeyt. (Leuven: Peeters, 2004), 103-120.

Eeckhout, Bart. 'Studenten bereid 'K' van KUL te laten vallen'. *Veto* 24.6 (1997) 1-2 (http://www.veto.be/pdf/jg24/veto2406.pdf).

Eisenstadt, Shmuel. 'Multiple Modernities', *Daedalus* 129 (2000) 1-30.

Francis, Pope. 'Apostolic Exhortation *Evangelii Gaudium* on the Proclamation of the Gospel in Today's World (24 November, 2013)'. *Acta Apostolicae Sedis* 105 (2013) 1019-1137 (English version: http://w2.vatican.va/content/francesco/en/apost_exhortations/documents/papa-francesco_esortazione-ap_20131124_evangelii-gaudium.html).

Gauchet, Marcel. *The Disenchantment of the World.* Trans. Oscar Burge. (Princeton: Princeton University Press, 1999).

Habermas, Jürgen. 'Religion in the Public Sphere'. *European Journal of Philosophy* 14.1 (2006), 1-25.

John Paul II, Pope. 'Encyclical *Redemptoris Missio*. On the Permanent Validity of the Church's Missionary Mandate (7 December, 1990)'. *Acta Apostolicae Sedis* 83 (1991) 249-340 (http://w2.vatican.va/content/john-paul-ii/en/encyclicals/documents/hf_jp-ii_enc_07121990_redemptoris-missio.html).

Lyotard, Jean-François. *The Postmodern Condition: A Report on Knowledge* (Theory and History of Literature vol. 10). Trans. Geoff Bennington and Brian Massumi. (Minneapolis: University of Minnesota Press, 1984).

Paul VI, Pope. 'Post-synodal Apostolic Exhortation *Evangelii Nuntiandi*' (8 December 1975). *Acta Apostolicae Sedis* 68 (1976) 5-76 (http://www.vatican.va/holy_father/paul_vi/apost_exhortations/documents/hf_p-vi_exh_19751208_evangelii-nuntiandi_en.html).

Pontifical Council for Inter-religious Dialogue. *Dialogue and Proclamation:*

Reflection and Orientations on Interreligious Dialogue and the Proclamation of the Gospel of Jesus Christ (19 May 1991), *Acta Apostolicae Sedis* 84 (1992) 414-446 (http://www.vatican.va/roman_curia/pontifical_councils/interelg/documents/rc_pc_interelg_doc_19051991_dialogue-and-proclamatio_en.html).

Silberman, Israela, E. Toray Higgins and Carol S. Dweck. 'Religion and World Change: Violence and Terrorism versus Peace'. *Journal of Social Issues* 61.4 (2005), 761-784.

Sleiderink Nora and Nelis Jespers. 'Dossier K'. *Veto* 44.3 (2017) 19-20 (http://www.veto.be/pdf/jg44/veto4403.pdf).

Taylor, Charles. *A Secular Age*. (Cambridge, MA: Harvard University Press, 2007).

Tylor, Edward B. *Primitive Culture, Researches into the Development of Mythology, Philosophy, Religion, Language, Art and Custom*, 2 vols. (Mineola, New York: Dover, 2016) (reprint of the 2nd ed. 1873).

Üffing, Martin. 'Catholic Mission in Europe 1910-2010', in *A Century of Catholic Mission*. ed. Steven Bevans SVD (Regnum Edinburgh Centenary Series 15). (Oxford: Regnum Books, 2013), 34-43.

Vatican Council II, The Basic Sixteen Documents. Trans. Austin Flannery O.P. (Northport, N.Y. and Dublin: Costello Publishing and Dominican Publications, 1995).

Walldorf, Friedemann. *Die Neu-Evangelisierung Europas*. (Gießen: Brunnen Verlag, 2002).

Exploring the Five Marks of Global Mission: A British Perspective

Cathy Ross

This volume is about mission in secularised contexts in Europe. One common mark of all European countries is that they are experiencing a drop in religious belonging but religion is not disappearing. In England, the Anglican Church is the established church and attendance is declining. The Church of England Research and Statistics Department's "Statistics for Mission 2016" baldly states: "Over recent decades, attendance at Church of England church services has gradually fallen. These trends continued in 2016. Most key measures of attendance fell by between 10% and 15% between 2006 and 2016."[1]

Yet religion is not disappearing, nor is Christian faith. The Anglican Church has therefore been exploring how to reach out in such a setting and to proclaim the Good News. In this paper I will offer some reflection on how the Five Marks of Mission have influenced such approaches in the Church of England and on the learnings from some practitioners.

A Brief History

The Five Marks of Mission have been widely used in the Anglican Communion over the past 30 years and have a history of evolution, reception, and change.[2] I will not detail all the history here but just give a brief overview, which is pertinent to the discussion of how the Five Marks of Mission have been influential in the development of missional thinking in the Church of England.

The Five Marks of Mission in the Anglican Communion and the publication of *Mission-Shaped Church*[3] in England in 2004 have been significant in putting

---

[1] https://www.churchofengland.org/sites/default/files/2017-10/2016statisticsformission.pdf accessed 28 January 2018

[2] For further reading on the history of The Five Marks of Mission, see Jesse Zink, "Five Marks of Mission: History, Theology, Critique", *Journal of Anglican Studies,* Volume 15, Issue 2, November 2017, pp.144-166; Cathy Ross, "An Exposition and Critique of the Five Marks of Mission in Ecclesiology in Mission Perspective/Ekklesiologie in missionarischer Perspective", *Contributions to the Seventh Theological conference within the framework of the Meissen Process of the Church of England and the Evangelical church in German* (Evangelische Verlaganstalt: Leipzig, 2012), 146-170.

[3] *Mission-shaped Church: Church Planting and Fresh Expressions of church in a changing context.* (London: Church House Publishing, 2004)

mission at the forefront of Anglican life and practice in the past 30 years. Back in the 1980s it seemed that the Church of England's engagement in mission was almost moribund. A gradual realisation was beginning to emerge that the church needed to move from a focus on a pastoral model to a more clearly defined focus on mission and its practice. Various Anglican reports claimed that the dominant model within the Church of England was a pastoral model and that there needed to be an urgent move from a pastoral approach to giving mission its proper place.

In 1984 the Anglican Consultative Council (ACC-6) met in Nigeria and proposed four "dimensions" of mission:

1. To proclaim the Good News of the Kingdom
2. To teach, baptise and nurture new believers
3. To respond to human need by loving service
4. To seek to transform unjust structures of society[4]

By 1988 the Lambeth Conference embraced these four dimensions as the mission of the church. In 1990 the ACC-8 suggested adding a fifth "affirmation". The report states:

> We now feel that our understanding of the ecological crisis, and indeed of the threats to the unity of all creation, mean that we have to add a fifth affirmation:
>
> (e) To strive to *safeguard the integrity of creation* and sustain and renew the life of the earth.[5]

Eventually these "affirmations" were adopted by the Church of England's General Synod in 1996 and at the Lambeth Conference of 1998 they were identified and endorsed as The Five Marks of Mission in our Communion. In my opinion, the Five Marks are a not a perfect or complete definition of mission. "They do not say everything we might want to say about mission in today's world. … However, they are also rich with potential and they do form a good working basis for a holistic approach to mission."[6] Paul Avis has noted that worship is missing – "there is no mention of worship offered to God and particularly of the Eucharist as the centre and summit of worship."[7]

However, even in 1996 the Five Marks were beginning to be reviewed and by 1999, one year after their official endorsement by Lambeth, the report of MISSIO called for them to be revisited. This report claimed that the first mark of mission, evangelism or proclamation, encapsulates what mission is about.

---

[4] ACC 1984. Anglican Consultative Council Standing Commission on World Mission, *Giving Mission its Proper Place – Report of the Mission Issues and Strategy Advisory Group*.

[5] ACC 1990. *Mission in a Broken World, Report of ACC-8 Wales 1990*. (London: Anglican Communion Office), 101.

[6] Andrew Walls and Cathy Ross (eds.) *Mission in the 21st Century, Exploring the Five Marks of Global Missio (*London: Darton, Longman & Todd, 2008), xiv.

[7] Paul Avis, *A Ministry shaped by Mission.* London (London: T & T Clark, 2005), 16.

This is certainly an ongoing and live discussion within the Church of England with the current Archbishop of Canterbury trying to redeem the 'e' word. Evangelism and witness are two of the Archbishop's current priorities and he wishes to renew and restore confidence in the concept and practice of evangelism. He defines evangelism as: "showing others – through our words, actions, attitudes and interactions – how God has offered every one of us a new start."[8]

The Five Marks of Mission have continued to be revised, with the addition of an emphasis on reconciliation added in 2012 at the request of the churches in Burundi and Canada. So, the current iteration is:

- To proclaim the Good News of the Kingdom
- To teach, baptise and nurture new believers
- To respond to human need by loving service
- To transform unjust structures of society, to challenge violence of every kind and pursue peace and reconciliation
- To strive to safeguard the integrity of creation, and sustain and renew the life of the earth[9]

Janice Price, World Mission Policy Adviser for the Church of England, affirms that they have been used in many dioceses, deaneries and parishes as well as around the Communion. "They have given churches a practical language and image of mission that can be applied locally as well as globally."[10] This is important as it has helped to break down the division between mission at home and abroad. It has helped the Anglican churches to acknowledge that mission is from anywhere to anywhere. It has also helped the churches to understand the holistic nature of mission. Price confirms that they "have been instrumental in shaping the mission imagination of the Church of England".[11]

Importantly they have also been influential for young people. Price writes, "The Five Marks are being used to shape perceptions of what mission means for new generations of younger Christians who are exploring and finding their vocation in taking part in God's mission."[12] Indeed, a recent publication on the Five Marks of Mission (by Regnum) is by a group of young Anglicans who wrote their reflections on mission around this framework. The young writers agreed that the Five Marks were indeed a helpful framework and not a straitjacket. In the preface to this volume, then Archbishop Rowan Williams reflects on the practice of mission as articulated by these young Anglicans:

---

[8] http://www.archbishopofcanterbury.org/pages/evangelism.html, accessed 24 January 2018.

[9] http://www.anglicancommunion.org/identity/marks-of-mission.aspx, accessed 24 January 2018.

[10] Janice Price, *World-Shaped Mission, Exploring new frameworks for the Church of England in world mission.* (London: Church House Publishing, 2012), 10.

[11] Price, *World-Shaped Mission*, 11

[12] Price, *World-Shaped Mission*, 11

> All the writers here are deeply aware that what they are fundamentally talking about is the work of *God.* They are not discussing programmes that we may or may not want to take up but exploring the nature of the great current of diving transforming love in which we are swept up and which sustains us when we fail or stumble.[13]

The Five Marks of Mission appear on the Anglican Communion website as bullet points rather than numbered, as if to move away from any prioritisation and to focus on its holistic approach to mission. However, they are preceded by two intriguing statements on the Anglican Communion website, which seem to mirror a dilemma about the exact nature of the relationship between mission and evangelism:

> The Five Marks of Mission are an important statement on mission which expresses the Anglican Communion's common commitment to, and understanding of, God's holistic/integral mission.
>
> The first mark of mission, identified at ACC-6 (the sixth meeting of the Anglican Consultative Council in 1984) with personal evangelism, is really a summary of what all mission is about, because it is based on Jesus' own summary of his mission (Matthew 4:17, Mark 1:14-15, Luke 4:18, Luke 7:22; cf. John 3:14-17). Instead of being just one (albeit the first) of five distinct activities, this should be the key statement about everything we do in mission.[14]

We endorse and are committed to holistic mission but the first mark is a summary of what all mission is about. These two statements express the tension and ambiguity found in discussions on mission in the Church of England – in parishes, mission agencies, theological colleges.

Let us now consider the more recent influence of The Five Marks of Mission on one of the most significant reports and subsequent movements in the Church of England today.

Mission-Shaped Church

The *Mission-Shaped Church* report (*MSC*) has been very influential in the Church of England and has sold more than 27,000 copies – an extraordinary number for a church report. The Five Marks of Mission formed an important part of the reflection behind this report. In its introduction the report outlines its two key themes: "that the Church is the fruit of God's mission, and that as such it exists to serve and to participate in the ongoing mission of God".[15]

---

[13] Cathy Ross (ed.), *Life-Widening Mission, Global Anglican Perspectives.* (Oxford: Regnum, 2012), ix.

[14] http://www.anglicancommunion.org/identity/marks-of-mission.aspx, accessed 24 January 2018.

[15] Price, *Mission-Shaped Church*, xii.

This report echoed The Five Marks of Mission by developing five values for a missionary church. These were published in the *MSC* and claim that a missionary church is:

- Focused on the God the Trinity and that worship lies at the heart of a missionary church.

This is an interesting value as worship is not one of the Five Marks of Mission.

- Incarnational and seeks to be shaped by the culture in which it is located.
- Transformational and exists for the transformation of the community it serves.

Recent missiological thinking, picking up the theme of hospitality, might wish for more reciprocity and mutuality here. It might be challenged to wonder who is the host and who is the guest and how the church itself might be transformed by being in a particular community.

- Disciple-making through calling people to faith in Christ and developing a Christian lifestyle in that context.
- Relational by forming a welcoming and hospitable community of faith.[16]

MSC has provoked robust critique. Perhaps one of the most thoughtful came from Professor John Hull. One of his most trenchant critiques is around the theology of *missio Dei.* He reminds us that mission is indeed God's mission and that "[T]he effect of this revolutionary thinking was to readjust the relationship between church and mission".[17] He claims that "*Mission-shaped Church* continues to view mission through the lens of the church instead of viewing the church through the lens of mission."[18] Another caustic critique is found in *For the Parish b*y Davison and Milbank. They claim that Fresh Expressions of Church has a consumerist approach to culture, a weak ecclesiology and a lack of respect for Anglican tradition.[19]

Notwithstanding these critiques, this report has been enormously influential in the practice of mission in England and beyond. One of its offspring has been the "Fresh Expressions of Church" movement, a term first used in the *MSC.* This is an ecumenical movement and refers to the following: "Fresh Expressions are new forms of church that emerge within contemporary culture and engage primarily with those who don't go to church." According to the website, there are now more than 3,000 Fresh Expressions active around the world. There are many different types of Fresh Expression: alternative worship, café church, cell church, community development plant, messy church,

[16] Price, *Mission-Shaped Church,* 81-2

[17] John Hull, *Mission-Shaped Church A Theological Response.* (London: SCM, 2006), 30.

[18] Hull, *Mission-Shaped Church,* 31.

[19] Andrew Davison and Alison Milbank, *For the Parish: A Critique of Fresh Expressions.* (London: SCM, 2010).

midweek church, network church, new monastic community, missional community, school-based church, traditional church plant – to name a few.[20]

Here are four key features that distinguish and unite Fresh Expressions (FX) quoted from their website:

- **A Fresh Expression is fresh!** New, original, pioneering, innovative, different… you get the idea. A FX is not a re-brand or update to an existing model – it is a NEW thing that has developed because of a particular culture or context. They can be a network or a gathering, and they often don't look like 'church'.
- **A Fresh Expression has its own identity.** It isn't a tag-on or optional extra for people already involved in church, nor is it a bridge for those outside the church into joining 'the real thing'. Fresh Expressions *are* the real thing for the people they engage with.
- **A Fresh Expression is mainly for people who don't 'go to church'.** 'Un-churched' (those who've never been) or 'de-churched' (those who left for whatever reason) – FXs tend to grow to serve and make a space for these folks.
- **A Fresh Expression journeys with people.** They make discipleship a priority – valuing people's different faith journeys and supporting them as they wonder, explore and encounter.[21]

Recent research by Church Army researchers across 20 dioceses in England showed 1,109 FX with 50,000 members. It also showed that they are small with their average size being 50. Three quarters began in the past ten years. Their evidence shows that attendees are 21% non-churched and 20% de-churched. One third of leaders are lay and FX are as likely to be led by women as by men. FX are proportionally more present on needy estates than the overall distribution of parishes. 28% continue to grow numerically and 55% maintain the growth gained. They claim:

> Evidence suggests that for every person sent out to be part of beginning a fresh expression of church, now there are more than two and a half more people. Nothing else as a whole, in the Church of England, has this level of missional impact and the adding of further ecclesial communities, thereby fuelling ecclesial imagination.[22]

This is exciting and challenging. The movement is young – not even 15 years old yet – but has grown, changed and become more reflexive during its young life. The FX movement picks up the language and concepts of mission

[20] See "Encountering the Day of Small Things" for a fuller list. https://churcharmy.org/Publisher/File.aspx?ID=187469.

[21] https://freshexpressions.org.uk/about/what-is-a-fresh-expression/ accessed 28 January 2018.

[22] For the full report and analysis, see https://churcharmy.org/Groups/286719/Church_Army/web/What_we_do/Research_Unit/Current_research/The_Day_of.aspx, accessed 24 January 2018.

and makes it part of ordinary vocabulary and practice. An introductory book on FX and Pioneer Ministry, *Fresh!*, explains: "Fresh Expressions are intentionally missional, outward-looking Christian communities called into being to make the love of God known in an increasingly secular society. … They have a deep sense of being sent, of apostolicity."[23]

Fresh! also offers three theological reasons why FX and pioneer ministry are central to our Christian faith: it roots us in the apostolic ministry of the New Testament, the Christian tradition is about being fresh and God is a God who pioneers fresh expressions of church. An apostolic theology requires us to bear witness to Christ and to establish communities of believers. The authors assert that the three persons of the Trinity are pioneers and that they bring into being that which is fresh, not stale. "Freshness is the hallmark of what they do. The interplay of the three persons of the Trinity is for the purpose of mission."[24] So the challenge is to be innovative and creative as we witness to Christ in our various contexts.

Pioneer Ministry is part of the FX landscape. The Church of England understands a Pioneer as: "Pioneers are people called by God who are the first to see and creatively respond to the Holy Spirit's initiatives with those outside the church; gathering others around them as they seek to establish new contextual Christian community."[25] Another definition offered by a pioneer herself is "A pioneer is someone who sees future possibilities and works to bring them to reality."[26] Pioneer ministry is also growing and having an impact in the Church of England. The numbers of pioneers are gradually increasing, and there are more conferences, publications on pioneering and resources being put into it. As I write this the lead story on the FX website is about Tim Watson, "A Week in the life of a Pioneer", outlining a variety of involvements in the local community from Trash café to worship services in the local school to Sunday church in a local café.[27] Tim is a pioneer minister on the south coast of England and he explicitly refers to The Five Marks of Mission in his approach to ministry. He affirms that they offer a holistic approach to mission and they offer a wider perspective on how to go about getting involved in a community. It means that he can be creative and innovative in how to engage in mission in this context and the Five Marks of Mission allow for witness in many manifestations. Tim writes:

> In the process of deep listening to the community it has been important to try to listen to the extended community, not just church congregations or those with

---

[23] David Goodhew, Andrew Roberts and Michael Volland, *Fresh! An Introduction to Fresh Expressions of Church and Pioneer Ministry.* (London: SCM, 2012), 76.

[24] Goodhew et al, *Fresh!*, 34-35.

[25] https://www.cofepioneer.org/pioneermeaning/, accessed 24 January 2018.

[26] Beth Keith, in Jonny Baker and Cathy Ross (eds.), *The Pioneer Gift, Explorations in Mission (*London: SCM, 2014), 1.

[27] https://freshexpressions.org.uk/stories/, accessed 31 January 2018.

> associations with the church, but those in the wider community. Being attentive to listen for forgotten or unheard voices, listening to local statistics, but also listening and valuing local stories and anecdotes. … there is a concern about social isolation and loneliness. With that in mind we sought to rent an ex-tattoo shop for a drop-in social space. Our offer was not accepted and so we await further properties coming up for rent.[28]

FX freely acknowledges their obligation to the Five Marks of Mission as a way of understanding mission.[29] The former Bishop of Gloucester acknowledged the debt the existing church owes to this movement as he has seen "existing churches being reshaped for mission".[30] This holistic understanding and approach to mission is evident in FX. Indeed, the authors claim, "One of the gifts of fresh expressions to the wider Church may be the discovery of fresh ways in which this holistic understanding of mission can be realised in practice."[31]

Missional communities and emerging church are also an important part of this landscape. Michael Moynagh writes about new expressions of church and describes "four tributaries" that have emerged as a response to the new situation of post-Christendom in the global North. These are: church planting, emerging church, fresh expressions of church and missional communities.[32] He claims that these all coalesce to create new contextual forms of church that are "missional, contextual, formational and ecclesial".[33] Each of these streams claims that it is trying to reach people who are mainly outside the church, to focus on discipleship, and to embed a contextually appropriate faith community among those with whom they live and serve. There has been an increasing appreciation, as Steve Bevans has reminded us that "the church does not have a mission, but the mission has a church".[34] This means that the church comes to be the church as it engages in mission; that mission is constitutive of the church itself. This kind of thinking that has pointed to the importance of context, the recapturing of the *missio Dei* and that the church is missionary by its very nature, a renewed focus on a holistic approach to mission, and the influence of The Five Marks of Mission have all been vital for the recent understanding and practice of mission in Anglican churches.

---

[28] Tim Watson, "Listening and the Five Marks: the Beginning of Mission with a Local Community", lecture given at "Bearing Witness", A conference at Ripon College Cuddesdon, 30 September 2017. Quoted with permission.
[29] Goodhew et al, *Fresh!*, 79
[30] Goodhew et al, *Fresh!*, 103.
[31] Goodhew et al, *Fresh!*, 81.
[32] Michael Moynagh, *Church for Every Context, An Introduction to Theology and Practice. (*London: SCM, 2012), x-xii.
[33] Moynagh, *Church for Every Context,* xiv.
[34] Stephen Bevans and Roger Schroeder, *Prophetic Dialogue, Reflections on Christian Mission Today (*Maryknoll: Orbis, 2011), 15.

Beautiful Witness

I would now like to give some examples that highlight not only the tension but also the close relationship between evangelism and mission. In 2016 I was involved in a research project entitled "Beautiful Witness: Practical Theologies of Evangelism in the Church of England" funded by Durham University and the Evangelism Task Group of The Archbishops' Council. This project interviewed eight practitioners around the country about their understanding and practice of evangelism.[35] We discovered that evangelism is a tricky word – some like it and some do not. Some are happy to see evangelism as the only aspect of mission, some see mission as a wider concept. We found a range of perspectives from our practitioners in this small research project and that the borders between evangelism and mission are porous, blurry and messy – as you might expect. In what follows I will summarise a few common themes. Although these themes do not map directly onto The Five Marks of Mission, I believe it is because of the appropriation of the Five Marks that these themes have emerged.

1. Listening to the local context

Clearly, context is vital. All the practitioners, who were in a variety of contexts from new church plants in poor or more middle-class contexts, prison ministry, to more recognisably Anglican parish ministry, commented on the importance of listening to and knowing their context. All of them know their contexts well, they live there – an incarnational approach – and they listen to and observe what is going on in their contexts. They are attentive and observant. They had researched their contexts. They know about levels of unemployment or affluence, housing statistics, demographics, the history of the place, industries and businesses coming and going, the people of influence as well as the underbelly and the unseen and powerless in their places and spaces. Listening, learning and observation – being attentive to the context is vital for all of them.

2. Creativity and imagination

This was a common theme among all the practitioners. The couple in Hull spoke of the importance of love, imagination and courage. Picking up on the theme of the Holy Spirit as a pioneer, they were challenged to act in ways that did not stifle the Holy Spirit and to find freedom in that. They described the need to be able to read the Bible, engage in worship that expressed the needs and desires of that community and not to impose middle-class values on it.

Another practitioner spoke about doing mission with "a twinkle in our eye" – so that there is a sparkle or a little joke – and that says something about God.

---

[35] This was also the theme of an edition of ANVIL journal in 2017 in which you can see interviews with the practitioners and read further articles on the theme. See https://churchmissionsociety.org/resources/beautiful-witness-anvil-vol-33-issue-2, accessed 24 January 2018.

One of her aims is to be out in the public square, to ensure that Jesus is represented in the public space – whether it is the raft race, the carnival, the flower show. She described how for three years they had made and given away non-alcoholic cocktails at the annual flower show. Each year they gave their cocktails different names. One year they had names such as life in all its fullness, or forgiveness. So, they had people come to their stall in the flower show and ask "can I have some forgiveness please?" People saw the little joke, but it was also meaningful. The forgiveness cocktail had the flavour of something fresh and clean and if they wanted to they could have a conversation about what it means to be forgiven. This represented who God is – simple, gentle, invitational. She explained that it is not about pressurising or pestering people into buying something or signing up to something but rather it is metaphorically enacting something that is true about God and giving them a flavour of Jesus. This is counter to the consumerist culture. Here the church is giving away with no expectation of return and is modelling a generous God.

Another couple introduced the concept of "Edge Sunday" to their church. Three times every year, they do not meet to worship but rather they organise themselves into groups to go out and bless the city. They might offer a pop-up BBQ or café, clean the streets or offer to pray with people. They see this as a way of serving others and reminding themselves that the church is not about us but must have a missional impetus to go. They believe in taking risks, having a go and cultivating a culture of expectancy.

All of these are good examples of exercising our gifts of creativity and imagination.[36]

3. God is already at work in people's lives

This was a concept that all the practitioners affirmed. Back in 2003, then Archbishop Rowan Williams was saying, "Mission, it's been said, is finding out what God is doing and joining in."[37] We have heard this said so often now that it has almost become a cliché. However, these practitioners were able to affirm this and see this principle at work. One of the practitioners discovered this among a group of young mums who wanted to meet to discuss spiritual things. Another discovered it among mums at the school gate who were willing to meet on a Friday morning in the school to bring their own questions and issues about life. Another remarked that gradually it became obvious that God is at work here and that it may not be the hard earth that they were expecting. Gradually they began to see faith in unexpected places as the Holy Spirit

[36] Will Gompertz, BBC Arts Editor, claims in *Think Like an Artist… and lead a more creative, productive life* ((London: Penguin, 2015) that we all have creative talent and he wants to harness it to help us solve some of the major world issues. Replace in his argument artist with witness or evangelist and note how we could apply them in our mission.

[37] http://rowanwilliams.archbishopofcanterbury.org/articles.php/1826/archbishops-presidential-address-general-synod-york-july-2003. Accessed 21 June 2018.

opened their eyes to faith that was growing in unexpected ways. They were challenged at the resourcefulness of people in this particular context and how resilient people are when faced with adversity. Gradually as they began to listen and learn, and to get to know the place, they began to appreciate the beauty that was there and to see how God was already working in people's lives. As one practitioner put it, "God is in the rubble" and if we keep trying to tidy things up, we risk stopping what God can do.

4. Reciprocity and mutuality

One of the practitioners spoke movingly about allowing people to serve them and making themselves vulnerable. They were all aware of the reality of the power dynamics when engaging in mission and evangelism and were determined, as far as possible, not to allow unequal power dynamics to undermine relationships. They are also aware that it takes time to build relationships and trust. All the practitioners confirmed that it is a long journey of getting to know people, becoming friends, sharing stories, building trust together. One couple commented on the stream of short-term teams who had come into the community to try to do good, which turned the community into a project to be done to. Jean Vanier has commented on this:

> Befriending a person with a disability or alcoholism isn't going to provide an instant solution to their difficulties. But this friendship can lead to a mutual transformation by touching the place where God lives in each one of us. We can then begin to work *with* people who are fragile instead of simply *for* them.[38]

Jesus modelled powerlessness and vulnerability by being a guest in our world, by letting go and being among us in our place and space. This radically changes the power dynamics. So often in mission, the receiving person or culture is seen as needy, vulnerable, in need of help. We have to turn this on its head. We need to be in relationship with them and learn to see the resources and spirituality inherent in that community and context.

What I think these stories illustrate is that for mission to be contextual we need a broad and generous understanding of mission. This is what the Five Marks of Mission offers us – an understanding that allows us to be expansive in our engagement in mission. We do not need to be confined by an evangelism-first perspective, because there are many ways of coming to Christ. Mission has been likened to "a cut diamond of which no single facet can display its beauty and complexity".[39] We need many angles and approaches to mission according to the context. I believe that the Five Marks of Mission, although not a perfect summary, does allow for a range of witness that is contextual, creative, holistic and can be appropriated for each and every context.

---

[38] Jean Vanier, *Signs of the Times, Seven Paths of Hope for a Troubled World (*London: DLT, 2013), 119.

[39] Quoted in Avis, *A Ministry,* 16.

Conclusion

All the cited examples show how pioneers and individual Christians attempt to reach out and give witness to Christ in a secularised world. I believe that the increased focus on mission, partly brought about by the adoption of The Five Marks of Mission and their influence on movements such as FX and Pioneer Ministry, gives us cause for hope and expectation. The FX movement is not yet 15 years old (officially), so it is young, energetic, able to be flexible and to experiment. Some of its critics charge it with fragility, smallness, little theology and the fact that some communities come and go. In my opinion, fragility, smallness and change are at the heart of the Gospel. There is a vulnerability at the heart of our faith; indeed, the Cross stands as a reminder of that vulnerability. Each manifestation of growth has the fragile status of an ingrafted olive branch that by its very nature can be removed. Much of Jesus' teaching on the growth of the Kingdom is about its veiledness, its unpredictability and the sheer length of time maturity can take. Yes, we can have confidence that the Kingdom grows, but we may need a greater humility when we talk about particular manifestations and whether they are expressions of growth or decline. It is also vital to remember that the effectiveness of Christianity within a culture depends on proper translation, contextualisation and the development of local theologies. At its best, I believe this is exactly what the FX movement is trying to do in a secular context that needs to experience the Gospel afresh.

Along with Pope Francis, I have a dream:

> I dream of a "missionary option", that is, a missionary impulse capable of transforming everything, so that the Church's customs, ways of doing things, times and schedules, language and structures can be suitably channelled for the evangelisation of today's world rather than for her self-preservation.[40]

[40] http://w2.vatican.va/content/francesco/en/apost_exhortations/documents/papa-francesco_esortazione-ap_20131124_evangelii-gaudium.html, paragraph 27.

Emerging Churches as Survival of the Fittest? Some Reflections about the Search for Missional Procreation in the Dutch Secular Context

Gerrit Noort

Introduction

Are emerging churches nothing less than the survival of the fittest in a secular context? Statistics underscore that the Netherlands is a highly secularised country and that traditional churches are rapidly becoming irrelevant for its secular citizens. More than a century ago, in 1899, virtually all Dutch citizens were church members. In that year only 2.3% of the population was not religiously affiliated.[1] In 1970 church membership had dwindled to 75%, however, and in 2005 to 45%.[2] According to recent research, 68% of the population now has no religious affiliation.[3] It is expected that this figure will rise to about 72% in 2020. Christians will then constitute about 14% of the population and Muslims 8%.[4]

These rather striking figures, however, are not what we will consider in this article. What we will focus on is that, in spite of these statistics, a significant number of new Christian faith communities have recently emerged in secular Dutch society. Against the trend of an ongoing decline of institutional churches they surprisingly seem to succeed in attracting secular Dutch citizens, be it on a limited scale.

From 1990–2008 at least 281 new Christian faith communities were initiated in the Netherlands, not counting the many newly shaped Christian migrant churches[5] or 'confessional' church plants.[6] And between 2013 and

---

[1] J. van Eijnatten, F. van Lieburg, *Nederlandse Religiegeschiedenis*, Hilversum 2006, 330.

[2] J. Becker, J. de Hart, *Godsdienstige veranderingen in Nederland*, SCP Den Haag 2006, 29.

[3] A.P.J. Bernts, J. Berghuijs e.a., *God in Nederland 1966-2015*, Ten Have, 2016.

[4] Bernts, Berghuijs, *Godsdienstige veranderingen*, 52-53.

[5] This article will not include a discussion of Christian migrant churches in the Netherlands that have largely emerged since the 1980s. For an overview, see M. Jansen, H. Stoffels (eds.), *A Moving God: Immigrant Churches in the Netherlands*, Zürich/Berlijn, 2008; R. Calvert, *Gids voor christelijke migrantengemeenschappen in*

2017 the mainline Protestant Church in the Netherlands (PCN)[7] initiated 92 new missional faith communities. The report *Fingers Crossed* (2017), on lessons learnt and challenges after eight years of pioneering in the PCN, enthusiastically states that the new emphasis on pioneering missional projects has now gained momentum and is accelerating. Feelings of both elation and concern are expressed. There is joy, because about half of the approximately 10,000 participants in the new faith communities didn't have any recent church involvement. There is concern as well, because many of the pioneering initiatives are fragile and may not be sustainable in the long run. In that respect the title of the report, *Fingers Crossed*, is telling.

The new faith communities may be procreative, but can they be regarded as vessels that will ensure survival in the secular age? The report doesn't answer that question but contends "that it is realistic to expect that ten percent of the faith communities within the Protestant Church will be pioneering places in the near future". The issue, according to national coordinator of the pioneering projects M. Vellekoop, will then be how the emerging communities can find an enabling environment within the framework of the institutional church.[8] The church should make sure that it empowers the new communities and that they are not smothered in church regulations and institutional interests.

In what follows we will trace Dutch perspectives on church planting and aim to identify challenges to the further development of the emerging churches. We will start by briefly sketching post-war thinking about mission in the context of the Netherlands. This will provide the necessary background information that will enable the reader to better understand the current emphasis on shaping new churches in the Dutch secular context.

Rotterdam, Rotterdam 2007. SKIN, the platform of Dutch migrant churches, provides ample information on its website. See http://skinkerken.wixsite.com/skin.

[6] M. Vellekoop, 'Nieuwe kerken in een nieuwe context: Onderzoek naar gemeentestichting in Nederland en de rol van contextualisatie', Master thesis, Free University, Amsterdam 2008. Confessional church planting here refers to planting churches that are 'purer' than the existing ones (cf. Stefan Paas, *Church Planting in the Secular West*, Grand Rapids, 2016, 48). Others use the term 'sectarian' church planting, emphasising the desire to duplicate "congregational expressions of deeply held convictions about doctrinal and ecclesiological matters" (cf. S. Murray, *Church Planting. Laying Foundations*, Scottsdale 2001, 94).

[7] In Dutch: Protestantse Kerk in Nederland (PKN). This mainline unified Protestant Church was instituted in 2004 and incorporated two reformed denominations and the Lutheran church in the Netherlands. The church now has about 2 million members and is the largest Protestant denomination in the Netherlands.

[8] M. Vellekoop, 'Keeping our fingers crossed', in *Fingers Crossed. Developments, lessons learnt and challenges after eight years of pioneering*, Protestantse Kerk in Nederland, Utrecht January 2017.

Post-war Emphasis on Local Mission

Because of its history of colonialism, a long line of Dutch theologians reflected on the missionary calling of the church. Among them was Gisbertus Voetius (1589–1676), the first Protestant theologian who discussed the purpose of mission and defined it as the conversion of the non-Christian peoples (*conversio gentium*), gathering the converted (*collectio*) and planting the church (*constitutio ecclesiae*). For centuries, basically until 1945, theological reflection on mission primarily focused on mission work in the Dutch colonies. Adherents of primal religions ('animists') in those distant territories were by and large approached as 'blind heathen' who needed to be Christianised and civilised.

Though Dutch mission societies in the nineteenth and early twentieth century regarded the Netherlands as a Christian country, they also recognised a missionary obligation to Dutch citizens. This was caused by serious concern about the many 'baptised heathens', church members with only rudimentary knowledge of the Christian faith and praxis. When the Dutch Missionary Society (*Nederlandsch Zendeling Genootschap*) was established in 1797, this was explicitly referred to in its opening address.[9] For that reason the society not only recruited missionaries for work in the colonies but also for evangelistic ministry in the Netherlands. This domestic work, however, did not have church planting as its goal, but instructing church members in the Christian faith through preaching and teaching.

When in the nineteenth century conservative Christians started to severely critique the 'deplorable' situation of Dutch Christianity, this would eventually lead to the planting of new churches. This was the case in 1834 when new reformed faith communities were shaped, that several decades later would constitute the Christian Reformed Churches. And also in the 1880s, when Reverend Abraham Kuyper felt that the national reformed church was severely ill because of secular influences and could not be expected to recuperate. He therefore led the faithful out of the national church and established the Reformed Churches in the Netherlands (*Gereformeerde Kerken in Nederland*). These emerging churches upheld reformed orthodoxy and emphasised a *praxis pietatis* (1 Tim. 4:7b, "train yourself for godliness"). They intended to distance themselves from modern theology and "the spirit of Enlightenment". These emerging churches were not established for missional or contextual reasons. It concerned confessional church planting, with the clear motive to establish a purer church according to reformed doctrine.

After the Second World War new perspectives on mission in the Netherlands emerged. The devastating war had shocked believers to the core as they realised, to use the words of the South African missiologist D. Bosch, that they were all at best "Christo pagans" and that "the world" was fully present in

---

[9] *Aanspraak van het Zendeling Genootschap*, Rotterdam 1798, 13-14.

the churches.[10] The influential Dutch theologian K.H. Miskotte (1894–1976) already addressed this very issue in his 1939 publication on Edda and Thora, in which he observed that history was leading up to a battle between the realities of paganism (Edda) and the truth (Thora) that is shared by church and synagogue.[11] The church, therefore, should embark on a mission to break open Western syncretism and push for a clear choice between destructive myth and divine logos. Missiologist H. Kraemer (1888–1965) followed a similar reasoning in his well-known publication *The Christian Message in a non-Christian World* (1938), in which he placed 'Biblical realism' (the witness of prophets and apostles concerning the realities, that "challenges man in his total being to confront himself with these realities and accordingly take decisions") as a fundamental starting point and criterion over against the non-Christian religions.[12]

In the post-war context evangelicals and Pentecostals started to emphasise the need for planting new churches (see below). They did so for evangelistic reasons and for creating a contemporary type of faith community. The mainline Netherlands Reformed Church, however, emphasised the need for renewal of the existing congregations and for an ongoing Christianisation of the Dutch nation. Kraemer, having returned from missionary service in Indonesia in 1937, became a prominent figure in the church renewal movement and powerfully put mission on the agenda of the church. In doing so he made a plea for engaging in a constant dialogue of the church with secular society. The unique realism of God's revelation, he claimed, could only be fully shown in dialogue with the world.[13]

There was a difference of opinion in the reformed churches about the way mission in the Netherlands should be shaped. There were those who understood mission in terms of theocratic representation of the church in society. Others distanced themselves from any form of theocratic thinking and emphasised the need for an unconditional presence of the church in society. A few more words on these approaches are needed.

Characteristic for the theocratic approach of mission was the idea that not only church members should be instructed in the Christian faith but also the whole nation. This view started from the assumption that God's reign in secular society needed to be enlarged through an expansion of the church and through an ongoing (or renewed) Christianisation of the Dutch nation. The nation, not just the church, should be called into obedience to God. The government was expected to partner with the church in that missional effort. In that context Arnold van Ruler (1908–1970), another theologian that shaped post-war

[10] D.J. Bosch, *Transforming Mission*, New York 1991, 370.

[11] K.H. Miskotte, *Edda en Thora*, Nijkerk 1939, 10.

[12] H. Kraemer, *The Christian Message in a Non-Christian World*, London 1947 (2nd ed.), 64-66.

[13] B. Hoedemaker, *Met anderen tot Christus*, Zoetermeer 2000, 33-34.

thinking about mission in the Netherlands, held that both government and church – as the totality of the signs of God's Kingdom – should reign over the life of the people.[14] For him mission was *not* about reproducing churches or shaping new faith communities, but about constructing a "baptised nation" in which through "planting" law and reconciliation (not churches!) true humanity could surface.[15]

The second approach, mission as presence in society, was extremely critical of the concept of a covenantal national church and mission as ongoing Christianisation. This approach prioritised solidarity and serving, not insisting on obedience to God's law or on planting churches. Instrumental in developing this approach was the Reformed missiologist Johannes Hoekendijk (1912–1975), who is regarded as the third theologian who shaped post-war mainline Protestant Dutch missiology. He took a radically different approach than Van Ruler: the church in itself was not God's dwelling place and it could not be equated with the Kingdom. Churches should not be newly planted, but the existing ones should be turned 'inside out'. Churches should therefore embark on a pilgrimage and join people in their longings and struggles. A church that remains introverted and that exists over against the world serves no purpose. As such, he saw the church as a function of mission.

The approaches to mission of Kraemer, Van Ruler and Hoekendijk enabled Dutch churches to process that the Christian West had been naïve and too optimistic about Christian identity in a secular culture. Their approaches helped clarify that the church needed to be reshaped in terms of movement and pilgrimage. However, their frameworks hadn't sufficiently helped to rethink how the Gospel could be disclosed for the young secular generations that had gradually been de-churched and for Christian believers who wrestled with understanding and living the faith in a secular context. The urgent question became: 'How can we continue our faith tradition?' and 'How can we speak with others, including our own children, about the Christ of the Gospels?'

When in 1983 Amsterdam hosted an international congress of 3,800 itinerant evangelists from 133 countries, a national newspaper covered the event and printed an iconic picture on its front page: an African evangelist, in three-piece black suit, proclaimed the Gospel to a Dutch woman on the beach, holding a big Bible is his hands. This photo provoked discussion, as many Dutch Christians felt a certain unease. Wasn't this an entirely outdated way of doing mission? The Reformed Dutch missiologist and missionary Johannes Verkuyl (1908–2001), invited by Billy Graham to address the evangelists, observed that the evangelicals increasingly showed awareness of the coherence of proclamation, service, partnership and fighting for justice and that he hoped for a breakthrough in the evangelical-ecumenical relationships.[16] Remarkably,

---

[14] J.M. van 't Kruis, *De Geest als missionaire beweging*, Zoetermeer 1998, 115, 119.
[15] B. Hoedemaker, *Met anderen tot Christus*, Zoetermeer 2000, 35.
[16] 'Niet alleen zieltjes winnen', *Leidsch Dagblad*, 13 July 1983, 21.

Verkuyl did not show an awareness that a deficiency in ecumenical missiology needed to be addressed as well, namely the virtual absence of ecumenical reflections on shaping new missional communities as an authentic way of doing mission and practising discipleship. Though in the 1982 CWME affirmation *Mission and Evangelism* a clear reference to church planting can be found in paragraph 25, in Dutch mainline missiology of the 1980s the shaping of new faith communities was not given consideration.[17] It would take until well after the turn of the century before this was given serious attention. Mainline Protestant churches in the Netherlands would only then increasingly recognise that the changed context called for a renewed emphasis on contextual expressions of church and that they could no longer rely on the old parochial system of local congregations, as that system was rapidly eroding because of decline in church membership and selling off church buildings. In gaining an understanding they turned to the evangelicals and more conservative reformed denominations, as they had already put a lot of energy in planting new churches and reflecting on its mechanisms. In the next paragraph we will focus on this development.

Post-war Emphasis on Shaping New Faith Communities

In a 2008 Dutch publication on shaping new missional faith communities[18] it is submitted that although Moravians and Baptists shaped new Dutch faith communities in the nineteenth century, the major impulse for church planting can be observed in the 1960s and 1970s. Until the 1990s most of these initiatives were taken by the evangelical movement. Older Dutch denominations have only very recently started with church planting programmes. In his elaborate description of organisations and churches that are active in church planting in the Netherlands, missiologist Stefan Paas mentions that out of 18 only 3 have their origins in Europe. Of those three organisations, two only recently started their work in the Netherlands (Urban Expressions and European Christian Mission). The remaining 15 organisations, such as CAMA, Christian Associates, Greater Europe Mission and Victory Outreach, all find their origins in the US. Paas therefore submits as a matter of fact that, until recently, church planting in the Netherlands was an import product.

The first wave of church planting (1960s–1990s) can be characterised as a period in which hundreds of evangelical and Pentecostal congregations were

---

[17] CWME, *Mission and Evangelism. An Ecumenical* Affirmation, 1982, par. 25: "It is at the heart of Christian mission to foster the multiplication of local congregations in every human community. The planting of the seed of the Gospel will bring forward a people gathered around the Word and sacraments and called to announce God's revealed purpose."

[18] G. Noort, S. Paas, H. de Roest, S. Stoppels, *Als een kerk opnieuw begint. Handboek voor missionaire gemeenschaps-vorming*, Zoetermeer 2008. This paragraph is largely based on what missiologist Stefan Paas writes on pages 84-91 of this handbook.

established in the Netherlands. As we have noted above, during this period the traditional churches hardly, or not at all, reflected on shaping new faith communities and still relied on their post-war analysis of mission as Christianisation and presence in society. The emerging evangelical congregations promoted a new model of being church and were outspoken in their evangelistic intentions. Donald McGavran's Church Growth Movement, according to Paas, was the main inspiration for this first wave of emerging churches. Saturation and reproduction were key words in the missional strategy.

In the 1990s a shift in thinking occurred. The first wave of church planting had acted as a wake-up call for the traditional churches, but it was also acknowledged that the reproduction and multiplication of churches would not turn the tide of secularisation. It was recognised that the secular context demanded new approaches that would truly relate to a modern, secular lifestyle and to contemporary values. Contextualisation and incarnation became buzzwords. There was an increasing awareness that church planting was not about evangelisation only, but that an integral contextual approach was needed that also incorporated service to the community.

It is in this context that the mainline Protestant Church in the Netherlands, at the beginning of the twenty-first century, sought renewal of its missionary programmes and started to consult with churches and organisations that already gained experience in the field of pioneering, such as the Christian Reformed Churches and the Anglican Church of England. The 2004 PCN report 'What contributes to Christian witness',[19] discussed by the synod, presbyteries and staff of the national office, led to a challenging process of redefining and reimagining the missional calling of the church, which intended to give renewed emphasis to communicating the Gospel message in a secular context.

A number of external and internal factors contributed to these discussions. Around the year 2001 a number of church members united in their criticism of the way PCN shaped its missional work. They felt that the emphasis on presence and solidarity, though very important, was one-sided and left little room for sharing the Gospel stories. Some wondered if the staff in the national office were in favour of intentional mission at all. J. van Butselaar, retired general secretary of the Netherlands Mission Council, publicly stated that in the Protestant Church mission seemed to be 'parked on a bench close to the back door,' suggesting that it would soon be escorted out of the building. Although this criticism was sharply responded to, in the end it resulted in a thorough process of evaluating the missionary quality of the mission programmes. A report, drafted and widely discussed in 2004, looked critically at the position of mission in the church order and evaluated whether or not mission programmes

[19] 'Wat bijdraagt aan het getuigenis', synod paper Protestant church in the Netherlands, 2004.

were in line with them.[20] The drafting group concluded that there was indeed a problem. They observed that the core identity of mission had been neglected for a long time. *Diakonia*, while being an integral part of God's mission, should be clearly distinguished from *kerygma* and *martyria*, the communication of the Word of God as such. The report called for a rediscovery of the centrality of mission and evangelism and for overcoming the sense of an embarrassed uncertainty that the Christian faith maybe was no longer relevant in a secular age. Second, the report stated that, in accordance with the church order, new paths should be identified to reach the unchurched and de-churched. This was the first time that the Protestant Church pointed to the need for church planting in the Netherlands, particularly in those areas where there no longer was a visible or contextual representation of the church. In the 2006 vision document of the Protestant Church we read in that context: "We really hope that the number of people who hear the Gospel will grow and will trust God. For these people we want to be church and be church with them. We want to reach out to people whom we cannot reach at the moment because the way in which we are church. Therefore, we will try to find new ways."

After 2006 the Protestant Church developed a significant missionary programme that focused on shaping new faith communities. The church appointed a team that specifically aims to initiate and coordinate local pioneering projects. Initiatives intend to create contextual new faith communities, which can fully interact with the needs and joys of people in secular society. Theologically the leaders of these initiatives have different backgrounds. Some have a strong reformed background, others are influenced by evangelical theology, others are liberal. This in turn influences the activities: they range from inviting people to become disciples of Christ to opening a home for divorced fathers so that they can live in proximity to their children; from starting an online faith community for the mentality group 'modern mainstream' (consumerist, rather traditional in values, focused on beautiful things) to shaping new multicultural faith communities.

Time to Evaluate

The autumn 2017 issue of the Dutch practical theological journal *Handelingen* was devoted to 'pioneering'. The issue describes trends concerning emerging churches in the Netherlands and offers a provisional evaluation. In one of its articles Vellekoop distinguishes between two generations of emerging faith communities in the Protestant Church, namely those initiated before and after 2013.[21] The first generation concerns church plants in areas without visible

[20] G. Noort, J. van 't Kruis e.a., 'Het verhaal gaat niet vanzelf', Protestantse Kerk, Utrecht 2004.

[21] M. Vellekoop, 'Pionieren vanuit de Protestantse Kerk in Nederland: een tussenstand', in *Handelingen. Tijdschrift voor praktische theologie en religiewetenschap*, 2017/3, 20.

representation of the church, such as new housing estates in (sub)urban areas. In these emerging communities the worship services on Sunday had a central place in the activities, even though it was acknowledged that these services had less 'missional potential' than activities on other days of the week. The second-generation church plants, however, do not place as much emphasis on starting worship services. The focus is much more on finding contextual, creative and sustainable forms of being a Christian community.

Finding sustainable forms had to be given serious thought, as the acceleration of the number of pioneering projects (in 2017 approaching 100 local initiatives) soon showed the limitations of the available funds. For first-generation projects an amount of €100,000 was available annually, which meant that a missionary worker could be appointed. For second-generation projects only €20,000 was made available (for a maximum of six years), implying that the role of volunteers, not the professional theologian or missionary worker, became more central in shaping the activities of the emerging faith community. Next to sustainability the *locus* in society became an issue in second-generation projects. These were to a much lesser degree determined by geography, and much more so by sociological factors.[22] The question became which sociologically defined groups of people were not in reach of Christian faith communities, even when churches were physically present in a certain geographical area. The second generation marked a shift from traditional geographic church planting to contextual and flexible ways of shaping new faith communities.

The report *Fingers Crossed* (2017),[23] offering the results of research in some 66 Dutch pioneering projects, shows that not all pioneering projects are centred around worship services. In 68% of the emerging communities worship services are conducted. Around 67% offer regular communal meals, 48% are involved in community service (*diakonia*), 45% offer artistic activities and 33% are engaged in the monastic tradition.

Significantly, 40% of the people who are actively involved in the emerging communities had no prior engagement in church life. And these participants are young too: the age group 20–40 years is classified as 'best represented' in 52% of the pioneering places. This, states the report, is "a significant feature and important to existing local congregations because this generation is often not present in existing local congregations".[24]

For church leadership another outcome is important as well: many who are in positions of leadership in these new faith communities have no academic theological qualifications. This is now the case in 17% of the pioneering teams. In 80% of the communities, however, there is either a team member with a

---

[22] M. Vellekoop, 'Pionieren', 20-21.

[23] *Fingers Crossed.* See http://lerenpionieren.nl/wp-content/uploads/2017/01/Fingers-Crossed-fresh-expressions-in-the-Netherlands.pdf.

[24] *Fingers Crossed*, 8.

theological degree at the level of higher professional education (30%) or with academic qualifications (50%).[25] Parallel to this we can observe that in 18% of the pioneering projects there are no paid staff. The work is done on a voluntary basis. To respond to these trends, learning communities are shaped at a national level to ensure that available space for pioneering also becomes an enabling environment.

Challenges: Space and Enabling Environment

Vellekoop readily admits that the journey of pioneering in the Protestant Church in the Netherlands has only just begun.[26] For that reason he is reluctant to draw any conclusions about the future of pioneering projects, but he is ready to mention some challenges. Next to the issue of sustainability, he refers to the challenge of realising an organisational structure for these pioneer places within the church as a whole. Most of the pioneering projects are started under the umbrella of the local church. But what happens when an emerging faith community claims adulthood? What then is its relationship to the 'mother church', how are its relationships to other churches in town shaped and how is the relationship to the synod organised?[27] Vellekoop is quick to answer that these issues are not easily solved, and he therefore calls for further research and theological reflection.[28]

A glimpse of what he means by that can be seen in a recently distributed PCN research programme on pioneering communities (September 2017), in which the church intends to cooperate with academic theological institutions.[29] This programme identifies eight fields of research that need attention in the years 2017–2020. Among the fields mentioned are 'soteriology in practice,' which focuses on the understanding and experience of salvation. What is good news to participants in pioneering projects? And how does that relate to the understanding of mission by the pioneers? Other fields of research focus on sociological issues: What is community and in what ways do people join (Christian) faith communities? Does membership contribute to shaping communities or should other means be found to provide space for involvement? And a final example of the fields researched: to what extent does a reflection on contextualisation in the secular context really play a role in the shaping of emerging communities? Or is it merely lip service while we still use trusted methods of duplication?

---

[25] *Fingers Crossed*, 7.
[26] M. Vellekoop, 'Pionieren', 22, 24.
[27] See also N. van Hierden (a.o.), *Over speelruimte en spanning. Praktijkonderzoek naar de relatie tussen bestaande en nieuwe kerkplekken*, Utrecht 2018.
[28] M. Vellekoop, 'Pionieren', 23-24.
[29] S. Stoppels, M. Vellekoop, 'Onderzoeksprogramma pionieren. Acht onderzoeksthema's rond pionieren voor de jaren 2017-2020', PKN, Utrecht 2017.

Some would argue that the real challenge of the new focus on pioneering projects and emerging missional communities is that it may light the fuse in the ecclesial powder keg. This is what Hans Schaeffer and Henk Geertsema, both members of the Free Reformed Churches (*Gereformeerde Kerken vrijgemaakt*, GKv), observe in a recent article. They submit that the current reformed emphasis on church planting has to be understood in the context of a search for reformed identity in a time of rapid social and ecclesial change.[30] Since its inception this reformed denomination, established in 1944 as a secession of the Reformed Churches in the Netherlands (GKN), had a self-understanding of having a clearly outlined reformed identity that was highly critical about the secular world. This idea of having a clear reformed identity changed in the 1990s, however, when theological diversity emerged in the conservative Free Reformed Churches because of living in a secular context and decreasing demarcation lines between denominations. It was in this context of emerging diversity that the church made space for church-planting initiatives. These church plants sometimes developed in a (theological and liturgical) direction that was not expected by the 'mother church'. This would even lead to a much-debated case in which a pioneering community would leave the denomination that had initiated and nurtured it. Differences had become too big to bridge.[31]

The question for the Free Reformed Churches, in this context of diversity, became: What is a good missional method (criteria), what are good missional results (goals and expectations) and what exactly is the reformed identity of the church plants (identity)? The discussions on the reformed identity of the church plants reflected discussions on the identity of the denomination as a whole (e.g. about the ordination of women). Church plants in that sense ignited a discussion on reformed identity. Some were not happy with ecclesial experiments, whereas others welcomed them as signs of much-needed renewal. According to Geertsema and Schaeffer, pioneering projects became the litmus test for reformed identity.[32] The emerging ecclesial and missional practices became a challenge to reformed orthodoxy. The authors conclude that at the start of the pioneering projects clear contours of reformed identity were assumed, but in the end existing codes of what it entails to be reformed could not be used in a normative way. They evaluate the history of Free Reformed church planting (some 40 projects) as an indication of a church in transition. The challenge, they state, is to ensure that the transition will not end in a 'locked-in' situation of stagnation and a dying old system. They make a plea for understanding church planting and the related discussions as a part of the search for a new identity.[33] Emerging faith communities should not be a cause

---

[30] H. Schaeffer, H. Geertsema, 'Gemeentestichting als lont in het kruitvat', in *Handelingen. Tijdschrift voor praktische theologie en religiewetenschap*, 2017/3, 55-65.
[31] This was the case with the pioneering project StroomWest in Amsterdam.
[32] H. Schaeffer, H. Geertsema, 'Gemeentestichting', 59.
[33] H. Schaeffer, H. Geertsema, 'Gemeentestichting', 60-64.

for difficult and unproductive discussions and identity issues but should much rather be reinterpreted in terms of creating an enabling environment, as experimental space for transition towards renewal. The challenge, they contend, is to evaluate the pioneering projects in order to rediscover and renew the identity of the church.

A certain unease of denominations with their church-planting initiatives, such as in the Free Reformed Churches, is not limited to conservative churches. Nienke van Hierden and Sake Stoppels observe a similar development in the mainline Protestant Church in the Netherlands, where experiences in pioneering projects directly challenge the church order and its underlying theological premises.[34] Innovative and creative pioneers are not very likely to abide by given sets of ecclesial regulations of church life. They look for what works and what effectively contributes to shaping a new faith community in a secular context. When pioneers have to implement decision-making mechanisms, when it has to be determined who can be part of a leadership team or who can baptise new believers, the issue of church order surfaces.[35] Van Hierden and Stoppels observe that the synod of the Protestant Church created a lot of space to facilitate pioneering projects. According to some the created enabling environment has actually become too large a space, as they feel it leads to an unhealthy competition of the old existing faith community and new emerging communities. The 'old' community matters, is what they say. Their opponents will hold that new experiments are needed to revitalise the old communities, or to offer an alternative for secular people, Christians and those of other convictions alike, who are no longer interested in participating in the old ways of a traditional Christian faith community.

Van Hierden and Stoppels argue that existing denominations as such may well be about to blast themselves into oblivion because of their emphasis on pioneering, as they are convinced that the emerging new faith communities will not develop a strong relationship to the mother church.[36] But that, they write, has both positive and negative aspects: the "old denominational ways" may no longer be visible in the new communities, but in them we can clearly see the "renewing power of the Gospel of Jesus Christ".[37] They therefore make a plea for recognising the newly emerged faith communities as spaces where the 'both-and' can be practised. It is our calling, they contend, to create a network of pioneering communities and traditional congregations in which believers interact meaningfully in mutual dependence. Believers, both in traditional congregations and in newly shaped communities, should respectfully address

[34] N. van Hierden, S. Stoppels, 'Verbinding zoeken op de grens', in *Handelingen. Tijdschrift voor praktische theologie en religiewetenschap*, 2017/3, 69.

[35] See also G. Noort, 'Kerkordelijke overwegingen bij gemeentevorming', in G. Noort e.a., *Als een kerk opnieuw begint*, Zoetermeer 2008, 335-359.

[36] N. van Hierden, S. Stoppels, 'Verbinding zoeken op de grens', 71.

[37] N. van Hierden, S. Stoppels, 'Verbinding zoeken op de grens', 71.

common questions, issues and responsibilities that relate to our missional calling. This 'both-and' should also be safeguarded in church policy and church orders, so that the voice of pioneers and pioneering communities is heard and taken seriously.

Fit to Survive?

In this article we have shown that in post-war Dutch perspectives on mission in a secular context the emphasis gradually shifted from underscoring the importance of Christianisation and presence to making space for shaping new contextual faith communities. As shown, this focus on church planting can no longer be regarded as an evangelical prerogative. Also, conservative reformed and mainline Protestant churches are engaged in this endeavour and experiment with a wide range of theological and missional approaches.[38] This development is not going unnoticed and discussions on the direction pioneering takes and what it will mean for the church will continue for a long time.

At the beginning of this article we provocatively asked if the new emerging churches are a tangible representation of church that is able to adapt to secular times and that therefore may be well suited to survive the secular age. This, of course, remains to be seen. One thing is sure: the new churches are contextual, attractive and procreative. But are they sustainable? Vellekoop was reluctant to answer that question and he kept his fingers crossed. It is important to remind ourselves of the long history of modern (Western) mission in other continents, which points to the value of the three-self formula: churches that are self-governing, self-supporting and self-propagating are sustainable and fit for survival. From mission history we learn also that it is important to be involved for the long haul. Funding a pioneering project for a project cycle of three years only will not do. Apparently, the Spirit is patient and takes more time to build communities of disciples.

Maybe the newly emerged churches point to the survival of the fittest in the secular age. But then we need to remind ourselves that it remains to be seen if the old churches, with their old ways, are *not* fit to survive. Old denominations have, for hundreds of years, been able to ensure an enabling environment for witness and *diakonia*, for celebrating the mystery of the Gospel and initiating people in the Christian faith. Two mega churches that were recently built in the small town of Barneveld, centrally located in the Dutch Bible Belt, may serve to illustrate this point. Church members who worship in these strict Calvinistic churches, seating respectively 1,400 and 2,500 people, even cause traffic jams on Sunday mornings when they arrive in masses to fill the pews. In spite of their intentional non-contextual faith practice that distances itself from secular society, these conservative congregations continue to attract young families.

---

[38] Cf. O. Blok, M. Vlaardingerbroek (eds.), *Survivalgids pionieren*, 2016; M. Reinders, *Heilig Vuur*, 2016.

While many have, both in past and present, predicted that religion – including the existing churches – would vanish, we now recognise that the secularisation hypothesis had its flaws. Religion in Northwest-European secular society is even back at centre stage, because of the migration of Muslims and Christians from the global South to our secularised North and because of debates about the role of religion in society. Emerging Christian faith communities in the Netherlands are not only contextually responding to secular culture but they also find themselves in a multi-religious society.

The old churches, then, though slow to change, may be more adjusted for survival than is often suspected. The new emerging churches on the other hand, while contextual and flexible, may not be sustainable or may turn out to be too fluid to survive. Whatever our hopes and expectations, as believers we may rest assured that both old and new churches are moved by the Spirit to embark on the road of discipleship. Ultimately it is not adaptability and contextuality that determines who is best suited to survive. It also hinges, humanly speaking, on committed discipleship and working with others for the common good of all. The 'both-and' approach seems a wise road to travel.

Cognitive Dissonance as a Missiological Challenge and Opportunity: An Evangelical Perspective on Western Europe[1]

Lars Dahle

> The issue between the atheist and the believer is not whether it makes sense to question ultimate fact, it is rather the question: what fact is ultimate? The atheist's ultimate fact is the universe; the theist's ultimate fact is God.
>
> John Lennox[2]

In the late 1990s Lesslie Newbigin claimed that developing a missiology of Western culture is "the most urgent task facing the universal church at this time".[3] Michael W. Goheen recently expressed this as a threefold task: a theological task of faithfully articulating the Gospel in the Western context, an ecclesiological task of exploring the missional identity of the church in the West, and a cultural task of probing the stories and fundamental assumptions of Western culture.[4]

This missiological agenda is highly relevant for Christian witness in secularised Western European contexts. The narratives and experiences that many confessing Christians are sharing from such settings are clear indicators of alienation and marginalisation. One such story from Northwestern Europe made a huge impact at the Tokyo 2010 global mission conference:

---

[1] This article is part of a wider project, where I am exploring Christian mission as the three-dimensional global task of "bearing witness to Jesus Christ and all his teaching – in every nation, in every sphere of society, and in the realm of ideas" (*The Cape Town Commitment*, 'Foreword', https://www.lausanne.org/content/ctc/ctcommitment#foreword). The emphasis here is on the third dimension (i.e. "in the realm of ideas") in the Western European context. See further L. Dahle, 'Mission in 3D: A Key Lausanne III Theme', in M. S. Dahle, L. Dahle and K. Jørgensen (eds.), *The Lausanne Movement: A Range of Perspectives* (Oxford: Regnum, 2014), pp.265-279.

[2] John Lennox, *God and Stephen Hawking: Whose Design Is It Anyway?* (Oxford: Lion Hudson, 2011), p.68.

[3] Lesslie Newbigin, 'Culture of Modernity', in *Dictionary of Mission: Theology, History, Perspectives*, eds. Karl Müller et al. (Maryknoll, NY: Orbis Books, 1997), 98.

[4] Michael W. Goheen, *Introducing Christian Mission Today: Scripture, History, and Issues* (Downers Grove: InterVarsity Press, 2014), 297-329.

> Stefan Gustavsson of Sweden gave a Macedonian call ("Come over and help us," an allusion to Acts 16: 9) about how to evangelise secular Europeans, the "prodigal sons" of Christianity today… He pointed out that the Christian church in Europe is rapidly diminishing…; the gospel is not viewed as good news – many think it's been tried and found false… Furthermore, he claimed, Europe is a mix of the modern and the postmodern… He concluded: "The advent of postmodern thinking has not diminished the need for apologetics; it has doubled it. Now the Christian church has two major challenges to deal with: The concept of truth (that there is such a thing as attainable truth) and the content of truth (that it is the Christian message, not naturalism, which is the truth)."[5]

In a subsequent, recent publication, Stefan Gustavsson expands on the shared experiences of many Christians in such deeply secular contexts. He proposes *cognitive dissonance* as a helpful explanatory model, i.e. psychological experiences of conflict resulting from incongruous beliefs and attitudes held simultaneously. We may summarise his cultural analysis as follows:

> God is taken for granted within our Christian churches, and sermons may describe his love and goodness. But the existence of God is hardly ever justified, it is only presupposed. The Bible is quoted and applied, but no reasons are given for the selection and credibility of the biblical books. Jesus is being worshipped, but no explanation is presented for his uniqueness and his salvation. Prayer, liturgy, and mission are only seen as Christian traditions, and thus never argued for in relation to the wider secular context.
>
> Our culture at large, and especially the educational system, however, views God as absent. Prayer is only a psychological exercise. The Bible is an irrelevant ancient text which contains some literary gems. Science has replaced faith in God. Christianity is not unique, but only one alternative among many worldviews. Jesus is an inspiring humanist. The Christian faith can no longer be seen as

---

[5] Allen Yeh, *Polycentric Missiology: 21st-Century Mission from Everyone to Everywhere* (p.84). (Downers Grove: InterVarsity Press. Kindle Edition), pp.83-84. "After [Gustavsson's] presentation, the entire consultation (most of which represented the fruit of European missionary sending in past centuries) began to intercede for this once Christian continent that is now itself in need of pioneer missionary effort – a phenomenon being referred to as 'reverse mission'. At the same time, many non-Western mission leaders remarked that the very trends which contributed to the decline of the church in Europe are beginning to affect their countries as well." (David Taylor & Young Cho, 'Tokyo 2010: Analysis and Reflection on the Global Missions Consultation', in Kirsteen Kim & Andrew Anderson (eds.) *Edinburgh 2010. Mission Today and Tomorrow* (Oxford: Regnum Books, 2011), 307.)

objectively true; it may function as a source of personal inspiration or as a kind of spirituality which may lead to increased well-being.[6]

Thus, many confessing Christians in Western Europe (and beyond) are faced with a demanding cognitive dissonance between Christian stories, beliefs and truth-claims within the church and dominant secular narratives and arguments in the wider culture.

Following on from Gustavsson's perceptive analysis, *this article explores how dealing with cognitive dissonance is a key missiological task in many Western European contexts.* This exploration is carried out in three parts after an introductory presentation of the classical theory of cognitive dissonance; *first* by describing some of the key cultural factors behind this challenging experience for many confessing Christians, *second* by discussing and outlining an appropriate Christian response to this challenge, and *third* by considering cognitive dissonance as a potential missiological opportunity.

Revisiting the Theory of Cognitive Dissonance

The American social psychologist Leon Festinger published *A Theory of Cognitive Dissonance* in 1957. He claimed in this seminal publication that the relationship between any pair of cognitions may be consonant (in harmony), dissonant (in disharmony) or irrelevant. Festinger noted that there is a human preference to hold consonant cognitions. Since it is psychologically uncomfortable to hold contradictory cognitions, the unpleasant experience of dissonance motivates a person to change their cognition, attitude or behaviour.

Festinger summarised his theory as follows: "The presence of dissonance gives rise to pressures to reduce or eliminate the dissonance. The strength of the pressures to reduce the dissonance is a function of the magnitude of the dissonance."[7] Furthermore, he outlined three methods that people use to reduce cognitive dissonance: "(1) They can change one or more of the cognitions or behaviours. (2) They can add new cognitions that alter the magnitude of the dissonance. (3) They can reduce the importance of the cognitions causing dissonance."[8] It has recently been observed that Festinger's pioneering theory "still provides much explanatory, integrative, and generative power".[9]

When applying these insights to the cognitive dissonance experienced when faced with conflicting fundamental Christian and secular truth-claims, we also

---

[6] Stefan Gustavsson, *Trenger troen forsvares? En programerklæring for kristen apologetikk* (Oslo: Lunde Forlag, 2016); my translated summary of Gustavsson's argument on pp.26-27.

[7] Leon Festinger, *A Theory of Cognitive Dissonance. Vol. 2.* (Stanford, CA: Stanford University Press, 1962), 18.

[8] Morvan, Camille. *An Analysis of Leon Festinger's A Theory of Cognitive Dissonance* (London: Routledge / The Macat Library), 36-37 [Kindle Edition].

[9] Morvan, *An Analysis*, 61.

need an appropriate understanding of the nature and function of worldviews. In view of our present missiological concerns, the following definition offered by James Sire may be helpful:

> A worldview is a commitment, a fundamental orientation of the heart, that can be expressed as a story or in a set of presuppositions (assumptions which may be true, partially true, or entirely false) which we hold (consciously or subconsciously, consistently or inconsistently) about the basic constitution of reality, and that provides the foundation on which we live and move and have our being.[10]

This leads to three key observations central to the purpose of this article. *First*, Christian and secular truth-claims both relate to the level of fundamental personal commitment. At this level, an ultimate change of beliefs and convictions is demanding. *Second*, Christian and secular truth-claims may be expressed both as competing stories and as conflicting sets of presuppositions. *Third*, Christian and secular truth-claims offer contradictory perspectives on faith, reality, humanity and values. It is quite understandable in view of these observations that simultaneous deep exposure to Christian and secular truth-claims may lead to challenging experiences of cognitive dissonance for many confessing Christians.

Experiencing Cognitive Dissonance as Christians: Key Cultural Factors

There are at least four central cultural factors involved in generating deep experiences of cognitive dissonance for confessing Christians in many Western European contexts.

First, the significant cultural factor of the educational system and the academy should be mentioned. What is being communicated about religion in general and Christian faith specifically in many of these settings? How does that challenge young Christian believers? A recent doctoral dissertation in Gothenburg may provide us with some key answers. After having observed the discourse on religion and worldviews in upper secondary school religious education classes in Sweden, Karin Kittelmann Flenser summarised her major findings as follows:

> The findings indicate that a secularist discourse was hegemonic in the classroom practice and implied norm of talking about religion, religions, and [religious] worldviews as something outdated and belonging to history. A non-religious,

[10] Sire, James W. *Naming the Elephant: Worldview as a Concept* (Downers Grove: InterVarsity Press, 2015; 2nd ed.), 141 [Kindle Edition].

atheistic position was articulated as neutral and unbiased in relation to the subject matter and was associated with being a rational, critically thinking person.[11]

It seems plausible to presume that such a reductionist secular discourse is predominant in the educational system in many countries in Western Europe. This secular discourse is reinforced by highly influential secular paradigms in the academy, as noted by Gustavsson:

> In the natural sciences, naturalistic interpretations are offered for the Big Bang theory and the evolution theory. In the discipline of literature, postmodern hermeneutics excludes absolute Christian truth-claims. In the study of history, the Christian church is presented as an oppressive institution which has supported slavery, the suppression of women, and homophobia. Within psychology, God is explained away as being projected in our image. In the social sciences, all religion is seen as products of the social contexts. In gender studies, real distinctions between men and women made in the image of God are excluded. Within post-colonial studies, 'the Christian West' is portrayed as the exploiter. In religious studies, the search for God within and the similarities between various religions are emphasised.[12]

Because of these dominant secular paradigms in textbooks and teaching in many European schools and universities, young confessing Christians are being deeply challenged in such educational and academic settings at the foundational worldview level. This leads to a widespread experience of cognitive dissonance, evident from many observations in youth and student ministry contexts. Such experiences may be compared to trying to have one foot in each rowboat, when two adjacent boats are drifting apart.[13] It should also be added that Western Europe affects the rest of the world with its

---

[11] Karin Kittelmann Flenser, *Religious Education in Contemporary Pluralistic Sweden.* PhD thesis. University of Gothenburg, 2015, 6. https://gupea.ub.gu.se/bitstream/2077/40808/1/gupea_2077_40808_1.pdf [Accessed 23 February 2018].

[12] Gustavsson, *Trenger troen forsvares?*, 24-25. [My translated summary.] It should be added that such secular paradigms often contain elements of truth, which may be (re)discovered when the reductionist claims are relativised. This is what Peter Berger famously called "the relativizing of the relativisers"; see his *A Rumor of Angels* (New York: Doubleday / Integrated Media, 1970), p.42ff.

[13] "Enlightenment thinking pushed Christian believers toward the untenable position of one foot in the rowboat of their Christian worldview, and the other foot in a rowboat of their education which was shaped by Enlightenment ideas – with the two being slowly pulled apart. In this situation, believers felt a cognitive dissonance between the Enlightenment and Christian worldviews." (Greg Pritchard, 'A Global Vision of the Gospel (III)', www.EvangelicalFocus.com 4 February 2015) [Accessed 23 February 2018.]

predominant secular thinking, through its many influential secular perspectives and its often leading role as an educator.[14]

A *second* key cultural factor is the media, whether news, documentary, entertainment, creative or social media. Tim Keller points out that various media, especially in Western Europe and in the US, are key carriers of basic secular assumptions. These are influential background beliefs that our culture presses on us about the Christian faith and which make it seem so implausible:

> These assumptions are not presented to us explicitly by argument. Rather, they are absorbed through the stories and themes of entertainment and social media. They are assumed to be simply 'the way things are'. They are so strong that even many Christian believers, perhaps secretly at first, find their faith becoming less and less real in their minds and hearts. Much or most of what we believe at this level is, therefore, invisible to us as belief. Some of the beliefs … are: "You don't need to believe in God to have a full life of meaning, hope, and satisfaction."; "You should be free to live as you see fit, as long as you don't harm others.";"You become yourself when you are true to your deepest desires and dreams.";"You don't need to believe in God to have a basis for moral values and human rights.";"There's little or no evidence for the existence of God or the truth of Christianity".[15]

Thus, secular paradigms in most Western European schools and universities are reinforced by this widespread communication of explicit and implicit secular convictions in the Western media. This includes popular fictional stories where secular worldview perspectives are portrayed positively, Christians are being stereotyped, and Christian faith and practices are excluded.[16] "Put another way, there is now dissonance or a discrepancy between imagination (formed by the arts via TV and movies) and the truth from Scripture (proclaimed from the pulpit)."[17]

A *third* key cultural factor is the increasing presence of worldview pluralism in Western Europe, because of reduced Christian influence and increasing media exposure and immigration. Harold Netland raises the empirical question, "whether, when faced with intelligent, sincere, and morally good people who embrace different religious commitments, Christians do in fact experience

---

[14] See further Greg Pritchard, 'A Global Vision of the Gospel (II)', www.EvangelicalFocus.com 28 January 2015. [Accessed 23 February 2018.]

[15] Keller, Timothy. *Making Sense of God: An Invitation to the Skeptical* (New York: Penguin Publishing Group, 2016), 5 [Kindle Edition].

[16] Key popular examples from the fascinating world of television series include *The Big Bang Theory* (with its dominant scientism), *Modern Family* (with its plurality of family norms and lifestyles) and *Downton Abbey* (with its clear absence of Christian faith and practices).

[17] Darrow Miller, "Why Do Movies Influence Youth More Than the Bible?", 23 August 2012. http://darrowmillerandfriends.com/2012/08/23/christian-worldview-and-the-arts/ [Accessed 23 February 2018.]

'cognitive dissonance', a reduction in confidence in their own beliefs, and sense the need to justify their beliefs".[18] Netland himself answers affirmatively. It should be added that the fact of religious pluralism may be interpreted in different ways, whether the underlying perspective is secular relativism, religious syncretism, or the acknowledgment of alternative absolute truth-claims.

A *fourth* key cultural factor is the marginalisation of Christian faith and practice in Western Europe. This process is related to the previous three factors but needs also to be understood on its own terms. In the context of this article, it is natural to focus on the plausibility challenge in Western Europe.[19] This challenge consists of two parallel phenomena, i.e. Christian ideas are seen as less meaningful and Christian institutions are becoming more marginal. The first phenomenon is especially relevant for cognitive dissonance. It includes the following significant challenges in many of today's Western European societies:

> (1.) Christian ideas and images are often viewed through the cultural lenses of post-Christendom, i.e. through stories of mythical and factual abuses of power by churches and Christians throughout history.
>
> (2.) Biblical realities, concepts and images – such as God, Father, holiness, sin, love, salvation, cross, freedom and Jesus Christ – are not defined through the lenses of classical Christianity, also because of the loss of any given, traditional authority.
>
> (3.) The wider cultural milieu is a context where the Gospel is not usually seen or heard as a viable and relevant option, either in terms of reason (arguments) or in terms of imagination (stories).[20]

All the four major cultural factors outlined above contribute significantly to the experience of cognitive dissonance among many confessing Christians in Western Europe (and beyond[21]). As Netland points out, one should not "minimise the degree to which individuals, including [confessing] Christians, undergoing normal educational and socialisation processes in the West,

---

[18] Harold Netland, *Encountering Religious Pluralism: The Challenge to Christian Faith and Mission* (Downers Grove: IVP Academic, 2001), 273.

[19] A more comprehensive treatment of the marginalisation of Christian faith and practice in Western Europe includes the legal, the attitudinal, the plausibility and the credibility levels. See further Lars Dahle, 'Western Europe: Marginalization of Christians through Secularization', in Hans Aage Gravaas et al. *Freedom of Belief and Christian Mission* (Oxford: Regnum Books, 2015), 382-394.

[20] Dahle, 'Western Europe', 388.

[21] The global influence of Western secular worldviews through the academy and the media as key missional challenges will be explored in depth in future contributions.

struggle with basic Christian beliefs, intuitively sensing the need for justification".[22]

Responding to the Challenge(s) of Cognitive Dissonance: Key Strategies

As mentioned earlier, Leon Festinger argued that there are three basic ways to deal with cognitive dissonance. He described these as changing one of the cognitions, adding new significant cognitions, or reducing the importance of the cognitions. Festinger did not consider these approaches as mutually exclusive.

These three supplementary strategies illustrate a spectrum of responses from many confessing Christians when faced with the demanding experiences of cognitive dissonance, because of contradictory Christian and secular truth claims.

First, Christians may try to change one or more of the beliefs, opinions or behaviours involved in the dissonance. Because of the plausibility of secular convictions and political correctness in the wider Western European setting, Christians may be persuaded to give up – or downplay – key Christian doctrines such as the Trinity, God as Creator, Jesus as Lord and Saviour, and personal faith, witness and discipleship, thus accepting a secularist worldview. Alternatively, Christians may be encouraged to uphold key Christian beliefs with confidence, and thus challenge fundamental secular convictions as insufficient, inconsistent and undesirable.

Second, Christians may try to acquire new information or beliefs that will increase the existing consonance and thus cause the total dissonance to be reduced. If Christians continue to be deeply attracted to naturalism, individualism or relativism, they may gradually adopt such fundamental secular perspectives as plausible overall explanations. This may lead to an ultimate acceptance of secular worldview perspectives. On the other hand, Christians may be encouraged to expand their knowledge of the relevant premises, issues and facts, and pursue that new knowledge in accordance with classical Christian convictions. If so, the personal confidence in biblical truth claims will grow and the total dissonance will be reduced.

Third, Christians may try to forget or reduce the importance of those cognitions that are in a dissonant relationship. If Christians are suppressing or diminishing the significance of fundamental Christian doctrines, this may lead to a gradual adoption of secular beliefs and attitudes. Christians may also be downplaying the challenges from secular thought, which in turn may result in a Christian ghetto mentality with insufficient teaching and a problematic inward-looking ministry. On the other hand, if Christians become increasingly convinced of the authenticity, credibility and relevance of key Christian truth claims, the personal significance of secular convictions will be gradually

[22] Netland, *Encountering Religious Pluralism*, 273.

reduced. This latter strategy presupposes broad and credible justification of central Christian truth claims.

Such alternative and conflicting strategies may be seen all over Western Europe in churches, youth and student work, and children ministries. However, there is currently an increasing emphasis in many contexts on constructive apologetic strategies both internally and externally. As mentioned above, this includes encouraging confessing Christians *first* to uphold key biblical beliefs, *second* to expand the knowledge of Christian faith and relevant alternative worldviews, and *third* to offer broad and credible justifications of central Christian truth claims.

We can observe this new apologetic renaissance in various settings in Western Europe. In the university world, there is an increasing number of evangelical university missions with a clear apologetic edge, organised by student organisations such as IFES alongside the specialist university ministry FEUER.[23] The emphasis is on biblical material, persuasive public communication and a variety of creative approaches. This European-wide phenomenon includes the increasingly popular 'sceptics weeks' in Norway. There is also an increasing interest in Christian apologetics among a growing number of younger Christians, focusing on books, podcasts and social media by well-known and highly popular evangelical apologists such as John Lennox, William Lane Craig and Ravi Zacharias. The growing influence of The Oxford Centre for Christian Apologetics (OCCA), The European Leadership Forum (ELF) and the annual Norwegian Veritas Conference are all clear indicators of this development.[24]

The need for a holistic apologetic approach in a Western European context was emphasised in a recent research project at NLA University College (Norway) called "Why Jesus?"[25] carried out in the period 2012-2016.[26] The project was based on in-depth interviews with Christian youth workers and faith educators and on subsequent critical reflections on the interview findings in the light of recent relevant research on youth ministry, worldview formation and apologetics. This led to the development of a holistic apologetic strategy for youth ministries, which consists of three parts. The *first* component is a hermeneutical approach, which helps young Christians to identify traces of secular and religious worldviews in influential educational, academic and media texts around them. The *second* element is a didactic approach, which

[23] See further https://feuerreports.wordpress.com/about/. [Accessed 23 February 2018.]

[24] See further www.johnlennox.org, www.reasonablefaith.org, www.rzim.org, www.theocca.org, www.euroleadership.org and www.veritaskonferansen.no. [Accessed 23 February 2018.] For an illuminating case study, see Katelyn Beaty, 'Oxford's Unapologetic Female Apologist', *Christianity Today*, April 2015.

[25] In Norwegian: "Hvorfor akkurat Jesus?". This research project was funded by the national Christian faith education reform in Norway.

[26] See further https://www.damaris.no/hvorfor-akkurat-jesus/. [Accessed 23 February 2018.]

helps young Christians to see the consistency, the credibility and the relevance of a comprehensive Christian worldview based on central biblical truth claims. The *third* part is a formative approach, which allows young Christians to gradually mature and grow into a more confident Christian commitment within an affirmative Christian community.[27]

Cognitive Dissonance as a Missiological Opportunity: Turning the Tables

So far, in this article, I have primarily focused on cognitive dissonance as a challenge for confessing Christians when faced with the demanding tension between Christian and secular truth claims. However, we also need to explore how cognitive dissonance may serve Christian mission and apologetics positively, both *inwardly* in terms of discipleship and Christian growth in children and youth ministries and *outwardly* in terms of pre-evangelism and evangelism.

The internal apologetic strategy emerges out of Jesus' prayer for his disciples in John 17, where he describes the disciples' status as "being in the world, but not of the world, and sent to the world". Following on from this, Luciano Cid suggests that we need to create a formal and informal educational environment within church contexts in which children and youth "are presented with alternative perspectives specifically intended to cause what psychologists refer to as *cognitive dissonance*. That is, as adults who profess to be Christians, we should continually provide our children [and youth] with premises that can counterbalance the inaccurate viewpoints being offered by the world".[28]

If Stefan Gustavsson's assessment is correct, that many churches in Western Europe have largely neglected to recognise and address significant secular challenges, we need to take Luciano Cid's advice seriously. This includes identifying and challenging such key contemporary secular worldview perspectives as naturalism, secular humanism and pantheism, by introducing alternative premises, perspectives and arguments related to the Christian faith. We may call this Christian discipleship of the mind.

I have found this approach highly constructive in my own teaching, preaching and writing, especially related to The Communication and Worldviews Programme at NLA University College (Gimlekollen Campus, Kristiansand, Norway) since 2001. This includes exploring the following foundational statements about the Christian faith in open dialogue with students (and other young Christians outside the classroom): (1) Every worldview,

---

[27]Bjørn Hinderaker, 'En helhetlig religionspedagogisk tilnærming til sannhetsspørsmålet. Sluttrapport fra trosopplæringsprosjektet *Hvorfor akkurat Jesus?*', *Theofilos* 8.2 (December 2016), 277-288.

[28] Luciano Cid, "In the world, but not of the world. Cognitive dissonance and altering student perspectives." *The Inspired Home Educator. A Biola Youth Academics Blog.* 6 February 2017. http://youth.biola.edu/blog/in-the-world-but-not-of-the-world-cognitive-dissonance-and-altering-student-perspectives/. [Accessed 23 February 2018.]

including the secular ones, is based on faith commitments. Therefore, we need to challenge the popular view that claims that secular worldviews are based on science and facts, whereas the Christian worldview is supposed to be based on faith and feelings. (2) Many secular worldviews (such as naturalism and secular humanism) misinterpret science, overestimate human reason and underestimate morality, truth and religiosity. (3) Our human search for ultimate meaning, purpose and dignity can only be fulfilled partially through non-Christian worldviews, whereas it is only the Christian faith that provides a comprehensive fulfilment. (4) There are many good arguments for the credibility of the Christian faith, both for the belief in God as the Creator and in Jesus Christ as the unique Saviour and the risen Lord. (5) The central Christian truth claims about Jesus Christ invite us to respond to Him with personal trust, thus challenging our fundamental belief and behaviour.

The external apologetic strategy emerges out of Paul's insightful and provocative comment in Rom. 1:18, where he describes the heart of all unbelief as a way of "suppressing the truth". Os Guinness explains:

> As such, unbelief cannot be other than partly true and partly false, though each unbeliever will have responded to the tension by taking it in either of two directions. Some, usually the few, will have been more consistent in rejecting God, and therefore ended further from God and his full reality. Others, usually the majority, will have been less consistent in rejecting God, and therefore ended closer to God's reality.[29]

This biblical insight led Christian authors such as G. K. Chesterton[30] and Francis A. Schaeffer[31] to develop the broadly negative apologetic strategy of 'table-turning':

> This strategy turns on the fact that all arguments cut both ways. It therefore proceeds by taking people seriously in terms of what they say they believe and disbelieve, and then pushing them toward the consequences of their unbelief. The strategy assumes that if the Christian faith is true, their unbelief is not finally true, and they cannot fully be true to it. At some point the falseness shows through, and at that moment they will experience extreme cognitive dissonance, so that it is no longer in their best interest to continue to persist in believing what they believed

---

[29] Os Guinness, *Fool's Talk: Recovering the Art of Christian Persuasion* (p.112) (Downers Grove: InterVarsity Press, 2015), 112 [Kindle Edition].

[30] G. K. Chesterton, *Manalive* (Los Angeles: Indo-European, 2009), 73-78.

[31] Schaeffer expressed this in the following way: "The more logical a non-Christian is to his own presuppositions, the further he is from the real world; and the nearer he is to the real world, the more illogical he is to his presuppositions." (*The God Who Is There* (London: Hodder & Stoughton, 1970), 122.)

until then. When they reach this point, they are facing up to their dilemma, and they will be open to rethinking their position in a profound way.[32]

This apologetic strategy illustrates that cognitive dissonance may represent a significant missiological opportunity in pre-evangelism and evangelism, in the context of meaningful relationships with non-Christian family, friends, colleagues and neighbours. Peter S. Williams expounds on this in the setting of Western Europe:

> I agree that apologists should try to use common ground to lead the non-Christian into a discovery of cognitive dissonance inherent within their non-Christian worldview, revealing a felt need to which the Christian worldview can be addressed as a to-be-desired intellectual and existential resolution. However, to follow this advice one must be able to compare and contrast the Christian worldview with relevant non-Christian worldviews (so that one can build upon commonalities whilst critiquing differences).[33]

Thus, the Christian community needs to provide alternative Christian viewpoints on all areas of life and particularly on those that a given culture considers crucial. "This is not only needed to provide plausibility for the Christian worldview for non-Christians but also for Christians, who otherwise live in a continual tension of what the sociologists call 'cognitive dissonance'."[34]

In other words, as we have seen above, there is dual need among confessing Christians for an external and an internal apologetic strategy.

Concluding Reflections

This article has explored cognitive dissonance as a missiological challenge and opportunity in predominantly secular settings, from an evangelical perspective and with a specific focus on Western Europe.

I have presented a threefold argument: (1) The challenging experience of cognitive dissonance is because of key cultural factors such as secular paradigms in the academy and the media, the increasing presence of worldview

[32] Guinness, *Fool's Talk*, 109. It should be mentioned that Guinness underlines that the negative strategy of 'turning the tables' need to be complemented by the positive strategy of 'triggering the signals'. This latter phrase refers to what Peter Berger called 'signals of transcendence', i.e. "phenomena that are to be found within the domain of our 'natural' reality but that appear to point beyond that reality" (*A Rumor of Angels*, 53). Such experiences beep like a signal, impelling us to transcend our present awareness and think more deeply, widely and seriously.

[33] Peter S. Williams, "Apologetics in 3D' *Bethinking.org* https://www.bethinking.org/apologetics/apologetics-in-3d [Accessed 23 February 2018.]

[34] Benno van den Toren, *Christian Apologetics as Cross-Cultural Dialogue* (London: T&T Clark / Continuum UK, 2011), 187 [Kindle Edition].

pluralism and the marginalisation of Christian faith and practice; (2) An appropriate Christian response to this challenge includes upholding key biblical beliefs, expanding the knowledge of Christian faith and alternative worldviews, and offering broad and credible justifications of fundamental Christian truth claims; (3) Confessing Christians may use cognitive dissonance internally and externally as a constructive and creative way of challenging alternative worldviews.

The emphasis has been on the role of apologetics in Christian mission in such secularised contexts. This is not because apologetics (*apologia*) is more important than other key missional tasks, such as *kerygma* (preaching), *martyria* (witness), *didache* (teaching) and *diakonia* (service). The reason, however, is that apologetics seems to have been a largely neglected task within many Western European churches.

Thus, there is a need to reclaim biblical foundations and models of apologetics, to learn from historic and contemporary apologetic mentors, and to build a constructive apologetic culture inside Christian churches, fellowships and ministries, in order to equip for holistic disciple making and mission.[35]

[35] See further Lars Dahle, 'Truth, Christian Mission, and Apologetics: A Response and A Proposal', *Norwegian Journal of Missiology* 67.1 (March 2013), 21-38. http://www.egede.no/sites/default/files/dokumenter/pdf/NTM_2013_1_Dahle.pdf [Accessed 23 February 2018.]

In Search of Mission in A Secular Europe

Paul Bendor-Samuel

Introduction

This chapter asks, What is the future for mission in Europe and how might the mission of the Church develop?

Those involved in attempts to understand and plan for the future will be familiar with scenario planning, in which a range of possibilities are postulated. In a recent article, Pew Forum attempted to plot the growth of Islam in Europe, postulating three scenarios based on a variety of growth factors.[1] The scenarios all predict growing numbers of Muslims as a percentage of total population but offer widely differing rates of growth. Using the analogy, we can be certain that God continues to invite the church to participation in his mission. We can be less certain as to what this will look like and what the impact will be. The church is called to humble witness but with no guaranteed results. This need not disturb us. We are reminded of Jesus' words as he commissioned the 72 in Luke 10. They will be received in different ways, some in peaceful welcome, others with rejection but, says Jesus, even in rejection be sure of this 'the kingdom of God is near' (Luke 10:11). As we get started, let me say a few words about 'mission' and our context, 'secular Europe', since our perspectives on these deeply shapes the potential scenarios for mission in the future.

A Word on Mission

The word 'mission' is highly contested today and rightly so. It was not until the sixteenth century that the church began to use 'mission' in ways we do today. Michael W Stroope has traced this history, demonstrating its origins in Iberian diplomatic and military activity during the expansion of the Spanish and Portuguese western and eastern empires.[2] The word is freighted with unhelpful baggage, whether narrow reductionisms or as a symbol of imperial and colonial imposition. Stroope considers all use of 'mission' as anachronistic when used

---

[1] http://www.pewforum.org/2017/11/29/europes-growing-muslim-population/ (accessed 1 April 2018).

[2] Michael J Stroope, *Transcending mission: The eclipse of a modern tradition* (London: Apollos, 2017), 238-262.

to describe the activities of the church before the sixteenth century. Indeed, he makes a strong case for abandoning its use completely. The problem, however, is that no term remains baggage-free for long. Witness the evolution of the English words for disability over the past 30 years; from handicapped, disabled, special needs, specially abled and back to people with disabilities.[3] Each change was made with good intent but quickly became loaded with both positive and negative meaning.

Stroope's alternative, 'pilgrim witness', briefly sketched in the epilogue to his book, fails to reflect the richness of biblical concepts of mission. Our task is to constantly reinvest the word 'mission' with meanings that reflect the nature of God and his mission as revealed through the grand narrative of Scripture while making sense of this in our contexts. I am reminded of a recent conversation at the Oxford Centre for Mission Studies where I work. We held an open evening in which we shared stories of what our scholars and faculty are doing. At the close of the evening one of the visitors, a local resident, approached me and noted, "As a result of tonight I am going to have to revise my understanding of mission." "Oh," I responded, "how so?" Her reply, "I thought mission was shoving the bible down people's throats. Tonight I discovered it is about reaching out and supporting people." Perhaps not a perfect description of the fullness of mission but reflective of someone on a journey, willing to reimagine a word in the light of fresh evidence.

The richness of our mission is derived from the ultimate purposes of God, expressed in Ephesians 1:9-10:

> he made known to us the mystery of his will according to his good pleasure, which he purposed in Christ, to be put into effect when the times reach their fulfilment – to bring unity to all things in heaven and on earth under Christ.

God's mission, as Rene Padilla simply puts it, is that "everyone and everything should come under Jesus Christ as Lord".[4] This is the mission that Jesus, sent from the Father, continues to send us his disciples into the world to participate in. This vision of the ultimate purpose of God, where all things are reconciled and reintegrated under the Lordship of Christ, speaks of the kingdom reign of God in all its freedom, life and beauty. But this Kingdom does not exist in a vacuum. The Kingdom, as revealed to us in the Gospels, is not an abstract set of ideas or even the exercise of righteousness and justice but

[3] The positive shift through this journey has been the move from defining people as 'the disabled' (noun) to people with disabilities (a descriptor).

[4] Rene C Padilla, 'An ecclesiology for Integral Mission' in *The Local Church, Agent of Transformation,* Tetsunao Yamamori & Rene C Padilla (eds.) (Buenos Aires: Kairos Ediciones, 2004), 25.

it is localised in a person: Jesus of Nazareth. (Luke 11:20). To quote Newbigin, "The kingdom has a human face."[5]

The revelation of the mystery of God that Paul refers to leaves no room for the separation of the Kingdom from the King in mission. It is important to stress this since there is a popular understanding that 'secularism is the latest expression of the Christian faith'. Graeme Smith goes on to state, "Secularism is Christian ethics shorn of its doctrine."[6] Pilgrim witness, to use Stroope's term, must demonstrate justice, mercy and grace not as standalone humanitarian values but as signs of the goodness of God and his invitation to repentance and new life in Christ. After the resurrection, the people of God are called not simply to recognise that 'the Kingdom is near' but that the 'Kingdom has come' in the suffering, victorious and ascended Lord, Jesus of Nazareth. This is what we are witnesses to when we speak of mission in a secular Europe.

A Look at Context

Mission always takes place in specific contexts. In this book a range of European contexts are considered. Recognition and response to the specificity of context makes discipleship and theologising both meaningful and transformational. One of the challenges in offering perspectives on the future of mission is that secular Europe is neither monolithic nor static. Below I will offer a few broad brushstrokes on some of the changes taking place and the ways in which these present moving frontiers for mission. These frontiers may include ethno-socio-linguist communities, but my primary concern is the frontiers associated with a modern and postmodern age.

Frontiers of Affluence and Poverty

A secular, that is, non-religious worldview of society, appears to be strongly associated with cultures of material affluence.[7] The relationship is complex and possibly discomforting for those of us who seek both material ease and spiritual vitality. Nonetheless, from a Christian perspective the challenge of affluence in relation to discipleship is as old as the teaching of the founder and the practices of the early church.[8]

Europe is far from alone in experiencing changing religious adherence in a context of increasing affluence. In South Korea, 27.6% of the population now

---

[5] Leslie Newbigin, *Mission in Christ's Way: A Gift, A Command, An Assurance* (New York: Friendship Press, 1988), 9.

[6] Graeme Smith, *A short history of secularism* (London & NY: I B Taurus, 2007) 2. This book is a recommended text for UK A-Level students studying religion.

[7] Owen Chadwick, *The Secularization of the European Mind in the Nineteenth Century (*Cambridge: Cambridge University Press, 1974). 181.

[8] See Peter Brown, *Through the Eye of a Needle: Wealth, the fall of Rome and the making of Christianity in the West* (Princeton: Princeton University Press, 2012).

self-identify as Christian, making Christianity the most populous religion. This has happened not simply because of the growth of the church but through the dramatic decrease in those identifying with Buddhism, while more than 50% of the population acknowledge no religious affiliation.[9] Anecdotal evidence suggests that while 27.6% of the national population is Christian, the figure for those in their twenties is dropping fast. These changes are taking place in a society that has experienced dramatic economic progress and widespread prosperity.

That said, the onward march of prosperity is by no means assured in Europe. Anyone who has travelled in Asia will have seen the wealth in city after city, from Singapore to Seoul to Shanghai. Towering over the whole landscape, the Chinese economy is set for global domination. Currently the second largest economy in the world after the US, economists disagree as to when it will become the largest but do not dispute that it will happen.[10] Contrast this with Europe. One factor in the rise of extreme expressions of nationalism across Europe is the decreasing standard of living felt by many, with increasing levels of poverty. European statistics show that one in four Europeans suffer with one of three types of poverty: monetary, severe material deprivation or very low work intensity (underemployment).[11] Meanwhile, European states are under huge pressure created by both an increased need for, as well as higher expectations of, medical and social services because of an aging demographic.

Frontiers of Religious Pluralism

Extreme nationalism feeds on difference. Relative freedom of movement, gross global inequalities, war, famine and poverty have combined to create the conditions driving mass migration into Europe. Since 2010 more than one million migrants entered Europe from Sub-Saharan Africa alone.[12] As a consequence, the religious landscape of Europe is changing in complex ways. Some Christian migrants bring vigorous expressions of faith, initially expressed in separate diaspora churches but over time flowing over into the indigenous population (see Harvey Kwiyani in this book, chapter 13). Migration has brought many Muslims to Europe. In 2016, 4.9% of Europe's population was Muslim. Pew Forum research suggests this will rise to between 7.4% and 14%

---

[9] According to the 2015 South Korean census the Christian population is 27.6% (Protestant: 19.7%, Catholic 7.9%) 15.5% self-reported as Buddhist. (Population and Housing census p17.) Those reporting as without religion increased from 47.1% in 2005 to 56.1% in 2015. (Population and Housing Census, 2015, p15.) NB: This data exists in the Korean document but not the English version.

[10] http://www.worldbank.org/en/country/china/overview (accessed 14 April 2018).

[11] http://ec.europa.eu/eurostat/statistics-explained/index.php/Europe_2020_indicators_-_poverty_and_social_exclusion (accessed 14 April 2018).

[12] http://www.pewglobal.org/2018/03/22/at-least-a-million-sub-saharan-africans-moved-to-europe-since-2010/ (accessed 7 April 2018).

by 2050, depending on the pattern of migration rates. In some countries these rates could be considerably higher, with the more rapid growth predictions postulating Sweden to reach 30.6%, Germany and Austria close to 20% and the UK and France close behind. Clearly the religious landscape in Europe is shifting significantly.

Frontiers on Being Human

In one domain, at least, European society has entered a space not visited before: the radical reimagining of what it means to be human. This is being explored in at least three distinct areas: (1) human sexuality, technology, social media, (2) relationships, and (3) enhanced human experience. Although this chapter cannot address these issues in any depth, it is important to recognise how these issues very significantly affect the context for mission in Europe. A brief comment on each area.

That gender is an entirely social construct is now mainstream belief. In a remarkably short period the lesbian-gay movement has become the LGBTQIA+ (lesbian, gay, bisexual, transsexual, queer/questioning, intersex, asexual, + stands for anything not mentioned) movement, with new descriptors being added regularly. Its impact is not simply seen in what is considered God-honouring sexual behaviour but on how we educate our children, even in nursery school, and how we relate to one another. There are now multiple lists of what constitutes appropriate pronouns[13] and in June 2017 Canadian law criminalised the refusal to call someone by the pronoun of their choice. While recognising the complexity of the issues raised here, exactly where this exploration of what it means to be human will take society is far from clear.

Issues related to understanding human sexuality surface deeper questions about the future of secularism and mission in Europe. Is the assumption that we can separate the religious and secular sustainable? If so, where is the place for freedom of conscience in relation to individual action in the public square? Will freedom of conscience be increasingly circumscribed by society and the courts? Will it become increasingly difficult for some Christians, or other religious groups, to practise their faith faithfully?[14]

Frontiers of Technology

Finally, a comment on technology, human flourishing and mission in Europe. Three years ago I was given my first smartphone. It took me a few hours to

[13] See as an example the 10 different root stems and 50 variants offered at https://lgbtqia.ucdavis.edu/educated/pronouns.html (accessed 7 April 2018).

[14] See, for example, the change of heart gay rights activist Peter Tatchell writes about such issues http://www.petertatchellfoundation.org/ashers-gay-cake-verdict-is-defeat-for-freedom-of-expression/ (accessed 14 April 2018).

realise the potential for access to information, communication and data storage opened up to me, a few months to recognise the addictive nature of the device that had become my constant companion. Numerous studies have shown the extraordinary amount of time we spend on screen devices and how this is shaping the way we relate to one another.[15] Two hours per day on social media is considered average, with young people often online for far longer. An increasing body of research is demonstrating the addictive nature of internet and social media use, with all the clinical signs that attend addiction.[16] This may seem no different from any number of addictions afflicting society (substance abuse, refined foods, gambling, pornography, video gaming, shopping). Perhaps the small-screen challenge relates to the ubiquitous use and seemingly harmless nature of social media. It is still unclear how the prioritisation of virtual relationships over actual will impact our expectations and experience of relationships. This goes to the heart of the Christian understanding of the Gospel as restored relationship with God, each other and the whole of creation.

The use of technology to correct and improve our experience of life continues to develop rapidly. A few hours ago I walked to our local optician. I was concerned about some changes I was experiencing to my vision in one eye. Within minutes the ophthalmologist had not only taken high-resolution images of my retina but also scanned it to cellular definition, enabling her to assess whether the retina was starting to detach itself from the back of the eye. Technology has transformed medical practice. Bioengineering is at the forefront of this revolution, particularly since the discovery in 2012 of the gene-editing tool known as CRISPR. This, and other gene therapies, have been successfully used to intervene in various cancers in China, the US and the UK. While technology opens up remarkable possibilities it also raises deep ethical concerns, including the development of designer babies.[17]

Technology is not only being used to shape the formation of human life or the experience of being human. Transhumanism is the name adopted by advocates whose goal is to enhance the human organism itself through technology. Nick Bostrom is Professor in the Faculty of Philosophy at Oxford University as well as founding Director of the Future of Humanity Institute at

---

[15] Peter-Paul Verbeek, 'Devices of Engagement: On Borgmann's Philosophy of Information and Technology', book review of Borgmann, A. *Holding On to Reality: The Nature of Information at the Turn of the Millennium*. (Chicago: University of Chicago Press, 1999) https://scholar.lib.vt.edu/ejournals/SPT/v6n1/verbeek.html (accessed 7 April 2018).

[16] Daria J Kuss & Mark D Griffiths; Online Social Networking and Addiction – A Review of the Psychological Literature, *International Journal of Environmental Reseach and Public Health.* September 2011; 8(9): 3528–3552. https://www.ncbi.nlm.nih.gov/pmc/articles/PMC3194102/ (accessed 7 April 2018).

[17] See microbiologist Dr David King's article on consumer eugenics: https://www.theguardian.com/profile/dr-david-king (accessed 7 April 2018).

Oxford. He is convinced that artificial intelligence (AI) is our greatest opportunity, to be put at the service of human enhancement.[18] He sees the time coming soon when AI is more intelligent than human life and, therefore, our most significant threat. This form of humanism on steroids, driven by fear and concerned with the elimination of aging and death, may appear to belong exclusively to the cinema screen. Yet at a popular level it feeds powerfully into a secular worldview where God is not needed, we are masters of our own destiny and where imagination, virtual reality and reality become fused.

The Changing Context: Summary

We have briefly scanned some of the socioeconomic changes taking place across Europe. The experience of unparalleled general standards of affluence, comfort and security on the one hand; decreasing living standards and global economic power shifts on the other. The confident belief in the inexorable march of technological advance moving us ever forward to a better and longer life on the one hand; the struggle of states to deliver support to an aging demographic on the other. Seven decades of relative European solidarity and peace; increasingly militant nationalism, a resurgent Russia, questions over the viability of the European project. The uncertainties and vulnerabilities brought by waves of invited and uninvited migration, rapid social changes and the search for personal, ethnic and national identity point to the possible breakdown of social cohesion and worse. Perhaps this scenario is difficult to image but Europe has been here before.

All the above are inextricably linked to global shifts in socioeconomic, political and military power, environmental degradation, ethnic and nationalist identity crises, religious movements and more. The butterfly beats her wings in any number of places and Europe feels it.

What, then, of mission in secular Europe?

Looking Back in Order to Look Forward

As we peer into the future, I suggest we look back to an apparently very different context, that of the early church and in particular the post-apostolic, pre-Constantinian period. One could argue that the two eras are so different that little can be learned from that time for mission today in Europe. Living in the shadow of empire, where life was cheap, gross inequalities of wealth and power were normative and all kinds of pagan superstitions gripped people's lives; might this speak more readily to other contexts globally than secular Europe?

Despite the real differences I suggest Europe today shares one critical reality with that pre-Constantine period: a church that does not hold a privileged

[18] See https://nickbostrom.com/ (accessed 14 April 2018).

position within society. Although the legacy of Christendom lingers on, we should not confuse the vapours of a Judeo-Christian value system with living faith in the Crucified one. David Bosch apparently felt that he had paid insufficient attention to secularism in his magnum opus, *Transforming Mission.* Weeks before his untimely death, he gave a lecture, subsequently published as a short volume.[19] He closed his lecture by quoting Johannes Aagaard: "the days of mission triumfans have passed and the days of mission pressa have come… The decisive missiological questions to which we have to respond will often put us be the judges and the prosecutors".[20]

I propose that, for the first time in 17 centuries, the church in much of Europe has entered a place where it shares some of the marginality, suspicion, if not hostility, experienced by the early church. Mission that bears witness to the Lordship of Christ over everyone and everything has much to learn from a church that experienced *missio pressa.*

The Mennonite scholar Alan Kreider has written on the way the process of conversion changed during the first four centuries of church life. He considers the three principal identity markers of believing, belonging and behaving, demonstrating how the initial step shifted over time from behaving to believing.[21] Kreider argues that the changes reflected a profound change of understanding in the way the church was to go about her mission. In his later book *The Patient Ferment of the Early Church,*[22] Kreider explores this in much greater depth, demonstrating that, against all odds, the early church grew not because of her evangelistic or church-planting strategies but primarily through the quality of discipleship. We will look at each element: behaving, believing and belonging to see how this might inform twenty-first-century mission in Europe in the light of the contextual issues raised above.

Counter-cultural Behaving

Alan Kreider asserts that the early church was not organised for mission in the way we speak of it today. There was no strategy for evangelism, church planting or expansion. It simply happened.[23] It was what Roland Allen would later call "the spontaneous expansion of the church". For Allen, this occurs when the Holy Spirit is trusted by missionaries to do his work in and through

[19] David J Bosch, *Believing in the Future: Towards a missiology of Western Culture* (Atlanta: Trinity Press International, 1995).

[20] David J Bosch, *Believing in the Future*, 61.

[21] Alan Kreider, *The change of conversion and the origin of Christendom* (Eugene, OR: Wipf and Stock, 2007).

[22] Alan Kreider, *The Patient Ferment of the Early Church: the improbably rise of Christianity in the Roman Empire.* (Michigan: Baker Academic, 2016).

[23] Kreider, *The Patient Ferment*, 9.

the church.[24] For Kreider, church expansion in the early centuries was akin to a fermentation process; a quiet, invisible transformation taking place in society where the key was lifestyle change that contrasted radically with society expectations and norms. Kreider draws on the work of French sociologist Pierre Bourdieu, who writes about *habitus*. *Habitus* is more than simply behaviour, it is a way of being, of belief embodied in behaviour.

This totally counter-cultural lifestyle, while being hugely costly at times, also attracted people. Here were women and men who endured suffering with patient, confident hope. They lived as equals in a mixed community; slave and free, men and women, old and young and from very different ethnic groups. They were people of integrity; they could be trusted. This lifestyle didn't just happen. It was nurtured through a carefully developed process of catechesis. Someone was attracted by a Christian they knew. They wanted to join the community but before they could fully participate, they had to undergo a process of catechism focused on Christian behaviour. These behaviours were supported from scriptural commands, particularly the words of Jesus. The process could take up to two years or more. Only when the lifestyle was evident would a person be deemed ready for baptism and following that, entrance into the full worship of the church and teaching on the deeper truths of Christian faith.

This understanding of mission reflects a perspective on mission deeply embedded in the whole of scripture. Israel's calling was founded on covenantal obedience.

> "Now then, if you will indeed obey My voice and keep My covenant, then you shall be My own possession among all the peoples, for all the earth is Mine; and you shall be to Me a kingdom of priests and a holy nation." (Ex. 19:5.6)

Covenantal obedience leads to adoption as a "kingdom of priests and holy nation". In other words, the whole nation will be set apart for priestly duty. Since the Levites were set apart as priests within Israel, this national duty was to be played out on behalf of the nations. Israel would represent God to the nations, attracting the nations to the worship of YHWH through the quality of her covenantal obedience. Solomon demonstrates the same understanding of Israel's role at the dedication of the temple.[25] The surrounding nations will flock to Jerusalem, joining Israel in the one temple court to worship and pray. (1 Kings 8:41-43, 59-61). To contrast centripetal mission in the Old Testament

---

[24] Rolland Allen, *The Spontaneous expansion of the church and the causes that hinder it*. (London: World Dominion Press, 1927).

[25] The first temple had only one court. In contrast, the second temple had a wooden wall (the soreg), creating an outer court for Gentiles and unclean. By the time of Herod's temple, the Gentiles were even further removed by a stone wall around the central structure. This is probably what Paul refers to when in Ephesians 2:14 he declares that Christ has destroyed the dividing wall of hostility.

with centrifugal mission in the New Testament is to miss the point. God was establishing the continuing basis for participation in his purposes: ethics. Unless the people of God live like the people of God there is no mission.[26]

The early church understood this. Not many today would choose Isaiah 2:2 as a basic discipleship memory verse:

> In the last days the mountain of the LORD's temple will be established as the highest of the mountains; it will be exalted above the hills, and all nations will stream to it.

Yet this was a favourite the early catechist was expected to know by heart. A wide range of Old and New Testament Scriptures were used in catechism but especially the teaching of Jesus and the sermon on the mount, as recorded by Matthew. The thrust of Jesus' teaching is not simply intellectual assent to propositional truth (believing) but behaviour consistent with being his follower. It is about *habitus*. In following Jesus, the early church recognised that he not only taught but also embodied his own teaching. Kreider highlights a number of specific areas in which the early church lived counter-culturally.[27] We will note four here, each reflective of patient endurance then and of particular relevance to secular Europe today.

Non-violence

Jesus commands his disciples to reject anger (Matt. 5:21ff), submit in the face of hostility (5:33ff), to love, pray for and do good to enemies (5:43ff). The early church not only followed these instructions but also applied them to non-violent behaviour generally. They rejected abortion, were implacably against the practice of infanticide, which was widespread, and rejected the violence of the amphitheatre, the popular sporting area of the day. Within their community, non-violence was embodied in the kiss of peace, a practice begun at the time of the apostles (Rom. 16:16; 1 Cor. 16:20; 1 Pet. 5:14).

Sexual Continence

Jesus taught purity of thought (Matt. 5:27ff) and respect for marriage (5:31ff). When challenged over the practice of issuing a divorce certificate for any reason the man desired, Jesus referred his testers back to both creation (God made humans male and female and gave them marriage (Matt. 19:4-6) as well as the Mosaic law (19:8-9), which was understood to allow divorce for three

[26] Christopher J. H. Wright, *The Mission of God* (Downers Grove: IVP Academic, 2006), 331.

[27] See Kreider who, at one point, lists 19 components of Christian habitus. Kreider, *The Patient Ferment*, 122-123.

reasons: marital unfaithfulness, abuse and neglect.[28] In the early centuries promiscuity was widespread and publicly celebrated. Women were at best second-class citizens, vulnerable and largely unprotected. This was particularly so for slaves who made up between 15% and 40% of the Roman empire and were considered property. The sexual continence and respect for women of the early church was massively counter-cultural.

Integrity

Oath taking was an important part of everyday life. Kreider quotes the fourth-century lawmaker Lycurgus that oaths were the power that holds society together.[29] The ultimate oath was the oath of allegiance to the Emperor as Lord. The early Christians refused to participate, not simply because it was a denial of the Lordship of Christ or because the practice failed to produce integrity but because Jesus had forbidden it (Matt. 5:33). We know of those who were willing to die rather than take an oath. The refusal to take oaths was part of a deeper commitment to trustworthiness. Christians were known for their integrity in business.[30]

Simplicity and Generosity

The early church took seriously Jesus' constant teaching about the corrupting nature of material wealth. Wealth was symbolised in purple cloth, a dye that was hugely expensive. It is said that one of the reasons Constantine was only baptised on his deathbed was because he did not want to give up his wealth. The church combined a rejection of wealth with the practice of radical generosity, as demonstrated at Pentecost. This generosity went beyond sharing material goods to the sharing of themselves through care for the sick and dying even when there was risk of contracting disease themselves.[31]

This call to discipleship was not world denying. Bishop Cyprian (210–258 AD) was asked to provide guidance on the content on catechesis. He wrote a text that has become known as To Quirinus 3. In it he documents 120 statements, each supported by Biblical texts. The first, citing no less than 36 texts, is Precept 1: "of the benefits of good works and mercy".[32] As he says elsewhere, "We do not speak great things but we live them."[33]

---

[28] See David Instone-Brewer, *Divorce and re-marriage in the Bible: the social and literary context.* (Michigan: Wm B Eerdmans, 2002)
[29] Kreider, *The Patient Ferment*, 271.
[30] Kreider, *The Patient Ferment*, 100.
[31] Kreider, *The Patient Ferment*, 111.
[32] Kreider, *The Patient Ferment*, 162.
[33] Cyprian, *On the Good of Patience 3*, trans. G.E. Conway, FC 36 (1958) quoted by Kreider, *The Patient Ferment,* 296.

At a recent Conference on World Mission and Evangelism of the World Council of Churches, I was speaking with one of the senior leaders. I asked him to share what he saw as the trajectory of the WCC. He responded, "In the past we were divided by theology. Today we are divided by ethics and this will be far more dangerous for our witness." Dietrich Bonhoeffer saw this clearly and wrote about it in Nachfolge,[34] devoting the central third of the book to an exposition of the Sermon on the Mount. If the church is to engage in mission in secular Europe it will require a renewed and radical re-commitment to counter-cultural behaving. Behaving that reflects the call of Christ will provide a compelling alternative lifestyle: rejection of violence in its different manifestations, freedom from addictions, sexual continence in a society in which sexual practice is seen as integral to being human, protection for the most vulnerable, integrity and generous simplicity. We suggest there is much to learn from this period of history when the church was marginal, vulnerable and often despised.

Counter-cultural Believing

Historians propose different factors to explain the unlikely growth of the church in the first centuries. Ramsey MacMullen summarises it as force, initially the power of miracles and exorcism, replaced by the force of the state.[35] However, Kreider, as we have seen, believes that it was the irresistible power of changed lives as well as the transformative power and mystery of Christian prayer and the Eucharist that contributed to this exponential growth of the early church.[36] Michael Green, theologian and evangelist, saw the power of evangelism and apologetics as decisive.[37] Kreider is somewhat dismissive of Green, stating that the best treatment of second-century apologetics appeared in 1970 with the publication of Green's book *Evangelism and the Early Church.*[38] It may be that the early church produced no organised, strategic document on evangelism but the early church clearly engaged in spoken witness and reasoned defence of the faith.

Green shows that the concept of conversion was alien to the times. "Conversion, then, in our sense of an exclusive change of faith, of ethic and of cult, was entirely foreign to the mentality of the Graeco-Roman world."[39] This speaks to our own context, where personal ethics may be tolerated but the call to conversion is seen as intolerant and colonising. Green outlines a wide range

---

[34] Dietrich Bonhoeffer, *The Cost of Commitment* (London: SCM Press, 1959).

[35] Ramsey MacMullen, *Christianising the Roman Empire (AD 100-400* (New Haven: Yale University Press, 1984).

[36] Kreider, *The Patient Ferment*, 211.

[37] Michael Green, *Evangelism and the early Church* (Crowborough: Highland Books, 1984 edition).

[38] Kreider, *The Patient Ferment*, 10.

[39] Green, *Evangelism and the early Church*, 176.

of evangelistic approaches including public evangelism, preaching, teaching (which inspired witness), testimony and martyrdom, witness in the home by different members of the household, home meetings and hospitality, written texts, including the development of the Gospels and apologetic materials.

Some of these materials took on a polemical and harsh tone.[40] This is a reminder that behaviour and apologetic must be consistent. For those who seek to live by non-violence, by turning the other cheek and loving the enemy, our engagement cannot be strident and aggressive but humble, gracious and respectful.

Secular Europe provides a challenging context to Christian apologetics. This is not simply because "the areligious do not see themselves as areligious in an almost completely atheistic society" as Jørgensen points out in chapter one of this book. Nor is it just because spirituality is largely seen as a commodity to be kept strictly private, where spirituality is understood as anything that makes for personal well-being. The challenge arises from the profoundly different understandings of what it means to be human: as creature made in the image of God or evolutionary material en route to further adaptation. This challenge presents arguably the greatest frontier in mission not just in Europe but globally. Yet this is a frontier where the Lordship of Christ is needed, pointing the way forward as we seek to harness knowledge in the service of society rather than at the expense of wholeness and fullness of life. The challenge requires the alignment of counter-cultural behaving with believing as well as counter-cultural belonging.

Counter-cultural Belonging

In 1955, Donald McGavran wrote *The Bridges of God*[41] in which he developed the proposal that the early church spread through family networks acting as bridges between communities. The book launched a missiological approach that has been subsequently termed 'mission by management', because of an apparently uncritical application of a North American business model to mission with an obsession for strategy, speed and scale.[42] Nonetheless, McGavran identified the importance of social networks in the spread of the Gospel of the Kingdom. The church grows not just through behaving and believing but by belonging.

Kreider gives considerable attention to the counter-cultural nature of the early church community. He proposes that the kiss of peace symbolised better than anything else the radical nature of this community. In general, people of

---

[40] Green, *Evangelism and the early Church*, 280.

[41] Donald McGavran, *The Bridges of God: A study in the strategy of Missions* (London: World Dominion Press, 1955).

[42] Escobar, S 'Evangelical Missiology: peering into the future', in *Global Missiology for the 21st Century*. William D Taylor (ed). (Michigan: Baker Academic, 2000), 109.

different social class and gender would not kiss, although a servant might kiss the feet of the master and someone of higher status might kiss the hand of one above them socially. The kiss embodied social status.[43] The kiss of peace demonstrated a completely different order of community. The kiss followed the preaching of the word and preceded the Eucharist. Catechumen could not join the kiss and left the service after the word as they were not yet holy.[44] Once baptised they became a member of the community. Despite great difference in status, age, gender and ethnicity the kiss demonstrated, in a deeply intimate way, their new identity as one in Christ. It also provided the opportunity for reflection and reconciliation. It is not easy to live together as equals when the prevailing culture emphasises difference. The kiss occurred before the Eucharist, providing an opportunity to be reconciled before the meal, thus symbolising the reconciling sacrifice of Christ. In a Europe that is fractured and struggling for cohesion in the middle of great ethnic diversity, what might be the equivalent of the kiss of peace?

Many in secular Europe struggle for any sense of meaningful belonging. Isolation affects the elderly and the young. Single-parent families are common while the workplace often offers little in the way of team belonging, particularly in information technology-focused industries. As already noted, many of us spend hours in 'virtual' isolation, with friendships reduced to 'likes' and emoji trading. Europe remains deeply divided socioeconomically. In 2017 the Organisation for Economic Cooperation and Development (OECD) published a paper on the socioeconomic divide in Europe.[45] Among the findings:

- The gap between the rich and the poor is at an all-time high.
- There are high levels of household debt with 10% of households over-indebted.
- 17% of all EU 15–29-year-olds are unemployed and at risk of being permanently left out of the labour market.
- Immigrants in employment are twice as likely as native-born peers to be living below the poverty line.
- Unemployment is 50% higher among youth of migrants compared with their native-born peers.

In this context of division and isolation, the church has an opportunity to offer counter-cultural community in which there is "neither Jew nor Greek, slave or free, male or female" but rather oneness in Christ Jesus (Gal. 3:28) and where "you are no longer foreigners and aliens, but fellow citizens with God's people and members of God's household" (Eph. 2:19). As Harvey Kwiyani points out in chapter 13, diaspora churches have an important role to play in

---

[43] Kreider, *The Patient Ferment*, 215.

[44] Kreider, *The Patient Ferment*, 217-218.

[45] https://www.oecd.org/els/soc/cope-divide-europe-2017-background-report.pdf (accessed 8 April 2018).

mission in Europe. This will require a journey of exploration involving changes of attitude and practice within both the indigenous and diaspora churches.

This journey of exploration will not be confined to the integration of ethnic diversity into new forms of Christian community, urgent as this. Stefan Paas has surveyed the history and practice of church planting in Europe and is critical of many of the assumptions and practices of the past 50 years.[46] Nonetheless, he is a strong advocate, theologically and practically, for church planting that draws on widely diverse approaches within the older churches as well as in the new expressions. Speaking of church growth, he notes, "the crisis (sic: of Christianity in Europe) touches almost every area of belonging, believing and behaving, and since European Christianity is a rich pool of traditions, proposals for renewal will inevitably be numerous, contradictory, tentative and messy".[47] Older churches have the potential to respond to the 'echoes of Christianity' that are still embedded in the semi-consciousness of some who otherwise consider themselves non-religious. New movements will question whether 'church' is even a helpful term. Whether renewed churches in old orders or new wineskins entirely, mission in secular Europe requires the church to offer counter-cultural ways of belonging that flow out of our belonging to Christ and therefore to each other.

Conclusion

Christendom is long since over for Europe. It can be argued that the continent is not only post-Christendom but post-Christian.[48] The advantage of this label, says Paas, is that it wakes us to the reality of task and, we suggest, its opportunity. In this chapter, we have briefly looked at what we understand by mission, the broad canvass of contemporary Europe and how the early church, marginal and often despised, may provide signposts for the mission of the church in Europe today.

The church has a tendency to engage in various forms of reductionism, emphasising variously word, action, sign and symbol. Secular Europe can afford no reductionism. If we imagine behaving, believing and belonging as three legs of the stool of mission, we need all three fully and courageously expressed. Each element complements the others and incarnates the wholistic expression of grace and truth. Will mission that faithfully bears witness through behaving, believing and belonging turn the tide of secularism in Europe? We don't know but whatever the response, we will affirm, the kingdom of God is here.

---

[46] Stefan Paas, *Church Planting in the Secular West: learning from the European Experience* (Michigan: Wm B Eerdmans, 2016).
[47] Stefan Paas, *Church planting in the secular West*, 185.
[48] Stefan Paas, *Church planting in the secular West*, 188.

Part 3

Perspectives among Youth

Ecumenical Youth Organisations and Their Mission in Secularised Contexts

Zuzana Babicova and Pawel Pustelnik

Introduction

In this paper we are investigating the issue of mission in a secularised context. We take a dual perspective on the problem and consider it through the lenses of two youth organisations, in which we both have extensive experience as practitioners and agenda-setters. Additionally, we look at the Catholic perspective on the mission. The youth context dimension is derived from the work of the two largest ecumenical youth umbrella organisations in the EU, namely World Student Christian Federation – Europe (WSCF-E) and Ecumenical Youth Council in Europe (EYCE). The Catholic backdrop is provided through involvement with some of the recent framings of youth – mission intersection.

WSCF and EYCE Work

One of the questions that is often asked in the secular context towards the youth ecumenical organisations is "who are you?" This pertains mostly to a broader landscape of youth organisations that are based in Europe. EYCE, for example, is a member of the European Youth Forum, which is a platform of European non-governmental youth organisations and within that platform usually aligns with other faith-based organisations (see below). This means that there is a larger faith-based canvas within a strictly secular organisation. It seems that the faith-based organisations are clearly seen by the other members of the Forum as Church-related, value-driven entities. The mission of the youth faith-based organisations is then conceived by the partners themselves, which often leads to perceiving the ecumenical youth as less mission-driven and more value-driven. This is particularly visible against other organisations present as they all claim to have "a mission", however mostly understood as an agenda or set of priorities.

Understanding of the Mission in EYCE and WSCF EYCE's Mission

It may seem odd to today's members of the EYCE, but as reported by Thesenvitz (2015), "EYCE was an organisation in excellent relationship with a number of communist and socialist official party youth structures with a regular attendance also at their famous 'World Festivals of Youth and Students"' in places like Moscow, East-Berlin and Pyongyang, the Council was facing the need for a kind of thematic re-adjustment once the Cold War had come to an end in the early nineties." Established in 1968, EYCE focused in the early 1970s on problems connected with global cooperation with the Global South and also exploring the issues of decolonisation. The other part of the activities was addressing youth unemployment and poverty, which clearly meant that cooperation with secular organisations was essential (Thesenvitz 2015). Through the 1980s and early 1990s, themes like xenophobia, racism, intercultural relations but also for the first time inter-religious dialogue started to gain prime attention within EYCE. Over the years, EYCE has been maturing and learning how to redefine itself, responding to the rapid social and political changes.

Today, EYCE sees itself as "a strong network of young Christians from all over Europe who seek unity between Christians and are engaged in the work for justice, peace & the integrity of creation" (EYCE 2016). The EYCE mission is explained by the organisation itself: "as a Christian youth organisation, EYCE strives to represent young people in Europe as much as possible. EYCE works on an entirely ecumenical basis, and therefore considers itself to be part of the wider ecumenical movement. It wants to encourage Churches and Christian youth movements in Europe to strive towards the unity of all Christians. Its goal is not to form one church structure, but to look for a means to work together despite of different denominational viewpoints. This means working together to overcome such obstacles as nationalism, xenophobia, social exclusion and proselytism" (EYCE 2016). The strong ecumenical angle of EYCE is also embedded in the beliefs it holds: "EYCE believes that bringing people together is the best way to foster mutual understanding between different Christian denominations and traditions. It tries to provide young people with a place to develop an understanding of the different expressions of faith in different denominations and countries" (EYCE 2016).

WSCF's Mission

WSCF mission is "to empower students in critical thinking and constructive transformation of our world by being a space for prayer and celebration, theological reflection, study and analysis of social and cultural processes and solidarity and action across boundaries of culture, gender and ethnicity" (WSCF 2016).

Whom do we serve? WSCF was founded to serve students of various Christian denominations and this body is open to welcome all students and youth irrespective of faith traditions, while maintaining its core Christian ethos and grounding. This openness has been ever present in WSCF and continues to be in its work.

To be more concrete, what is ultimately the mission for WSCF based on the above-mentioned statement? WSCF has formed its role as a seeker of understanding for questions students and young people have, as a body asking questions important for us in our historic times as well as going back to "old questions" without taking it for granted and rediscover answers or further questions. Thus, WSCF is very much on the journey towards an understanding. To name a few examples to show the nature of this work: in the US in 1959 there was an ecumenical student conference titled Inquiry and Involvement on Strategic Frontiers, in 2005 an event titled Higher Education in Europe: Universities as Service Stations or Laboratories of Universal Questions, in 2015 in the Czech Republic there was a conference called How to make Multiculturalism Possible?, and in other parts of the global WSCF Federation as it is Asia, programmes were evolving around understanding of roots of women's oppression and their unequal status (much work in the 1980s and still ongoing). WSCF and its work is therefore based around questions related to the times we live in.

As the two sections above outline, WSCF and EYCE have different backgrounds and scope of activities. While WSCF can boast its global citizenship, EYCE focuses very much on grass-roots level campaigning and activities.

Secular Contexts in the Mission of EYCE and WSCF

Working in secular contexts is also what both organisations nowadays consciously choose to do – to undertake their mission in secularised contexts and be open towards others with a goodwill to work together. WSCF and EYCE have been historically allying with secular partners, e.g. activities with non-religious partners and inclusion of willing non-religious members in their work. The events that both organisations run (and sometimes run them together, for example a study session that took place in Budapest in May 2016) are often co-organised by the Council of Europe. This strictly secular partner is strategic for the work of both organisations as it assures a large proportion of funding, and even more importantly generously funds the travel costs for the event's participants. Given how widespread both WSCF and EYCE's networks are, this support is vital for keeping the relationships flourishing. Another important secular partner for EYCE is the European Youth Forum, which allows the organisation to reach out to broader audiences as well as make the ecumenical movement heard in the debate strongly dominated by non-religious organisations. On the other hand, the Youth Forum provides for a platform of dialogue with other religious organisations. Through the Forum, but not exclusively, EYCE was able to start various partnerships, such as with the European Union of Jewish Students (EUJS), and Forum of European Muslim Youth and Student Organisations (FEMYSO). Interestingly, a secular venue becomes then a facilitator of inter-religious exchange.

The work in the secular context poses some perils too. Both organisations depend financially to a large degree on funding from secular donors, which may have some impact on the way we do our mission. In the past, the European church-related organisations and churches themselves used to provide WSCF and EYCE with significantly more resources than today. Thus, religious organisations such as WSCF and EYCE had to find a way to operate in a non-religious funding context.

Does that mean that WSCF and EYCE may be pushed to merely mimic the secular world at the end? How does it affect our mission? As mentioned, both WSCF and EYCE strongly rely on the funding provided by the EU Erasmus+ programme or Council of Europe (Youth Department of the Council of Europe), which allows us first to run the offices through the operational grant. Second, most of our events (such as seminars, training sessions, conferences) are reliant upon the funding provided by the EU institutions. This also means that the events need to be organised within the framework recognised by the funding bodies and need to conform to the aims and objectives given. Although these usually are defined in a broad way, they have limits. The broad framework can look like a "youth citizenship, youth mobility and the value of human rights, democracy and cultural pluralism" (Council of Europe 2016). Although these are values that are promoted by a secular donor, both organisations believe these are inherent to our Christian mission. WSCF and EYCE work on them through the aforementioned action-oriented mission where the aims are clearly defined (as opposed to a mission focused on critical intellectual scrutiny). The question with limits given by our secular donors comes when both organisations would wish to undertake projects, which may be of an intellectual inquiry nature that would show marked questioning of values promoted by those institutions. The freedom of thoughts thus is supported, but freedom as to how far we can go with our thoughts has its limits. This has an impact on our mission when speaking of dependency on secular donors.

How, then, can we safeguard our ideals while struggling to attract essential funding? More concretely, EYCE has been headquartered in Finland until 1999 and its presence there has been heavily supported by the local churches. The funding was not conditional upon agreement on programmatic work and consequently gave EYCE a fairly comfortable position as far as forming its mission was concerned. The situation changed once the office was moved to Brussels and the funding structure needed to undergo changes. The same applied to the documents such as constitution of the organisation, which needed also to comply with the rules of Belgian law in order for the organisation to be registered as a legal entity. The spirit of the organisation remained unchanged, whereas the formal side of EYCE had to adapt to the new circumstances.

Catholic (Youth) Perspective

Before delving into the Catholic youth perspectives, the paper offers a snapshot of the secularisation process in Ireland, where both WSCF and EYCE are present. An interesting case of close intersection between what is generally considered a public sphere (education) and the religious can be viewed in Ireland, where the Catholic Church runs around 90% of state-funded primary schools (Sherwood 2016). Being a baptised Catholic is a requirement for children to be admitted to these schools. As reported in a survey commissioned by Equate, "almost half [of respondents] – 46% would not choose a Christian school for their child if they had a choice, and one in five is aware of someone who has baptised their child in order to secure a school place." (Sherwood 2016) At the same time, the number of non-Catholics grows. Between 2006 and 2011 the number of respondents in the census who declared themselves as atheist, agnostic grew by 50% and reached roughly 6% of the population (Central Statistics Office 2011). Ireland was also the first country in the world that voted on marriage equality through a referendum, when 62% of the population were in favour of new legislation. A legislation that is clearly opposed by the Catholic Church. The secularisation is also visible through falling mass participation as well as a dramatically reduced number of new priests being ordained. Ireland has long been considered the Catholic stronghold, but as the case above shows, the Catholic Church is navigating in a fast-paced, shifting environment at the moment.

How does the Catholic youth backdrop appear against these circumstances? Supreme Pontiff, with the support of the Roman Curia, based in the Vatican showcases a framework of strong centralisation. This is something that in youth is seen as rather a complicated and distant structure. The ex-pope Benedict XVI explains that "Religion must continually allow itself to be purified and structured by reason" (Habermas and Ratzinger, p.77). The discourse offered by Benedict XVI would be appealing to philosophers but to a much lesser extent to youth. The church is aware that the language it used to use needs to be updated and is looking for modern vocabulary to regain attractiveness within both its members and in secularised contexts. In this way for example, Pontiff Francis has focused the church's discourse on solidarity and finding common ground between Catholics globally. This has been also implemented in the World Youth Day (WYD) that took place in Cracow, Poland in July 2016, which reflects on the Beatitudes and in 2016 especially on the sixth one (Pope Francis 2015). The narrative is based on happiness, as the Pope explains blessings (Pope Francis 2015). The missional aspect of the WYD is also aiming at renewal of the idea of pilgrimage that has been deeply rooted in the Catholic faith practice.

Conclusion

This paper has briefly indicated how on one side the youth organisations are involving with mission in a secular context. It has signalled main issues such as access to funding, cooperation with secular organisations as well as within the secular/ised context. These challenges mean that the ecumenical organisations need to redefine themselves to fit into the agendas of more and more secularised public institutions. While some perceive it as a threat, it can be also argued that they present an opportunity to be active in other, less explored fields. It is also a platform for cooperation with partners that offer broad perspectives, even if their missions are conceptualised differently.

References

Central Statistic Office. 2011. Census 2011: This is Ireland. Available at: [Accessed 3 February 2016].

Council of Europe. 2016. Youth: Young people building Europe. Available at: http://www.coe.int/t/dg4/youth/Coe_youth/Structures_en.asp [Accessed 1 February 2016].

EYCE. 2016. About EYCE. Available at: https://www.eyce.org/who-we-are/about-eyce/ [Accessed 2 February 2016].

Habermas, J. and Ratzinger, J. 2006. The Dialectics of Secularization: On Reason and Religion. San Francisco: Ignatius Press.

Pope Francis. 2015. Pope's message to young people to prepare for World Youth Day in Krakow. http://worldyouthday.com/popes-message-to-young-people-to-prepare-for-world-youth-day-in-krakow [Accessed 2 February 2016].

Sherwood, H. 2016. Faith, hope and secularity: Ireland on brink of change as church power wanes. The Guardian Online http://www.theguardian.com/world/2016/feb/17/faith-hope-and-secularity-ireland-on-brink-of-change-as-church-power-wanes.

Thesenvitz, D. 2015. EYCE: a boat on the waves of modern history in Europe. Paper delivered at the EYCE General Meeting, 8 July 2015.

WSCF. 2016. Vision and Mission of the WSCF http://www.wscfap.org/globalmovement/vision.html [Accessed 15 February 2016].

(De)Secularisation from the Perspective of the Serbian Orthodox Youth

Tijana Petković

The religiousness of citizens in Serbia and their attachment to Orthodoxy and the Serbian Orthodox Church (SOC) during the twentieth century should be viewed from several different angles. The impact of the SOC over the years has been unequal, even diametrically opposite. To understand this, we will look at two forms, one that is stimulating for SOC, in which the relativity of people is positively evaluated and in which the SOC enjoyed a great reputation. On the other hand, we shall investigate a pattern that has aggravated the social position, the spiritual influence and the national character of the SOC.[1]

The Religious Situation in Serbia – Historical View

We should be aware that only during the twentieth century the religious situation in Serbia changed drastically. Society had a positive image of religion and church in Serbia before the First World War, religious values were an integral part of social values, church and state were very close in different perspectives; they collaborated and supported each other. The Serbian Constitution from 1903 determines Orthodoxy as an official, state religion, religious education is a mandatory school subject, and national holidays were celebrated with church rituals. Atheism was socially undesirable. Between the two world wars, the social position of the SOC changed. From the position of the state church and socially privileged church in the Kingdom of Serbia, it shifted to a position of equality with other religious organisations and communities in the Kingdom of Serbs, Croats and Slovenes (later Yugoslavia).

The destabilisation of religion started immediately after the Second World War. In Yugoslavia, socialism became the ideology and the religious situation changed dramatically. The case for Orthodoxy in Serbia was very different, since after the marginalisation of the church, the SOC lost most of its influence in society. This eventually led to the destruction of church houses and the murder of members of the clergy. The Constitution from 1946 separates the church from the state, and almost all the power the church once had over

---

[1] M. Blagojević, 'Religiozna Evropa, Rusija i Srbija:juče i danas', *Filozofija i Društvo*, 18 (Mart 2008), 235.

marriage or education was now taken over by the state institutions.[2] In socialist Yugoslavia, the SOC, therefore, did not face only enormous material and financial problems but also socialists made the religiousness itself a socially problematic, stigmatised phenomenon. State policy sought to distance religion and church completely from the political sphere.

The impact of the system has been observed for several years since its inception. Religiousness has become remarkably reduced, and its decline continued during the 1960s and 1970s.[3] At the end of the 1980s and beginning of the 1990s, changes started to bring back the situation from before the Second World War, so a declared theism developed from a declared atheism. In this structure, during the first decade of the new era, we have the relatively stable structure of faithful people. Previous sociological research and public opinion research in Serbia not only demonstrated a strong confessional, Orthodox consensus, declared religiosity and faith in God but also conceptual syncretism, amorphous religious consciousness, selectivity dogmatic belief in Christianity and certain religious practices.[4]

The increase of the nominal number of the religious people in Serbia in the 1990s can be caused by the breakup of Yugoslavia and national strengthening. However, religiosity remains a rural phenomenon, as in previous decades; the most religious are farmers and housewives.[5] Older respondents are convincingly the most religious in comparison to other generations. Pantić notes that desecularisation in the early 1990s took place through the re-socialisation of persons who were previously non-religious or atheistically oriented. This process also implied a socialisation of a youth that has adopted religious values without passing through a state-ordered process of atheist education. Later sociological research has confirmed that during the 1990s the religious situation in Serbia was interpreted in terms of the revitalisation of religion and the desecularisation of Serbian society.[6]

The Religious Situation Today

Today, people are ready to identify themselves in religious terms; the number of atheists has been radically reduced and the fundamental religious beliefs of

---

[2] Also, in the next two Federal Constitutions, from 1963 and 1974 belief in God was proclaimed as a private matter, the churches were guaranteed freedom of religious practice rituals, but only in religious premises and yards around the churches. L. Radulović, 'Bog kao privatna stvar', *Etnoantropoloski problemi*, 9 (Januar 2014), 35-48.

[3] Dragomir Pantić, *Intenzitet religiozne i nereligiozne orijentacije u Beogradu* (Beograd: IDN, Centar za istraživanje javnog mnenja, 1974).

[4] M. Blagojević, 'Religijsko-konfesionalna identifikacija i vera u Boga građana Srbije', *Filozofija I Društvo,*23 (Januar 2012), 44.

[5] Blagojević, 'Religiozna Evropa', 245.

[6] Blagojević, 'Religiozna Evropa', 248.

Orthodoxy have been revitalised. Religious education was reintroduced in 2001 in state schools, after being banned in 1952.[7] Indicators of religious self-identification are at a high level, the most important belief, in God, is present in more than 50% of the population surveyed. Other dogmatic beliefs are not so widespread, but given the statistics of about 40 years ago, there is definitely progress. Indicators of traditional attachment to the church, such as baptisms, weddings, funerals, are brought closer to the results of the confessional identification of the population, while the indicators of religiosity and association with religion are the weakest, but still in the direction of desecularisation.[8] The church today must focus its efforts on helping its members develop moral habits and find ways to connect beliefs and actions; the church also must insist on the universality of the Christian Gospel, which embraces and interprets the private and the public dimensions of human life in history.[9]

Comparative research will be presented in three different tables: how many people are religious, and how many of them are practising certain religious ceremonies. Personal religious self-declaration of students in the years 1985 and 2013, and the general population of 2010 (in percent of all interviewed students) – see overleaf.[10]

Students today declare themselves as religious in a very large number, especially when we compare with the number from 1985. Overall, students first identify with the dominant confession in Serbia – with Orthodoxy and an extent of this identification almost completely corresponds to the data on affiliation with Orthodoxy from general research of the population in 2010. According to this indicator, we might not conclude, as before, that students are one of the most atheistic social groups, although maybe we could mention that the explanation of this phenomenon is not the first case. During socialism, even today, we should not ignore the conformism of students, acceptance of the prevailing way of thinking, and a former status of the stigma. Of course, the same is true for the second indicator, where we view the results in the tables: religious self-declaration of students today records a cardinal jump compared to the results from the mid-1980s when there were not a whole 3% undecided believers. Today in Serbia, 56% of students are conventionally religious, as members of traditional religious communities. In the past, there was a

[7] Rastko Jović, 'Religious education-challenges and perspectives in contemporary society: Western Balkans/Serbia', *Astra Salvensis*, 5, 9 (2017), 11.

[8] Mirko Blagojević, "Savremena religioznost studenata i desekularizacija srpskog društva" in Mirko Blagojević, Jelena J. Maksimović and Tijana Bajević (eds) *(Post)sekularni obrt: Religijske, moralne i društveno-političke vrednosti studenata u Srbiji (*Colografx, Beograd, 2013), 28.

[9] Emanuel Clapsis, *Orthodoxy in Conversation* (WCC Publications, Geneva, Holy Cross Orthodox Press: Brookline, Massachusetts, 2000), 144.

[10] Blagojević,"Savremena religioznost studenata", 33.

difference between the typical religious personality of the female sex and the typical male atheist. Nowadays, this difference is almost imperceptible.

Religious self-declaration / year of research	Students/ 1985, đorđević[11]	General population/ 2010, hkc, ca[12]	Students/ 2013, cres[13]
Religious, member of the traditional religious Community/believer	2,9	77,9	55, 8
Indifferent to religion / ambivalent position	16,2	3,9	9,5
Not religious /unbeliever	51,2	10,7	6,9
Agnostic			5,5
Convinced atheist	29,7	3,1	5,6
Total no. of religious people	2,90	77,9	69,2
Total no. of unreligious people	80,9	13,8	18,0

People, in addition to dogmatic beliefs (Holy Trinity, Jesus Christ as the Son of God, Paradise, Hell), also believe in certain parts of non-Christian, pagan or postmodern movements and religions.[14] Accepting the beliefs of other religions with the faith of the confession to which it belongs is called religious eclecticism,[15] and it is today very often characteristic of contemporary, postmodern religiousness. Although non-dogmatic belief in God is primarily represented by non-religious and indecisive students according to the statistic.

---

[11] Dragoljub B. Đorđević, *Studenti i religija, Građa iz istraživanja* (IIRO, Zbivanja:Niš, 1987), 1-128.

[12] Sociological experiential research titled "Religion of the citizens of Serbia and their relation to European integrations" was designed by the Christian Cultural Center (HKC) from Belgrade and implemented with the financial support of the Konrad Adenauer Foundation in Berlin and Belgrade and the Center for European Studies from Brussels on a representative sample for The Republic of Serbia, without Kosovo, of 1219 respondents in 2010, with additional examination of three confessional subgroups (Islam, Judaism, and Protestantism) in the first half of 2011. M. Blagojević, 'Religijsko-konfesionalna', 45.

[13] Center for religious studies of the Institute of Philosophy and Social Theory conducted in cooperation with the Belgrade office of the Foundation Konrad Adenauer and the Center for European Studies from Brussels Researching Religious, Moral and Socio-Political the values of the student population in Serbia, on a proportional basis a quota sample of 1056 students. TijanaBajević, Radule Perović, Ana Zotova, "O metodologiji" in Mirko Blagojević, Jelena J. Maksimović and Tijana Bajević (eds), *(Post)sekularni obrt: Religijske, moralne idruštveno-političke vrednosti studenta u Srbiji,* (Colografx, Beograd, 2013), 7.

[14] According to CreS statistics from 2013, 19% of students believe in astrology and 14.1% believe in magic. Blagojević,"Savremena religioznost studenata", 40.

[15] Blagojević, "Savremena religioznost studenata", 39.

The church's ritual practice represents the heart of the church's faithfulness and shows the level of connection of the faithful with the church activities, fulfilment of religious obligations and duties, which is an indispensable condition of salvation in Christianity. Therefore, indicators that show participation in ceremonies (baptisms, marriages, requiems, a celebration of holidays) are equally relevant as evidence of religious change as well as indicators of the current attitude towards religion (liturgy, church visits, confessions, prayers, fast).

Liturgy (mass, Jumu'ah)[16]	Students 2013	Students 1985	General 2010
Once per month	9,2	0,3	17,1
Few times per year	35,7		40,9
Never	51,2		42,0
Fast before the holidays			
Regularly	26,3	0,3	27,4
Sometimes	38,5		45,7
Never	31,5		24,2
Confession			
Often	6,2	0,1	7,3
Rarely	16,5		18,0
Never	73,3		64,7
Communion			
Yes	48,7		36,6
No	42,2		56,8

Let's see what gives us information about the traditional student relationship according to religion and church today in Serbia in relation to the earlier period:

Baptism[17]	**Students 2013**	**Students 1985**	**General 2010**
Yes	79,5	36,6	82,5
No	12,6	49,3	11,0
Celebration of religious holidays			
Ordinarily	76,8	3,7	91,8
Sometimes	13,8		
Never	5,7		
Requiem			
Yes	80,6		87, 3
No	14,8		8,0

16 Blagojević, "Savremena religioznost studenata", 51.
17 Blagojević, "Savremena religioznost studenata", 53.

The traditional connection is the most abundant and strongest connection of the people with religion and church in Serbia.

According to the modalities of religious self-declaration, in the research of the Christian Cultural Center in 2010, there are mostly traditional believers[18] who participate in ceremonies and honour their customs, but they are not active in the religious community (38%); believers who accept all the teachings of their religion (33%) are in second place.[19]

Even though there was a prediction that religion will disappear, a different turn of events took place. The latest results of the research are showing the trend of desecularisation in Serbia, especially after the time of socialism from the 1970s and 1980s. The rise of traditional religiosity, in addition to confessional, is increasing by a small amount. Although at first glance those percentages do not seem impressive, an increase over the 1990s is noticeable. For even better results, the church must meet the challenge of being simultaneously mystical and prophetic, socially active and spiritual, it must unite theology and ethics, liturgy with life.[20] Berger stated that religion does not only disappear, but it's more and more present in everyday politics and public life, and religion never vanished, but it was only invisible in our society.[21] That is definitely the case with the Balkan states, which Grace Davie named "an exception in comparison with the relative indifference of most Western Europeans according to the serious acceptance of religion".[22]

Bibliography

Bajević, Tijana, Perović, Radule and Zotova, Ana. 'O metodologiji.'In (Post)sekularni obrt: Religijske, moralne i društveno-političke vrednosti studenata u Srbiji. Eds Mirko Blagojević, Jelena J.Maksimović and Tijana Bajević. Colografx, Beograd, 2013.

Blagojević, Mirko. 'Religiozna Evropa, Rusija iSrbija:jučei danas.' Filozofija i Društvo18 (2008).

[18] When we speak of traditional, or cultural believers, we mean those who maintain a lesser or greater intensity of their relationship with the church, but they mostly partly or completely lack some of the elements of faith, most often churchiness. They are not eschatological oriented, but mainly towards the past, with the elements of natural religiousness and religiousness from the earlier periods of spirituality. Z. Krstić, 'Tradicionalni vernici kao pastirski problem i izazov', *Sabornost,* 5 (2011), 119-29.

[19] Z. Kuburić, 'Verovanje i pripadanje u savremenoj Srbiji', *Religija i tolerancija,* 10, 18 (July–December 2012), 12.

[20] Clapsis, 'Orthodoxy in Conversation', 135.

[21] Ivan Markešić, "Sekularna država i kršćanstvo. Mogu li u budućnosti jedno bez drugoga?", in Dragoljub Đorđević, Predrag Stajić and Dragan Todorović (eds.), *Hrišćanstvo u 21.veku* (Prometej, Leskovački kulturni centar, JUNIR:Novi Sad, Leskovac, Niš, 2014), 300.

[22] Grejs Dejvi, "Evropa: izuzetak koji dokazuje pravilo?" in Peter Berger (ed.), *Desekularizacija sveta* (Mediterran Publishing: Novi Sad, 2008), 100.

Blagojević, Mirko. 'Religijsko-konfesionalna identifikacija i vera u Bogagrađana Srbije.' Filozofija I Društvo 23 (2012).

Blagojević, Mirko. 'Savremena religioznost studenata i desekularizacija srpskog društva.' In (Post)sekularni obrt: Religijske, moralne i društveno-političke vrednosti studenata u Srbiji. Eds Mirko Blagojević, Jelena J.Maksimović and Tijana Bajević. Colografx, Beograd, 2013.

Clapsis, Emanuel. Orthodoxy in Conversation. WCC Publications, Geneva, Holy Cross

Orthodox Press: Brookline, Massachusetts, 2000.

Dejvi, Grejs. 'Evropa: izuzetak koji dokazuje pravilo?' In Desekularizacija sveta. ed. Peter Berger. Mediterran Publishing: Novi Sad, 2008.

Đorđević, B. Dragoljub. Studenti i religija, Građa iz istraživanja. IIRO, Zbivanja:Niš, 1987.

Jović, Rastko. 'Religious education-challenges and perspectives in contemporary society: Western Balkans/Serbia'. Astra Salvensis 5, 9 (2017).

Krstić, Zoran. 'Tradicionalni vernici kao pastirski problem i izazov.' Sabornost 5 (2011).

Kuburić, Zorica. 'Verovanje I pripadanje u savremenoj Srbiji.' Religija i tolerancija 10, 18 (2012).

Markešić, Ivan. 'Sekularna država i kršćanstvo. Mogu li u budućnosti jedno bez drugoga?' in Hrišćanstvo u 21.veku. Eds Dragoljub Đorđević, Predrag Stajić and Dragan Todorović. Prometej, Leskovački kulturni centar, JUNIR: Novi Sad, Leskovac, Niš, 2014.

Pantić, Dragomir. Intenzitet religiozne i nereligiozne orijentacije u Beogradu. Beograd: IDN, Centar za istraživanje javnog mnenja,1974.

Radulović, Lidija. 'Bog kao privatna stvar.' Etnoantropoloski problemi 9 (2014).

Part 4

Europe – and Beyond

Migrant Churches in a Secular Europe

Harvey Kwiyani

In this essay, I will discuss the context of migrant churches in Europe and how they wrestle with secularism that, for many of them, is a foreign phenomenon. I use the story of African churches in Europe to demonstrate why migrant churches find secularism problematic. I also explore how they are making efforts to adapt to make sure that their churches outlive them by finding appropriate ways to evangelise Europeans while they also continue to explore ways to effectively disciple the second-generation migrants. Overall, I suggest that even though migrant churches find it difficult to understand European secularism and to operate in Europe's secular contexts, they are resilient and will eventually discover ways to evangelise and make disciples in Europe.

Behold the New European Christians

There is a growing presence of migrant Christians and churches from around the world in Europe. In many European cities, migrant churches represent the growing sector of Christianity. Afro-Caribbean churches started to appear in Britain in the 1950s. African congregations sprouted in Europe in the 1970s. Later, in the 1980s, African denominations and church networks began to appear in Europe. Between 1990 and 2010, African churches proliferated in every major European city, especially in those European countries that had colonies in Africa – France, Britain, Belgium, Portugal and others. There exist now several thousands of African and hundreds of Latin American and Asian congregations in Western Europe. Migrant churches have become a significant and enduring part of the religious landscape in Europe. Their impact is unquestionable. Migrant Christians are slowly becoming the new European Christians.

Most non-Western Christians living in Europe would never have seen the real-life outplay of secularism and the effects of secularity before they migrated to Europe. Of course, many – especially those who engage in mission conversations – would have heard of the 'problem' of secularism or secular humanism in Europe and how it has suffocated Christianity in the continent. They would have been told, as Jonathan Chaplin puts it, that "secular humanism is now by far the dominant 'soul' of Europe, but whether or not that claim is accepted it is clear that maintaining a mutually respectful relationship between these preeminent European traditions remains a major challenge".[1] In my case, when I prepared to come to Switzerland from Malawi in 2000, I received a great amount of information about how secular humanism had replaced Christianity in almost all countries in Europe. However, it was not until I landed in Saint Gallen, Switzerland, that I began to understand what my teachers meant – and I felt that whatever they had told me was an understatement. Nothing could have prepared me for the shock of seeing a post-Christian society. I left Malawi at the peak of a massive spiritual revival, and everywhere I went in Switzerland, Germany – the lands of the Reformation – and Austria. Christianity seemed almost non-existent. The magnificent cathedrals (both Protestant and Roman Catholic) served as a testimony to the glory of the good old days when people flocked to church and Christianity was at the centre of European society. Now, most of the cathedrals doubled as museums. Most Europeans, even those who are nominally Christian, live as if there is no God. They live the true life of Charles Taylor's *buffered self.*[2] Secularism did not only make the public sphere neutral, it pushed Christianity to the margins.

The experience I had in Saint Gallen in 2000 is not unique to me. Over the past decade, I have spoken with a few hundred African pastors and church leaders in Europe. I have *interviewed* almost 200 African pastors in Europe the Diaspora – and the story is always the same. They all find secularism overwhelming and its impact on European cultures a lot worse than anything they could ever anticipate. Just like me, they believe that nothing they heard or read before migrating could have prepared them for what they saw once they started work in Europe. Further conversations with other non-Western missionaries working in Europe reveal similar sentiments. Not only does secularism shock us as migrant Christians in Europe but it also challenges everything we thought we knew about Europe. Even more, it often forces us to retreat into our own congregations that are usually established by migrants for other migrants.

More often than not, migrant Christians do not know how to respond to secularity as it is outside the realms of imagination for many non-Westerners. The very fact that people can choose to live without religion is hard to understand for many non-Westerners, especially those for whom religion means everything. I hear many migrant pastors wonder, "How can a person live without some form of religion? When they engage in worship as all humans do,

[1] Jonathan Chaplin and Gary Wilton, eds., *God and the EU: Faith in the European Project* (Routledge Series in Religion and Politics, Abingdon: Routledge, 2016), 272.

[2] In *A Secular Age*, Charles Taylor says a typical Westerner is a "buffered self"; an invulnerable self, isolated and protected from any sense of the transcendent, essentially living in a world without God or spirits because they do not exist or they are too far away (and if they exist, they are neither needed nor welcome anyway). See Taylor, Charles. *A Secular Age*. Cambridge, MA: Belknap Press of Harvard University Press, 2007.

what do they worship if they do not recognise the existence of God?" European secularism baffles non-Western migrants largely because religion is still on the rise outside Europe. On a worldwide scale, religion is on the rebound, coming back stronger and more adaptive. Peter Berger was right when he, in 1999, declared that the world is actually as furiously religious as ever[3] – a statement that debunks a great deal of the secularisation theories of the 1960s. It is also a statement that seeks to highlight that of the major religions in the world, it is only European Christianity that is in the state of critical decline. Elsewhere in the world, religion is on the increase. The Centre for the Study of Global Christianity at Gordon-Conwell Theological Seminary suggests that the proportion of people attached to the world's four biggest religions – Christianity, Islam, Buddhism and Hindus – rose from 67% in 1900 to 73% in 2005 and may reach 80% by 2050.[4] Christianity continues to grow at an exponential rate around the world, but especially in Africa where Todd Johnson suggests there now exist more Christians than in Europe – 600 million of them in Africa (up from 10 million in 1910 and 500 million in 2010) against 550 million in Europe.[5] In addition, of course, it is no news that Christianity is growing in other non-Western contexts such as Latin America and parts of Asia (such as China and South Korea). However, Christianity is also still growing in other Western contexts such as North America. To some extent, it is true that secularism, as it is known today, is a European phenomenon. Indeed, while people everywhere else are becoming increasingly religious, Europe's engagement with religion, especially among indigenous Europeans, continues to diminish. Institutional or organised religion is looking increasingly irrelevant as more people identify themselves as non-religious.

Secularism and the African Thought

To effectively paint an image of how migrant churches are responding to secularism in Europe, I will use the stories of African churches, and I do so for two reasons: (1) African Christianity in Europe falls in the line of my ongoing research that, in various manifestations, has continued for more than a decade and (2) African churches form the most visible brand of migrant churches in Europe. In addition, the experiences of the Africans in Europe are not too dissimilar to those of the Latin Americans and the Asians. Of course, there will be difference depending on who we talk to and where they are located in Europe, but in broad terms, the attitudes that many Africans hold towards

---

[3] Peter L. Berger, *The Desecularization of the World: Resurgent Religion and World Politics* (Grand Rapids, MI: W.B. Eerdmans, 1999), 2.

[4] John Micklethwait and Adrian Wooldridge, *God Is Back: How the Global Revival of Faith Is Changing the World* (New York: Penguin Press, 2009).

[5] Todd Johnson et al., "Christianity 2018: More African Christians and Counting Martyrs", *International Bulletin of Mission Research* 42, no. 1 (2018).

religion (especially the spirit world) are similar to those we see in some parts of Latin America and Asia, and consequently, their experiences of secularism in Europe are alike. As such, whether you are talking to a Brazilian in London or a Nigerian in Berlin, an Indian in Rome, or even a South Korean in Helsinki, the general outline of their response to secularism is the same – they find it strange, they do not know how exactly to respond to it and they are concerned for their children for whom secularism is their native culture.

The fact that Africans are very religious people has been well documented. Indeed, religion predates Christianity across the continent. When the missionaries arrived bringing the Gospel of Jesus Christ in the nineteenth century, they found thriving complex religious systems that had existed for centuries, and were, in most cases, more expansive than the Christianity they were bringing. For many Africans, the worldview of the Christianity brought by the missionaries was small and could not fully account for their day-to-day life. John Mbiti was right when he said in the 1960s that Africans are notoriously religious.[6] In addition, their religion encompasses everything they do – there is no aspect of their lives that is not touched by religion. A whole generation of African theologians, from Placide Temples and Alexis Kagame to Jesse Mugambi and Kwame Bediako, have explained how, for the African mind, there is no dichotomy between the religious and the secular or the spiritual and the material. Mbiti himself added that:

> Because traditional religions permeate all the departments of life, there is no formal distinction between the sacred and the secular, between the religious and the non-religious, between the spiritual and the material areas of life. Wherever the African is, there is his religion; he carries it to the fields where he is sowing seeds or harvesting a new crop; he takes it with him to the beer party or to attend a funeral ceremony, and if he is educated, he takes religion with him to the examination room or in the university; if he is a politician, he takes it to the House of Parliament.[7]

In his 2013 book entitled *What Is Not Sacred?* Laurenti Magesa adds that:

> In Africa, there is an essentially 'transcendental' perception of all life because all reality is situated in the sacred realm, which is a spiritual sphere. A person's life is their religion, so that 'religion' or 'spirituality' for that matter, is not identifiable as a separate institution but permeates the whole society … The spiritual is not opposed to the physical or material … both are intricately merged … The sacred

[6] John S. Mbiti, *African Religions and Philosophy* (Garden City, NY: Anchor Books, 1970), 1.
[7] Mbiti, *African Religions*, 2.

dominates and infuses the life-world although there are 'dense moments in the life of the people where the spiritual is maximally present.[8]

Jacob Olupona observes that:

> For adherents of African traditional religions, such a separation (between the religious and the secular) is neither desirable nor possible because religious belief informs every aspect of life – including birthing and death, marriage, family dynamics, diet, dress and grooming, health care, the spending and saving of money, interactions with one's friends, and, of course, governance.... Indeed, religion in Africa remains the pulse of the private and public spheres, placing a strong emphasis on moral and social order in families, clans, lineages, and intra-ethnic interactions. As such, it pervades the daily affairs and conduct of African societies.[9]

Religion is important to African peoples – it covers everything. Most African cultures still have their foundation on the belief that the world is much larger than what can be seen. Even outside Christianity, religious myths, symbols and rituals are part of daily existence. As the Christian population has grown in Africa, most of its new adherents have come from traditional religions and have found, especially in Pentecostal Christianity, ways to make Christianity reach all aspects of their life. Many converts bring along the zeal with which they devoted themselves to their old religions and expect Christianity to be more powerful than their traditional religions. It is not unusual for Christians to have to negotiate the spirit world of Christianity and supplement it with the spirit world of traditional religion. Spiritual problems need spiritual answers and cannot be fully resolved otherwise.

Consequently, their Christianity permeates all aspects of their life. Their faith is bold and loud, and it is lived out on the public sphere. Their long Sunday worship services are only charging stations where they refill their spiritual energies to empower them for their Christian witness throughout the week. There is not a space in their life where their Christian faith does not reach. The name of Jesus can be seen on any imaginable place: building and offices, homes, minibuses and canoes. The Gospel is preached in the offices, trains, buses, market squares, and almost everywhere there is a gathering of people. Africans take their religion everywhere: in the fields, in the classrooms, on the plane and in the Diaspora. Where an African is, even in Europe, there is also their religion. An African without their religion is like a fish out of water.[10]

---

[8] Laurenti Magesa, *What Is Not Sacred?: African Spirituality* (Maryknoll, NY: Orbis, 2013), 24.

[9] Jacob K. Olupona, *African Religions: A Very Short Introduction* (New York: Oxford University Press, 2014), 2.

[10] While it is possible for some Africans to deny allegiance to religion, they live in a world where they cannot escape its grasp at all. The communities to which they belong will most probably involve religion at one level or another.

Thus, secularity is generally a foreign concept to African Christians. The separation of the secular from the sacred does not make sense to most Africans.

Making Sense of Secularism in Europe

It is generally accepted that religion is important to African migrants in the Diaspora, be it in Europe or North America.[11] For this reason, most African migrants do not find Western secularism attractive. Even if they do not identify as Christian, because of their religious history in Africa, they tend to be sympathetic to religion. For many African Christians, migration is a religious experience that intensifies their Christian devotion or, in some cases, leads to religious conversion. In the context of secularism in Europe, religion becomes even more critical for Africans. It provides migrants with a coping mechanism in the face of all the isolation and adversity that they face in Europe where both anti-migration politics and racial discrimination are commonplace. It is usually when they meet fellow Africans in a religious atmosphere – in African congregations or at the mosque – that they can let their guard down, pour out their hearts to one another and to God, and live a few moments of abundant life. In singing the Lord's song in a strange land in the company of fellow migrants, they find both social and spiritual solace they cannot find anywhere else.

On the other hand, the secularism that surrounds the Africans in Europe often scares them into even more religious devotion. They see what could become of them and their children if they do not pray or fast enough and they would rather do what they can to avoid it. Laurenti Magesa explains why this is the case:

> In the worldview of practically all African cultures, the exchange of energies as a necessary condition for the possibility of all existence involves, most importantly, the well-being of the human vital energy and is necessary for the well-being of the rest of the created order. In a sense, the welfare of the universe depends on the health of human beings. The behaviour of human community is the foundation of the status of all existence. It bears reiterating that life's positive growth and development, or, conversely, its disintegration and death, depend on how the human vital force communicate with other vital forces. Consequently, human beings bear ultimate responsibility for universal harmony because they represent creation as conscious of itself, its most manifest spirit. By disturbing the equilibrium of the universe, humanity eventually destroys itself … Thus, the idea and structure of human society are essentially part of a worldview that is fundamentally holistic, sacred, and highly integrated.[12]

---

[11] See Jacob Olupona and Regina Gemignani, *African Immigrant Religions in America* (New York: New York University Press, 2007).

[12] Magesa, *What Is Not Sacred?*, 29.

Living in a place where the equilibrium of the universe is lacking pushes Africans to seek to restore it, even if it is just for their families and communities. Furthermore, there is a growing sense in which Africans have begun to think of Europe as a pagan continent. It is not unusual anymore to hear Africans describe Europe as a "dark continent". For them, of course, the spiritual darkness currently engulfing Europe is worse than whatever darkness Europeans saw in Africa 200 years ago. I hear many Africans ask in connection to the religious atmosphere in Europe today, "*Who is the heathen now?*" – a fair question in the light of current religious affiliation statistics in the two continents. This identifying of Europeans as heathens comes with every negative thing that Europeans attributed to Africa in the 1800s – including the need to evangelise and civilise Europe for a truly civilised person will also be religiously awake. These supposedly godless Europeans need to be converted again to the religion that they brought to Africa some 150 years ago. This rhetoric reflects the same attitudes that European missionaries and colonialists showed when they tried to Christianise Africa. Unfortunately for the Africans, most Europeans are not keen to engage with Christianity yet – especially the Pentecostal/Charismatic type of Christianity that is characteristic of African churches in Europe.

Even where African Christians engage with European Christians, there continue to exist many barriers that keep them separate. On the one hand, Africans are generally suspicious of Europe's Christianity that does not seem to engage the spirit world in an expressive manner like they do. They say it is too whitewashed in the river of the Enlightenment to be of any use. To the extent that it can be without explicitly engaging with the spiritual world, it is said to be secularised – it is a Christianity that lacks a lively sense of the sacred. Often, they describe it as dead.[13] On the other hand, most European Christians are not warming up to the loud and emotionally charged all-night-praying type of Christianity of the Africans. They find its lack of intellectual stimulation unforgivable and its emotionalism disturbing. In addition, more often than not, European Christians do not want to follow African leaders even when they are qualified.

Consequently, we have many African congregations in Europe. This phenomenon of migrant churches in Europe comes largely out of the migrants' refusal to secularise or to embrace European Christianity. In some parts of Europe, African Christians represent the growing sectors of Christianity. The London Church Census of 2012 suggested that black Christians account for more than 48% of church attendance in the city even though black people form only 13% of London's population. In some areas of Europe, migrant Christians have become the representative faces of Christianity. I have met young British

[13] Of course, this critique has been around since the early days of African independent churches in the late 1800s. It was foundational to the emergence of African independent churches in the late nineteenth century.

boys and girls who have grown up to believe that only black people can be Christians because all the Christians they know are black.

Adjusting to Secularism

I have, so far, argued that migrant Christians find secularism hard to understand as most of them come from contexts where religion covers all of life. I have also suggested that migrant Christians form their own congregations because, on the one hand, they despise secularism and do not want to take part in it and, on the other, they would rather worship with fellow migrants as European Christianity seems too secularised. While there is a tendency to retreat from the threat of secularism – the threat that they and their children will be secularised – and to retrench in their own migrant churches, many foreign Christians have started to realise that they cannot avoid it for long. Many have begun to look for ways to engage Europeans in spite of or because of their secularism. Many understand themselves to be the missionaries sent by God to re-evangelise Europe and, therefore, must seek to preach to the Europeans, secularised as they are. Failure to evangelise Europeans means that migrant churches have no future. Only local Christians, be they white Europeans or second-generation migrants, can effectively keep their churches going. I will now discuss how some migrant churches are engaging in evangelism and taking care of the second generation for the sake of their mission in Europe.

Nigerians Evangelising in London

The challenges of secularism are particularly manifest in the struggles that migrant churches have to negotiate to effectively evangelise beyond their fellow migrant communities. For most migrant churches in Europe, evangelism is both a hard chore and an uphill struggle. Even though their evangelistic zeal continues to burn fervently, the tactics and strategies that worked well in Africa do not work effectively among Europeans who are hardly interested in religion. Distributing tracts on the high street or knocking on people's doors for evangelism, no matter how long they do them, do not seem to grow churches. Whatever styles of evangelism they are using does not seem to help them connect with Europeans. Many migrant church leaders are beginning to realise they need to change tactics if they are going to be effective in ministry among secular Europeans. As such, their evangelism strategies are changing.

I have been involved in a phenomenological research of African congregations' engagement in mission in Europe since 2012. One congregation's story has stayed with me. A Nigerian congregation of the Redeemed Christian Church of God in East London was faced with a challenge; for economic reasons, members were moving to other parts of London while their younger-generation members left the church for other churches in their borough. They would close the church down in a few months.

After a season of prayer and discernment about how best to engage in mission in their town, they decided to ask, "What does the good news sound like to the people around us?" and "How best can we share it with them in a manner that they can understand?" They decided to experiment with a few ideas: television and social media ministry, after-school clubs, free music lessons, summer barbecues and block parties – all of which yielded little success. However, they realised that within a one-mile radius of their church, there were many elderly people living alone at home. Social workers in the congregation suggested that many elderly people living alone experience high levels of loneliness. In a missional discernment meeting, the congregation's pastor asked the members what the good news to such lonely elders can be. Before long, they agreed that, first and foremost, the good news to such lonely people is the unconditional love and companionship of Jesus, which is, of course, expressed through Christian neighbours being Jesus' "hands and feet" – not as a means to gain an audience to preach but really taking that companionship in itself as part of God's mission in their city. They stated that "Jesus, for the lonely in our neighbourhood, is a faithful friend that stays by our side forever", and made a commitment to be that friend to their lonely elderly neighbours.

The congregation sought training from experts in social work and guidance from their local council (which provided licences to the church to befriend and support the lonely elderly in the area). Thus, a *befriending ministry* was born. Within a few months of this, they had made many new friends in the neighbourhood, most of whom had asked about the faith, and quite a few had become Christians through their efforts. Their church got used to having visitors – mostly non-African – almost every Sunday because of this new thrust of community engagement. The congregation itself feels more at home in the community than it ever did. The congregation's pastor told me that they had three takeaways from the experience. The first is that evangelism is possible even in secular Europe. It generally takes longer and requires patience, but if you build bridges of trust with the people, they will listen to the good news. Second, they concluded that evangelism is necessary for, as the pastor told me, "a church that does not engage in evangelism is only waiting to close down". Most African churches in Britain know this. To survive in Britain, they must face the challenge to evangelise beyond their own African immigrant communities and to disciple their younger generation (which, in the context of Britain, is also a form of cross-cultural evangelism). Third, they learned that evangelism in the context of Europe must be relational. To be able to reach Europeans, migrant churches have to *relationally* move closer to European culture. All the other strategies will only do well if they complement relational ways of evangelism.

Second-Generation Migrants and Secularism

Everything I have argued so far applies to the lives of first-generation migrants. Their children – the second-generation African migrants in Europe – have no way of escape. These children of the migrants must find ways to be Christian in the secular context they call home. As a result, whether they like it or not, migrant Christians will eventually have to face the impact of secularism on their faith or that of their children. Thus, the greatest challenge currently facing migrant church leaders in Europe is the 'faith of the second generation'. Many migrant pastors are concerned about the effects of Europe's secular culture on their children. This is a universal challenge affecting Africans, Asians and Latin Americans alike. Consequently, many of them are currently trying hard to figure out how best to pass the faith on to the younger generation of their church members, if for no other reason at all to keep their children in their churches and ensure that their churches and ministries outlive them. Many have realised that once their children leave their homes – either for university or just moving out to be independent – they either go to other churches or stop going to church altogether. The general consensus among them is that second-generation migrants are not very keen to stay in the parents' churches. If they go to church, they would rather go to other youthful or youth culture churches like Hillsong where they will feel more at home and meet other youths who share their passions and culture.

That second-generation migrants are not staying in their parents' churches should not be a surprise. Apart from the fact that the parents' churches are shaped for a different audience, one of the major factors behind this challenge is that the second-generation migrants have grown up in a secular culture where most of what their parents take for granted does not stand at all. While most of the parents were raised in the faith in a context of spiritual revivals, were discipled in active Christian student organisations at school, and were taught to pray and wrestle with the evil spirits in prayer, migrant children in Europe are exposed to a different worldview. Without proper apologies, the younger migrants find it difficult to build bridges between the religious cultures at home and the secular cultures in the public sphere. Quite often, they lack the understanding of why their parents pray and worship the way they do. They do not conceive of the spirit world like their parents do. They become influenced more by Western schools of thought and theology.

The future of migrant churches in Europe – and their wrestling with secularism – depends almost exclusively on how well the second and third generations of the migrants will be discipled (and trained for the work of the ministry). Of course, in a general sense, we know that the future of any Christianity depends on how the faith is passed on from one generation to another. In the case of migrant churches, by the time the second generation passes the baton on to the third generation, their Christianity will have ceased to be a migrant Christianity. It will have taken on the spiritual characteristics of the new homeland. It is because of this that we believe that migrant congregations do not last more than two generations especially here in Europe.

In response to this threat that secularism poses to migrant churches, African migrant churches are beginning to turn over leadership to the second generation. Through the phenomenological research mentioned above, I became aware of a Malawian pastor in Nottingham, UK, who has just made his 20-year-old daughter the senior pastor of the church he founded 10 years ago. He has stayed on as an assistant pastor and his responsibilities include mostly mentoring the young leadership and praying for them. They have intentionally given leadership to the younger generation – none of the leaders in the church is older than 30. Thus, all leaders in this migrant church have grown up in Britain. They have grown up with African Christian parents and have learned of African spirituality, but they also understand British culture. This switch in leadership has made the church attractive not only to other younger-generation migrants but also to British youth. That pastor may have found the key to effectively engage European secularism – African spirituality communicated to Europeans in European vessels. That may be the future.

Conclusion

Secularism, no matter how we define it, has serious implications on how God's mission is carried out in Europe. It is not only creating an atmosphere of neutrality. It is marginalising religion, especially Christianity, and in so doing makes Europe a mission field. In this day and age, a good portion of God's missionaries in Europe will be foreign Christians from different parts of the world. Part of what these migrant Christians bring into the European mission field is their Christianity that is shaped by a worldview different from that of the Europeans, and this type of Christianity may be the answer to the spiritual needs in Europe. The first few decades of the presence of migrant churches in Europe are characterised by non-engagement and retreat as they try to figure out how best to respond. However, they are resilient learners. They will find ways, and if they do not, the second generation will.

Bibliography

Adogame, Afeosemime U. *The African Christian Diaspora: New Currents and Emerging Trends in World Christianity.* London: Bloomsbury Academic, 2013.

Berger, Peter L. *The Desecularization of the World: Resurgent Religion and World Politics.* Grand Rapids, MI: W.B. Eerdmans, 1999.

Chaplin, Jonathan, and Gary Wilton, eds. *God and the Eu: Faith in the European Project*, Routledge Series in Religion and Politics. Abingdon: Routledge, 2016.

Hanciles, Jehu. *Beyond Christendom: Globalization, African Migration, and the Transformation of the West.* Maryknoll, NY: Orbis Books, 2008.

Johnson, Todd, Gina Zurlo, Albert Hickman, and Peter Crossing. "Christianity 2018: More African Christians and Counting Martyrs". *International Bulletin of Mission Research* 42, no. 1 (2018): 20-28.

Kwiyani, Harvey C. *Sent Forth: African Missionary Work in the West.* American Society of Missiology Series. Maryknoll, NY: Orbis, 2014.

Ludwig, Frieder, and J. Kwabena Asamoah-Gyadu. *African Christian Presence in the West: New Immigrant Congregations and Transnational Networks in North America and Europe.* Trenton, NJ: Africa World Press, 2011.

Magesa, Laurenti. *What Is Not Sacred? African Spirituality.* Maryknoll, NY: Orbis, 2013.

Mbiti, John S. *African Religions and Philosophy.* Garden City, NY: Anchor Books, 1970.

Micklethwait, John, and Adrian Wooldridge. *God Is Back: How the Global Revival of Faith Is Changing the World.* New York: Penguin Press, 2009.

Olupona, Jacob, and Regina Gemignani. *African Immigrant Religions in America.* New York: New York University Press, 2007.

Olupona, Jacob K. *African Religions: A Very Short Introduction.* New York: Oxford University Press, 2014.

Taylor, Charles. *A Secular Age*. Cambridge, MA: Belknap Press of Harvard University Press, 2007.

Perspectives from the Global South: Europe the Exceptional Case?

Marina Ngursangzeli Behera

Introduction

In the early theories on secularisation, in the wake of the 1970s, the assumption was that modernity processes would affect a waning away of religion. Democracy, the development of societies and the spreading of sciences would transform the social fabric of societies that were considered traditional and affect the faith and belief systems of their people. In the end the modern worldview would transform the worldview of people considered an impediment on their path to a modern society and enlightened reason/ rationality.

One piece in this mosaic was the growing influence of the scientific atheism of the block states where religion was fought (the countries of the Soviet Union, China, Cuba and some other socialist countries). The collapse of the block system after 1990 gave way to a surprising resurgence of religion, religious communities and their influence on societies and politics, to the extent that wars in the Balkans and events such as the genocide in Rwanda/Burundi could easily be labelled as religious wars. With growing globalisation it became evident that religions were not waning, instead their influence was growing.[1] In the debates about these events and the changing perceptions of the role of religion, it has now become obvious that one can observe elements of secularisation as societal processes that nevertheless did not result in a waning of religion but in a changing of its role.

One can argue now that Europe is the exceptional case or even distinctive and not any longer the model describing the path that all the other societies would follow. One could also argue that India is an exceptional case,[2] and that

[1] For details see Johnson, Todd M., and Kenneth R. Ross (eds.), *Atlas of Global Christianity 1910-2010* (Edinburgh University Press, 2009).

[2] Aycan Tasyurek has rightly stated that it is not possible to describe or understand secularism in the Indian context in terms of separation between church/religion and the state (Donald Smith and Charles Taylor), nor as a private-public sphere distinction (Jose Casonova) because religion is diffused into both private and public spheres in India and

even in comparison to most South Asian countries, modern India stands out as officially being secular since 1976 with the inclusion of the term in its constitution. There never was the risk of a waning of religion. With its large sections of people following a broad variety of belief systems and practices that are lumped under 'Hinduism' and strong minorities, e.g. Muslims and Christians, the emerging political system took another direction: to establish secularism as the equality of all religions in Indian society and secularism got redefined in a unique Indian way. It is not about giving up religion or the absence of religion, but the respect for all faiths. The idea of secularism in the context of India is much more complex not only because of the huge population with diversities but also the complexity lying behind its application.

Any attempts to locate and situate the Asian contexts and specifically the Indian contexts within the European/Western understanding would be misleading and a futile attempt as European/Western secularism in its varied forms and patterns cannot be applied in its totality to other parts of the world. This is not to deny that there can be and are some links that could be made. One area where a link could be made is to look at how the historical event of Imperialism, which has often been overlooked, had contributed to the development of critical thinking and the cultural identity of the West. Thus, modern intellectual history, the development of its thought processes, is inextricably linked to the history of its encounter with non-Christian cultures through the colonisation process. The imagery in constructing the frame of intelligibility of the West that universalises itself has as its historical backdrop the encounter between European and non-European cultures. Through the work of comparison, the shape of the West and the non-West were thus co-dependent and co-emergent. This comparative relation continues to be isomorphic.[3] The Indian Constitution of 1950 originally did not have the term secular, though there was agreement on the nature of the Indian state adhering to secular principles. It was only introduced through the 42nd Constitutional Amendment in 1976. Since then, there have been those who appreciate the inclusion of the term in the constitution, and those who repeatedly criticise it as being of foreign origin and therefore not suitable for the Indian context. The problem seems to lie in its application. Moreover, in India it is impossible to try to translate or substitute the term 'secularism' into any of the Indian languages. In India secularism in general is understood by its antonym 'communalism',

---

is not just 'private belief' (John Locke). See Aycan Tasyurek, "Secularism in India" at www.academia.edu/5404273/Secularism_in_india.

[3] The theory of co-dependent and co-emergent of the West and the non-West is well argued by Gil Anidjar, who drew insights from Talal Asad and Edward Said. See Gil Anidjar, "Secularism", in *Critical Inquiry*, Vol. 33, No.1 (Autumn 2006), 52-77, published by the University Press, Chicago. For more details see Asad, Talal, Formations of the Secular: Christianity, Islam and Modernity (Stanford: The University of California Press, 2003); and Said, Edward W., Orientalism (New York: Vintage Books, 1994 (1978)).

whereas in the Western context it is understood by its antonym 'theocracy'.[4] The achievements of Indian secularism have come under continuous scrutiny, especially when there are continuous conflicts and tensions among different communities in the name of religion.

This paper is an attempt to briefly look into the ideas and objectives behind the Indian Constitution in relation to the term 'secularism' and how it has been played out on the Indian scene since then. Its aim is to highlight that secularism in India is quite different from the European understanding and that it hence faces different challenges and offers different solutions.

The Indian Constitution and Secularism

The Constitution of India has played an important role in shaping religion through legislation, forming one dimension of the complexity of secularism in India. In the Indian state's constitution, secular and religion are inseparable, with both having significant roles. There is no state religion and the constitution secures all Indian citizens freedom of faith, belief and worship, which gives the constitution its Indian secular character: India's secularism is impartial to all religious groups. Secularism works both ways. First, religion is not allowed to interfere in the affairs of the state, and second, the state is prohibited from trying to control religion by using its coercive powers.

Mahatma Gandhi describes the correct attitude towards religion as *Sarva Dharma Sambhava*, equal respect to all religions, which is different from the European secularism, which is independent of religion. In fact, by propounding the theory of *Sarva Dharma Sambhava*, Gandhi continued the age-old Indian tradition that can be traced to the ancient saying of *Ekam Sadavipra Bahudha Vadanti* (Truth is one) as a foundation for modern India. Jawaharlal Nehru on the other hand unceasingly advocated a 'scientific temper' and perceived religion and superstition, caste and communalism as hindrance to a modern India force.

Most of the makers of modern India, influenced by European thoughts and practices, were fervent supporters of secularism as an ideology along with the ideals of liberty, equality and respect for human dignity. After India got its independence during the discussion that took place regarding the constitution, there was a shared understanding and agreement on the importance and necessity of establishing a secular state for an effective functioning democracy like it was well established in Europe. For India to follow the ideals of democracy, secularism was considered essential. At the forefront of such ideas was the first prime minister of the country, Jawaharlal Nehru. For him, having a secular state was a crucial mark of modernity: "We have only done

[4] Ravi Kiran Jain, "The Why & How of 'Secularism' in the Indian Constitution", 4 October 2017. See https://sabrangindia.in/article/why-how-secularism-indian-constitution. Accessed on 7 May 2018.

something which every country does, except for a few misguided and backward countries."[5] This was for him especially important because he also acknowledged that "It is an ideal to be aimed at and every one of us whether we are Hindus or Muslims, Sikhs or Christians, whatever we are, none of us can say in his heart of hearts that he has no prejudice and no taint of communalism in his mind or heart."[6]

At the same time, it was also recognised that there was ambiguity inherent in the terminology when applied in the Indian context. Questions regarding how secularism would be applied, whether it would be possible at all, and to what extent, were raised. Ambedkar asked the question as to "what should be the policy of the State, how the Society should be organised in its social and economic side are matters which must be decided by the people themselves according to time and circumstances. It cannot be laid down in the Constitution itself because that is destroying democracy altogether".[7]

So, people like Nehru, and B. R. Ambedkar, though stout supporters of the ideals of secularism, recognised the problems of including the word 'secular' in the preamble of the constitution. It was very clear that a strict application of the term secularism in the Indian Constitution was not at all possible in the highly religious context of India. Lokanath Misra's statement during the debate echoes the dilemmas that the drafters of the Constitution were faced with:

> I accepted this secularism in the sense that our State shall remain unconcerned with religion, and I thought that the secular State of partitioned India was the maximum of generosity of a Hindu dominated territory for its non-Hindu population. I did not, of course, know what exactly this secularism meant and how far the State intends to cover the life and manners of our people. To my mind, life cannot be compartmentalised and yet I reconciled myself to the new cry....Do we really believe that religion can be divorced from life, or is it our belief that in the midst of many religions we cannot decide which one to accept? If religion is beyond the ken of our State, let us clearly say so and delete all reference to rights relating to religion.[8]

H C Mookherjee, the president of the drafting committee, in the same line stated:

---

[5] Transcripts of Constituent Assembly Debates on 12 August 1949, Part I. http://indiankanoon.org/doc163623/. Accessed on 5 May 2018.

[6] Transcripts of Constituent Assembly Debates on 26 May 1949, Part I. http://indiankanoon.org/doc1663158/. Accessed on 5 May 2018.

[7] Transcripts of Constituent Assembly Debates on 15 November 1948. http://indiankanoon.org/doc/163623/. Accessed on 5 May 2018.

[8] Transcripts of Constituent Assembly Debates on 6 December 1948, Part I. http://indiankanoon.org/doc/1933556/. Accessed on 5 May 2018.

> Are we really honest when we say that we are seeking to establish a secular state? If your idea is to have a secular state it follows inevitably that we cannot afford to recognise minorities based upon religion.[9]

Understanding that "since 'Enlightenment Secularism', with its core principle of separation, founded on the Protestant conception of religion as essentially a private concern with which states had no legitimate business, was never going to work in a country where rulers and religious publics had been interacting from time immemorial, it was better not to use the term at all, than to use it fraudulently," wrote Ian Copland. Consequently, in 1950 the Constituent Assembly adopted Articles 25, 26 and 27 of the Constitution with the intention of furthering secularism. Though not formally inserted in the document, secularism was definitely embedded in the constitutional philosophy.

In 1976 with the passing of the 42nd Amendment of the Indian Constitution under the then Prime Minister Indira Gandhi, the spirit of secularism that was always part and parcel of the Constitution was formally inserted into its body – with the preamble stating India as a "Sovereign, Socialist, Secular, Democratic Republic", without any attempt to give specific meanings of the terms. The secular state has been defined in terms of three distinct but inter-related sets of relations between the state and the people:

1. Guarantee of corporate and personal freedom of religious practices; (articles 25–28 of the Constitution)
2. No discrimination in favour of or against an individual because of his or her religion; (preamble and article 15 of the Constitution)
3. The separation of the state from religion – no right to promote or interfere with any religion.

Secularism in India can thus be understood as the state not having any recognised religion unlike a theocratic state, and all religions are treated equally. The state does not regulate the relationship between man and God and one can practice one's religion without the intervention of the state. Freedom of religion and worship are constitutional guarantees as the fundamental rights of the citizens of India. The state is expected to guarantee individual and corporate religious freedom and deal with an individual as its citizen irrespective of their religious faith. Secularism in India is an attitude, a way of life that does not spill intolerance among followers of different religions.

Writing in the *Swaraj* in 1971 Gandhi declared:

> Secularism is an ill understood word, if a State declares that its government shall be secular, it does not mean that its Rulers or Parliament will be agnostics or atheists. It does not mean that it dislikes and discourages religion. It means that persons of various religions will all be treated justly and without any

[9] Transcripts of Constituent Assembly Debates on 25 May 1949, Part I. http://indiankanoon.org/doc/790979/. Accessed on 5 May 2018.

discrimination based on religious differences. Justice to minority groups does not mean injustice to the majority.[10]

It means respect for all faiths, and not giving up faith, respect for all religion and absence of any kind of discrimination on this count. With constitutional mentions, secularism is a much more functional term in India. The demand for separation between religions and non-religious activities would be inapplicable in India because Indian civil society is strictly fused with religion and custom. It is also the venue where unity or a co-existence happens among diverse people.

Challenges and Problems

The idea of secularism in India is complex because of the complexity lying behind its application. Securing equalities, religious freedom and supporting secularism through a constitution does not eliminate all religious conflicts, continuing inequalities based on religion, ethnicity or economic state. The constitutional principle of secularism as the equality of religions has not been successful in securing the equality between Muslims and Hindus, holding society together.

The formula of *Sarva Dharma Sambhava*, the Indian variation of secularism, while aiding the organisation of representative democracy in independent India is not without its vices as it has also resulted in the Hindu majoritarian character of the modern India state, which prevents India's 'democracy' from truly being representative. Religious conflicts continue. The question of how representative Indian democracy really is, also includes the question of caste and reservation as lower castes have increasingly challenged the validity of Indian democracy where power is concentrated in the hands of the few wealthy higher-caste Hindus.[11] Here one touches on the aforementioned tension in the constitution: all religions are declared to be equal, but it included reservations for groups that are marginalised on the basis of ultimately religious grounds.

India had seen a large number of riots in terms of politics and non-politics since its birth. The thought of nationalism under Gandhi unified the people for a long time, and the legitimised secularism came only after independence. The

[10] Ram Jethmalani, The damage is irreparable: Hindutva on weak knees-I, *The New India Express*, 23 October 2000, 6.

[11] See Prakash Chandra Upadhyay, *The politics of Indian Secularism*, 2007 (New Delhi: Critical Quest, Cambridge University Press, 1992), 5. When lower-caste groups attempted to use the majoritarian vocabulary of community to demand social and economic justice, high-caste elites responded by calling upon merit, competition and efficiency – slogan of a market society – to justify their unwillingness to countenance further reservation. Yet in the Indian context, these bourgeois-liberal slogans have little appeal beyond the narrow circle of the dominant elites.

sustainability of secularism was questioned when the livelihoods of minorities were threatened by a misled majority.

There have always been two kinds of secularists in India: those who used secularism as a tool of nationalist politics, and those who consider it necessary to base both nationalism and democracy upon secular foundations based upon the separation between religion and politics. The second kind have been progressively marginalised, upheld by only the left-wing radicals and intellectuals, the former tradition grew increasingly hegemonic, through its accommodation of Hindu political idioms in the name of 'Indianness'.[12]

It must also be kept in mind that legislation was and is hugely affected by Hindu communalism. The Indian Constitution no doubt includes freedom of religion, the abolition of untouchability and the outlawing of all forms of discriminations. To establish national uniformity and peace, securing equality and religious freedom was necessary in a country made up of different religious groups. In the constitution there are also the reservations of seats in schools and colleges and jobs in civil services for citizens from scheduled castes and scheduled tribes. Though the state has made efforts to secure equalities for all its citizens and abolish inequalities based on religion and ethnicity, it cannot be ignored that to do that, terms that have their roots in Hinduism have been used. Traditional idioms used in politics have obscured the social and economic problems, preventing the possibility of finding a practical solution. The 'traditional wisdom' has also been used skilfully to describe and explain social disparities. Even class conflicts have been translated and presented in religious terms – *dharmic struggle.*[13]

The preamble of the Indian constitution states that India is a "Sovereign, Socialist, Secular, Democratic Republic." What was probably meant by 'sovereign' was the fact that India was no longer under the British 'Sovereign'. As Paulose Mar Gregorios states, "all nations are under the pressure of history to move forward from concepts of sovereignty and independence to a global society of autonomous states and mutually dependent under the conditions of justice, equality and mutually beneficial co-operation."[14] Gregorios similarly goes on to say that just as the word 'Socialist' does not in any way reflect our present socioeconomic reality and is in danger of heavy erosion,[15] so also the term 'Secular', basically meaning – in the Indian context as against the theocratic notions of a state as chosen by Pakistan after Independence and the resulting partition – that no religious communities would receive preferential treatment by the state, has not been very successful. Continuing in the same

---

[12] Prakash Chandra Upadhyay, Ibid., 6.

[13] How tradition has been used as a weapon to obscure social and economic has been succinctly pointed out by Prakash Chandra Upadhyay, Ibid., 13

[14] Paulose Mar Gregorios, *The Secular Ideology: An Impotent Remedy for India's Communal Problem*, ISPCK/Mar Gregorios Foundation (OTS), 33.

[15] Paulose Mar Gregorios, Ibid.

vein he points out that 'Democratic', which basically means power in the hands of the people to a certain extent is exercised through the vote. This, however, does not really empower the people as political parties appeal for votes on the basis of regionalism or religion, against which the constitution does not provide any safeguard.[16]

Increasing Hindutva politics, especially after the 1990s with the rise of the militant Bharatiya Janata party, caused a tangible crisis of secularism. The demolition of Babri Masjid on 6 December 1992 and the state-sponsored violence in Gujarat in 2002 when about 200 Muslims were killed after 59 Hindus were burnt alive in train coaches in Godhra, Gujarat has been considered the most recent crisis in secularism. These incidents have never been addressed properly by the police and judiciary. Inquiry commissions prepared reports that were either never made public or not followed by serious action. In most democracies, the kind of violence Gujarat experienced in 2002 would have resulted in attempts to identify those who were responsible for such atrocious acts and bring them to court. Sadly, there is no real evidence of this being done. The complexity of Indian secularism and diversity of religious and regional politics in India is also manifested in the Khalistan movement in Punjab, which sought a separate Sikh state in a Sikh majority religion, resulting in hundreds of casualties in the Golden Temple attack in 1985 – yet more evidence of the crisis that secularism is facing in India.

In these cases, religious identity was translated into culture and politics of communalism and communities fought for dominance and denied the equality of the religion of their opponents. There is another side to the ambiguity in the way secularism is understood, e.g. the way the state is involved in running temples and religious foundations. In states such as Tamil Nadu and Andhra Pradesh, there are established bureaucracies for temple administration and management of religious endowments, the enactment of the Hindu Code Bill in 1955 giving personal law for all Hindu citizens. It is quite evident that there is conflict between the Indian state's secularism and securing uniform civil code (through article 44) and the existence of multiple personal laws based on religion.

Building on this confusion are statements from people such as Sita Ram Goel, an ardent Hindu, who refers to the years immediately following independence of India as a time when Pseudo-secularism was introduced. He writes, "Prime Minister Jawaharlal Nehru who dominated the scene for 17 long years, promoted every anti-Hindu ideology and movement behind the smokescreen of a counterfeit secularism."[17] There is also the challenge that comes from the proponents of Hindutva who equate Hinduism with nationalism and secularism with Hinduism. This has a detrimental effect on the right to

---

[16] Paulose Mar Gregorios, Ibid., 34.

[17] Sita Ram Goel, *Pseudo-secularism, Christian Missions and Hindu Renaissance* (New Delhi: Voice of India, 1998), 4.

propagate, which has been granted constitutionally to the all religious minorities has been questioned and considered as anti-national, thus making one question the very nature of the republic – whether it has any relevance and meaning in such a context.

The interests of the secular polity of the country is ignored and weakened as political leaders make compromises with an eye on the vote banks, and minority groups are being appeased by political parties claiming to be secular while in reality they only sought political benefits. Religious minorities are relentlessly being coerced to seek for accommodation with the views and concerns of the majority for the sake of peace and harmony.

Conclusion

We can say that traditionalism and Indianess have played an important foundational role in the making of modern India. Even though the founding fathers of modern India rhetorically rejected anything that was considered alien and not Indian, they borrowed the Western model of representative democracy as the blueprint for the Indian nation state. In their attempts to retain tradition and Indianess, and in the process of inversion and translation of modern Western ideas into the language traditionalism have created the ever-lasting ambiguities that plague both the state and politics in India. Allowing and encouraging the project of building a modern secular nation state, and simultaneously upholding traditions such as the caste system and community, resulted in the former being distorted. In Gandhi's discourse the concept of nationalism, along with secularism and democracy, traverse the tortuous route of tradition so as to be flattened and redefined as an 'authentic' Indian value. Western nationalism was accompanied by a transition to a civil society and a democratic state in which religious behaviour was increasingly being marginalised and society was increasingly distanced from its religious and communitarian roots, and in which the world was assessed in empirical and rational terms, so that the secular rule of capital over society was legitimised through the primacy of market. In India on the other hand, nationalism provided and continues to provide legitimacy to a regime of landlords and big business and to the nation state by calling upon idioms of community, ethnics, religion and tradition.[18]

Secularism in India today is at the crossroads. Along with the mentioned issues come challenges that could be considered markedly different from those in a European context and arguably uniquely Indian. The European understanding of secularism as exclusion of religion from public life and a separation between state and religion does not work in India. As religion is intertwined in the daily lives of people in the country, almost everything is

---

[18] This has been well argued by Prakash Chandra Upadhyay. See *The Politics of Indian Secularism*, 18-19.

viewed from religious perspectives and standpoints. Attempting to exclude religion from daily and public life would result probably in more resistance and fights. Being confronted with the mentioned challenges calls for developing secularism in India as an attempt to deconstruct the association of religious identity politics with communalism and power aspirations.

In multicultural, pluralistic Indian society, such religious fervour has contributed to the rise of Hindu or majoritarian militancy in electoral politics and its consequences have begun to be felt in the judiciary and society at large.

Additionally, there has been a rise in the marginalisation and victimisation of religious and ethnic minorities. For example, Christian tribals have been made victims of violence, especially in states such as Odisha and Gujarat, where they are "requested" to (re)convert to Hinduism. Muslims are politically marginalised with less than 6% of MPs in the lower house of Parliament while representing 13.4% of the population. They also face discrimination in the job and housing markets.

The country's secularism also has close affinities with the pluralism, parliamentary democracy and federalism that have been cultivated for the past 64 years. However, there now appears to be a move away from multiculturalism towards a type of ethnic democracy exemplified by Israel and Sri Lanka where minorities are treated as second-class citizens. Such a move has implications for an adherence to the rule of law where the views and opinions of the majority are considered right. The claim of secularism as equality of all religions could be used in alliance with the individual citizens' right as counter arguments against the dominance of majoritarian communalism.

Added to this is the impact a liberalised economy is having on Indian society socially and economically. While job opportunities are opening up, ironically large sections of educated youth remain unemployable despite having obtained a post-graduate level of education, because of the quality of this education and the nature of the jobs available. This has resulted in large-scale migration of people from rural to urban areas and from one part of the country to another.

This has contributed to a sense of loss of identity, the growth of individualism – which has replaced the role family and community played in an individual's life – and the increasing isolation faced by individuals as they try to make sense of the increased competition in education, jobs and lifestyles.

On the one hand, attitudes towards religion are subtly changing, with an increasing number of urban youth considering religion an individual private choice and affair, while paradoxically on the other hand, a fear of loss of identity, culture and religious tradition because of modernity are also turning people to fundamentalist ideologies propagated in electoral politics.

The church's response to such a complicated situation demands that it reconsiders its role in Indian society, especially when these are challenges for which solutions cannot be found in a European context.

Indian theological curricula will need to formulate an Indian theological response that posits the Gospel message as relevant and addressing the needs of Indians, thereby breaking the impression long held by a vast majority of Indians that Christianity is a European import and out of sync with the challenges faced by Indian society. This becomes all the more important when we remember that the church in India runs some of the most reputed and sought after educational institutions and can thereby contribute, through secular education, to addressing these challenges.

How the Gospel message is made relevant to a complex context as this is what must occupy Indian Christians, whether a lay person or someone theologically trained.

Secularistion – Whose Discourse?

Esther Mombo

Whereas Christians and others in the West tell stories of how secularisation has affected Christianity and the church, there is currently very little secularisation discourse happening in Africa and we are not aware of dominant secularisation stories.[1]

In 1969, Mbiti observed that Africans were notoriously religious.[2] The context of this writing was bringing to light what African traditional religions were in the light of a changing society through colonial and Western mission Christianity. In 1986, Professor Ali Mazrui coined the term 'Africa's triple heritage' in which he names the heritage as Indigenous traditions, Islamic ways and Western tendencies. For him, Christianity is only part of what he called "Western tendencies". Similarly, in the phrase "Islamic ways" he meant much more than Islam as a religion. He was referring to the total Arab influence on Africa. Western tendencies refer to the total impact of the West on Africa.[3]

Christianity and Islam are known to be the major traditions today and they claim large followers. Historically, these two religious traditions came into Africa through the European-American and Arab expansion to Africa. Christian missionaries started mission work in Kenya, for example, and in the beginning made little headway. With colonisation and imperial expansion of the European nations after the Berlin conference of 1895, Christian missionary work began to expand rapidly.[4] The expansion of Christianity was aided by colonial and imperial movements because of the improvement of the infrastructure as it was the responsibility of the colonising nation to develop the nation they colonised. As well as this colonisation and imperialism were aspects of power and superior power to the local people's power. This was seen in economic, social and religious aspects. Africans followed the new ways because it was a way of survival. Christianity was adopted over against African

---

[1] Benno van den Toren & Willem J. de Wit: Secularization and Discipleship in Africa: Conclusions and Recommendations in Cairo Journal of Theology 2 (2015): 152-160 (http://journal.etsc.org/wp-content/uploads/2015/09/Cairo-Journal-of-Theology-2-2015-Van-den-Toren-and-De-Wit.pdf).

[2] John S. Mbiti, *African Traditional Religions and Philosophy* (Nairobi: EAEP, 1969), 1.

[3] Ali Mazrui, *The Africans: A Triple Heritage* (Boston: Little Brown, 1986).

[4] Berlin conference 1884–1885.

traditional religion for two reasons: it was the religion of the powerful and it opened up ways for upward social mobility in a changing society.

Despite the methodology of expansion and the motivation of the Africans, the observation today is that the heartland of Christianity is no longer in Europe but in Africa and Asia.[5] Philip Jenkins in his *The Next Christendom: The Coming of Global Christianity* writes:

> We are currently living through one of the transforming moments in the history of religion worldwide. Over the past five centuries or so, the story of Christianity has been inextricably bound up with that of Europe and European derived civilizations overseas, above all in North America. Until recently the overwhelming majority of Christians have lived in White nations, allowing theorists to speak smugly, arrogantly, of "European Christian" civilization. Conversely, radical writers have seen Christianity as the religion of the "West" or, to use another popular metaphor, the global North.[6]

Jenkins, like Walls, observes, "Over the past century, the centre of gravity in the Christian world has shifted inexorably southward, to Africa, Asia, and Latin America. No doubt there is a marked growth in Christianity in Africa."

The visibility of Christianity is seen in the use of names and symbols from the Bible in public spaces such as transport, shops, apartments, eating places, schools, hospitals, saloons, business premises, etc. As a sample I found in one street in an Africa city these names: the Shalom Saloon, the Ebenezer Holdings, Amazing Grace Apartments, Victory General Shop, Trinity Hospital, Bethsaida Hospital, Glorious Boutique Goshen Workshop, Elijah Hair Saloon, Goshen Fashion Shop, Jericho Metal Workshop, Tumaini (faith) Bar, Blessed Shelter Hardware, Unity Welding Shop, Provident General Store, Exodus Paints, Glory Paints, God's Blessed Shop; Rehoboth General, Glory Milk Bar, Eden Supermarket, Genesis Flats, Heavenly Hair Products, Anointed Fashions; Lazaro Apartments – the list can go on.[7]

Apart from its visibility is the question of the nature of this Christianity, which tends to be overtly conservative and Biblicist. But that is only "overtly". There is a great show of uncompromising moral concern on certain issues, especially those that touch the role and place of women or sex and sexuality. It appears as though most of the Christians oscillate between a strongly conservationist, Christo-centric theology, on the one hand, and the indefatigable hold of African culture on the other. In such a religious or Christian milieu, how does one discuss secularism? In this chapter I attempt to answer this question by sharing the perspectives as I see them from my context.

---

[5] Andrew Walls 'Towards Understanding Africa's place in Christian History' in J.S. Pobee (ed.) *Religion in a Pluralistic Society* (Leiden Brill, 1976), 180.

[6] Philip Jenkins, *The Next Christendom: The Coming of Global Christianity (*2002), 1-2.

[7] Esther Mombo 'Mission and Evangelism' in Kenneth Ross, J Kwabena (eds.) *Christianity in Sub Saharan Africa*. (Edinburgh: University Press, 2017).

Secularisation – Whose Question Is It?

The discourse on secularisation based on a model of philosophy that partitions with a paradigm of sacred and secular is not a question for Africans or that is not the way the question is formed. Shorter observes that:

> Sacred and secular represents two different ways of experiencing the same reality. In themselves they are not in competition or conflict. At the sacred level, reality is experienced as being under the governance of God, as the object of religious faith. The secular, on the other hand is the same reality construed as being accessible to humanity and under its control.[8]

Olulude, on the other hand, notes that:

> Secularism, despite popular belief is neither atheism nor a on religious belief system like humanism. It is a political movement that seeks the separation of religion and government and elimination of discrimination on the basis of religion.[9]

Both Shorter and Olulude show the complexities of secularism in Africa and how the discourse may be very contextual with regard to perception. The process of secularisation as noted above is a historical development as Africa has interacted with an outside world. The discourse of secularisation is not on abstract philosophical terms but in as much as it affects human lives and impacts on one's understanding and interpretation of the faith they hold in God. Even though Africa continues to be dominated by the technocratic, secularising culture of the North, the portrayed religiosity shows that the values of society, as well as the social dynamics are still rooted and shaped by religion. In this case one would argue that the contextual reality is that the sacred is in the secular and the secular is in the sacred. The issue is not an "either or" paradigm but a "both and" paradigm. As is the case, then, the interpretation of secularisation will be both contextual and on issues of life rather than abstract notions.

When Mbiti observed that Africans are notoriously religious, meaning one is born into this faith and grows in it and with it, this faith is inculcated into the daily life of the person from birth to death. With the advent of colonisation and Christianisation, people have chosen to add Christianity to the faith they held, not necessarily replacing it. Thus, the thinking and the philosophy behind their acquired faith remain African. The discourse on secularisation is both at the level of traditional thought and the challenges of modernity. It is both at the

---

[8] Aylward Shorter, *Secularism in Africa: Introducing a Problem*, https://sedosmission.org/old/eng/shorter.htm.

[9] Kunle Olulode, 'Up against the Wall – when secularism infringes on religious rights around the world'. In *Conscience. The Newjournal of Catholic opinion* (Vol. XXXVIII, 2017:4), 22.

level of dealing with old questions in a new environment. These may be questions of a political, social, economic and/or religious nature.

The impact of secularisation is what is visible rather than the abstract discussion on the same. Benno van den Toren and Willem J. de Wit, in their report about secularisation and discipleship in Africa, observe these forms or ways of seeing secularisation as including:

- Secularisation as desecralisation of nature and political authority
- Secularisation as the diminishing religious participation of individuals and communities.
- Secularisation as the withdrawal of different aspects of life and society from influence or religion.
- Secularisation as the changing authority of religion over individuals in which both the adherents to the religion and shape of one's religious life increasingly becomes an issue of personal choice and commitment.
- Secularisation as the use of religious means for secular goals.[10]

All these forms create a basis for the perceptions and fears of secularisation. The fears of secularisation are not on the diminishing numbers of adherents of religion as that is not the issue, since at the beginning of the section there seems to be an increased number of Christians. The issue is the nature of the Christian faith or the type and the impacts on the adherents.

Secularisation as a Challenge to Orthodoxy and Inherited Faith

When a group called the Atheist Society (AS) sought to be registered in Kenya in 2016, because it was their constitutional right, the religious traditions reacted with anger and implored the Attorney General to deregister the society. AS then challenged their deregistration at the High Court after the Attorney General yielded to pressure from religious groups to deregister them back in 2016 barely two months after it had been registered. Religious groups argued in a letter to the Attorney General that the society had made pronouncements that threatened peace, though others have insisted that this was an introduction of secularism, introduction of devil worship, free masonry, Satanism, sexual pervasion, drug abuse and other outlawed indulges. The High Court overturned the ruling and acknowledged that the earlier suspension of the society was unconstitutional and done in bad faith. In response to these allegations the leader of AS argued that the society was not about any of those issues they were accused of.[11] AS demanded the resignation of Attorney General Prof Muigai, whom they accused of bias and unfit to be the government's legal adviser as he proved unable to protect and defend the country's constitution

---

[10] Van den Toren & Willem J. de Wit: 'Secularization and Discipleship in Africa', 156.

[11] Ngasike Lucas Attorney General Githu Muigai suspends registration of atheists' society; Standard Media: 2016 May, https://www.standardmedia.co.ke/article/2000200192/attorney-general-githu-muigai-suspends-registration-of-atheists-society.

and protect minorities. AS gained momentum to challenge the term 'God'[12] in the Kenyan National Anthem and most recently, the teachings of religious studies in schools. Again, they claim that Kenya is a secular state[13] and thus, the term brings division rather than inclusivity. Second, similar teachings bring divisiveness among students.[14] This reaction by religious groups is a reflection of the perception that is popular with regard to secularisation. Some of the visible features of such 'discourses and acts' in large church traditions include the public defence of the authority of scripture, historic orthodoxy and the correct interpretation and application of the teaching of the scripture in matters not only of doctrine but also personal morality and ethics. The leaders of religious organisations are tasked with the reading and interpretation of texts in a way that reflects what to them is 'orthodoxy' and does not contradict 'the rule of faith'. Departure from this norm is interpreted as a departure from the historic faith and historic orthodoxy, and secularism is to blame for this departure.

Secularisation as Both Enhancing and Hindering the Voice for the Marginalised

As much as secularisation is blamed for acts deemed by some as against the received faith, secularisation gives a voice to some. The ones that secularisation has given empowerment to make their voices known are women. Women in Kenya and in African church congregations make up the majority of the worshippers but not the leaders.[15] It is the women who are impacted further with both positive and negative Christian teachings. Some of the Christian teachings are a hindrance to women's liberation, especially those that require 'women to be silent', 'women not to teach', 'women to be submissive'. This silencing of women has been used to affirm the status quo and at the same time viewed as women being in agreement with the teachings of the Christian texts. Inequality between men and women has continued to be a reality in both the religious and other spheres in society. Women are aware that both culture and tradition and texts have been used to justify their voicelessness. Oduyoye

[12] Daily Nation Atheists to petition House to remove 'God' from national anthem, October 17, https://www.nation.co.ke/news/Atheists-push-for-removal-of-God-in-national-anthem/1056-3418764-1d1j89/index.html.

[13] All Africa: Kenya: Atheists to Petition House to Remove 'God' From National Anthem, October 16, http://allafrica.com/stories/201610170372.html.

[14] Shiundu Lillian, Atheist in Kenya want ministry of education to abolish religious studies in public schools, in *Tuko Ke*, 2018: https://www.tuko.co.ke/264068-atheist-kenya-ministry-education-abolish-religious-studies-public-schools.html#264068.

[15] Esther Mombo and Heleen Joziasse, From the Pew to the Pulpit. Engendering the pulpit through teaching 'African Women's Theologies' in Men in the pulpit, women in the Pew? Addressing gender inequality in Africa. (eds.) H. Jurgen Hendricks, Elna Mouton, Len Hansen, Elizabeth Le Roux. Sun Press Stellenbosch 2012, 183-194.

observes that "women have to contend, however, with the fact that the western Christian culture and patriarchal ideology have seeped in, to the power of men or to endow men with power where they had none, while suppressing aspects of African culture that are favourable to women".[16] Mazrui, as noted above, discusses Africa's Triple heritage, for African women it is a triple patriarchy, which is observed by theologians such as Mercy Ouyoye as already shown. Although one may argue that Western education was a positive aspect because it acted as a vehicle for opening up space to women to engage and name aspects within both the Western and the African cultures issues of discrimination and marginalisation, secularisation has not fully helped with the emancipation of women. In this vein Lichuma has observed that:

> Secularism through the idolization of a private sphere of human rights and the deflation of some questions on human rights to this sphere, creates new forms of gender in equalities. Gender based violence is one of many examples of discriminatory matters that disproportionately and deeply impact women but which have remained buried in the private sphere.[17]

Secularisation for women is a double-edged sword, providing the space but not liberating enough.

Secularisation as a Contested Space

For religious people secularisation is brought to the fore when a matter being discussed is controversial and touches certain aspects of doctrinal teaching as noted above, such as worship of God or sexuality. Through various means including preaching and different forms of theological education, one delineates two perspectives on secularism. In preaching, secularisation is discussed at the level of materialism and how one should live a life of faith and not be attached to material things. As well as this, in some preaching, issues around politics and social justice are also discussed. A cross-section of preaching tends to fear certain forms of expressions of language such as the concept of 'human rights' and gender, to name just a few. This language is interpreted as unbiblical and a Western way of introducing aspects that are ungodly; it is also seen as a deviation from the inherited faith. When one looks at what the fears are about, it is not the language but a fear of discussing issues of power in gender relations. While theologically the same church would speak about creation in equal terms, they would enforce hierarchy in gender relations.

---

[16] Mercy Amba Oduyoye, *Introducing African Women's Theology* (Sheffield: Sheffield Academic Press, 2001), 28.

[17] Winfred Lichuma, 'No rights without remedies Gender inequality and secularism in Africa', in *Conscience. The New journal of Catholic opinion* (Vol. XXXVIII 2017:4), 21.

Historically there has been a tendency within the church to make secular concern a matter of somewhat marginal importance, in preparation for the 'other world', but in the world they build up an ecclesiastical order. The church then retreats to its own circle and creates a pseudo-world of religious validity in terms of its utterances through preaching. The type of preaching includes advice on how to live in this materialist world. This way of living appears not to be ideal; the way of living in the world is not withdrawing from it but engaging with the issues in the world. There are contestations in areas such as church and state, which emanate from what I noted about the separation between sacred and secular. There are those who have challenged this separation and argued for the prophetic role of the church, thus engaging with what is the secular.[18] The struggle to engage with social issues or not is an age-old one as the church is called back to its prophetic. In doing so, Christians struggle for the purity of both word and service even against their normal ministries.

In an age where some forms of technology seem to subvert 'religious values' of the people, the question on how to engage is not clear cut. Among the growing forms of Christian faith are those groups that approach secularism with a positive spirit, using it to preach about a God who wants his children to have the best food, clothing and shelter. The advocates of the prosperity Gospel further preach that God has met all the needs of people in the suffering and death of Christ. Every Christian, therefore, should now share in the victory of Christ over sin, sickness and poverty. A believer has the right to the blessing of health and wealth won by Christ, and they can obtain these blessings merely by joining a prosperity Gospel church and tithing to a God who multiplies whatever is given. The presentation of a miracle-working God through different mediums of communication appeals to those who are struggling with sickness and/or poverty as it requires no effort on their part to change their situation. For those who are doing well it is testimony to God's blessings to them. Even though technology is appropriated for material gain, engagement with the systems of injustice is limited.

The perception of secularism is also informed by the different forms of theology offered to some of those who take on roles of leadership. The types of theological education offered depend on the church tradition and the aims. Most churches are wary of forms of theological education whose pedagogy and content are heavily influenced by Western liberal categories. This is not a new phenomenon but one carried on from the colonial days when church colleges trained church leaders. This perception is based on the fact that secularisation is interpreted as anti-religion much more than a political stance that seeks to separate religion from the state. This separation is one in which people's freedoms are enhanced in the constitution and not privileging one religion over other forms of beliefs. It is exactly this that is frowned and resented in the

---

[18] John Henry Okullu, *Church and State* (Nairobi: Uzima, 1984).

preaching or theological teachings. Theological education is aimed at raising people's religiosity and increasing the number of converts. It is also meant to provide guidance to people on their spiritual life as opposed to the material wealth. There are those whose theology stresses less connection to the material world. There are those who encourage wealth creation and much wealth being a sign of blessings. Both these views are a sign on the contestation there is on how one lives for the sacred but in the secular. If the prayer of Jesus to his disciples in John 17:9,11, 14-18 is anything to go by then the challenge of how one lives in the world is a discourse for all people. The discourse can only be contextualised such that the questions raised receive the contextual questions. This is amid the realities of the globalisation and the global village. Each segment of the village experiences some aspects in a u inquest way and need to ask its question and provide its answers. This does not diminish connectedness but enriches the connections.

Conclusion

In this short paper I have tried to show several things, including the religious context of Africa as far as Christianity is concerned and its phenomenal growth. The discourse of secularisation has to be within this context. I have also shown that the discourse on secularisation exists but in a unique category. How does one live in a world that is increasingly materialistic, how does one who believed in God through Jesus Christ live in this kind of world? The discourse on secularisation still has the fears of Western civilisation and the challenges of it. The focus of the discourse is on how to maintain the numbers that profess the Christian faith but also the nature of the relationship with the world.

Epilogue: Thinking Two Thoughts

Knud Jørgensen

The contemporary narratives and experiences of this volume about *Mission in Secularised Contexts of Europe* prove that there is more, much more, than one narrative or experience. As a Norwegian friend and former politician keeps telling me when I ask a simple question: "You need to have at least two thoughts in your head at the same time." One contributor employs the term 'cognitive dissonance' to picture the conflict between a biblical worldview and a secular worldview. That may be helpful, but that is not what I refer to with thinking two thoughts because to me it is not an either-or. Rather it has to do with living with a broad understanding of mission (an expression used by Cathy Ross in her chapter).

Secularisation is a process inherent to the development of the Christian tradition, Wolters Hielke claims. Therefore, we welcome secularisation; it may set us free from the Constantinian prison and from the embrace of state churches. It opens the gates out of the cathedrals and our many Christian mausoleums. To be a secular Christian does no longer require that I am the custodian of a museum. Fresh air and fresh expressions, planting new Christian communities (e.g. in the Netherlands as Gert Noort talks about), living with diversity, complexity, multi-culturalism in the secular context of Hamburg, struggling with the indifference to religion in a context like East Germany, helping people to cope with reflexive modernity (Anthony Giddens' expression). A life marked by vulnerability, but also with glimmers of hope of renewal (Grace Davie); even where there seem to be no points of contact, the Gospel can be God's power to break up the stony asphalt – like the dandelion that breaks through the surface.

At the same time, I hear what Harvey Kwiyani and Esther Mombo are saying: How can anybody live without religion? (Which is not quite what secular people actually do.) What about powers and principalities? Is it simply for us secular Europeans to tell our African, Asian and Latin American sisters and brothers that we have come further along the road of wisdom? True, we cannot apply an African worldview to Europe, and I cannot bring my years in Ethiopia in the 1970s to Europe and just postulate that here is the real thing. But, to be honest, I do believe that this is *also* the real thing, so much closer to a biblical worldview – belief in prayer, God in the middle of my every day, victory over the evil powers, the blood of the lamb and signing myself with the cross. The migrants are the new European Christians; they will evangelise Europe, Kwivani says.

The chapters of this book indicate that it is more complicated than that. True, we need inspiration and renewal from churches in the Global South, but we also need to find our own way or ways in a world of indifference, selfies and vicarious religion. This has to do with contextuality, with rediscovering the biblical message's relevance in a secularised society, with hearing the Good News in a new way – maybe through dialogue with other worldviews, maybe through Alpha courses, maybe through diaconal praxis (combing dialogue and *diakonia*), maybe through witnessing to my neighbour about what I have seen and heard (1 John 1). The Good News does not begin with getting the message across, but with getting the message. Becoming feeble receivers rather than highly powered transmitters of the Gospel.

I have been re-reading the chapters of this volume while spending a week on the island of Patmos in Greece, the place where John the Theologian (as he is called here) received the visions from God and Christ about the end time. It is, if anything, a story where you need to think more than one thought at the same time. The visions, like the OT prophets, have two foci: the events of the present and the immediate future, and the ultimate eschatological event. Historical judgement becomes a type of, or a prelude to, the eschatological judgement. At least two thoughts at the same time – the blending of the preterist and the futurist: the beast is both Rome and the eschatological Antichrist.

Some of the seven letters to the seven churches could have been written to churches in the diverse European context. Do you recall the letter to Sardis (Rev. 3:1-6) – a church that suffers from the main problem of a deep spiritual apathy (which may have resulted from the softness and love of luxury of a secular society)? Outwardly it was a church well known for good works – it had the name of being alive; an outstanding reputation for life and vitality, but in the sight of God it was dead: a picture of nominal Christianity, outwardly prosperous, busy with religious programmes, but devoid of spiritual life and power. Well known as an active, vigorous Christian congregation, characterised by good works and charitable activities. But all these activities were a failure because they were only formal and external, and not infused with the life-giving Holy Spirit. Is this a picture of my church in Scandinavia? As I sit here on Patmos I sense the call of John: Remember what you received and heard; keep that and repent. Remember the early days when you received the Gospel and repent of the indifference into which you have fallen. Don't let the pagan environment soil your garments; don't adapt to the secular context in such a way that you lose the vibrancy of love and faith.

List of Editors and Contributors

Editors

Behera, Marina Ngursangzeli is from Mizoram, a state in Northeast India, and belongs to the Mizoram Synod of the Presbyterian Church of India. From 2005 to 2012 she served as an Associate Professor and Chairperson in the Department of the History of Christianity at the United Theological College (UTC) in Bangalore, India. From September 2005–2016, supported by the CWM, she held the chair of Ecumenical Missiology at the Ecumenical Institute, Bossey, a programme of the World Council of Churches and attached to the University of Geneva. She is presently serving as a Research Tutor and also as the MPhil Stage Leader at Oxford Centre for Mission Studies (OCMS), UK since 2017.

Biehl, Michael (Germany), b. 1956. Dr theol. from Kiel University, Germany, and an MA in Religious Studies (AMRS) from the University of Chicago, is currently head of Desk for Mission Studies and Theological Education at the Association of Protestant Churches and Missions in Germany (EMW). Before this, he served as the Director of Missionsakademie, Hamburg. He is an adjunct faculty (Lehrbeauftragter) for Missiology, Ecumenics and Religious Studies at the Department of Protestant Theology at the University of Hamburg. Editor or co-editor of several books in German and in English, including two volumes in the Edinburgh 2010 Series (Regnum).

Jørgensen, Knud, b. 1942. MTh from University of Copenhagen, PhD in Missiology, Fuller Theological Seminary. Journalist and theologian, served with Radio Voice of the Gospel, Addis Ababa, Ethiopia, the Lutheran World Federation, Geneva, the International Mass Media Institute, Kristiansand, Go out Centre, Hurdal, Norway, Norwegian Church Aid, the Mekane Yesus Seminary, Addis Ababa, and the mission foundation Areopagos. Dean of Tao Fong Shan, Hong Kong until 2010. Adjunct professor at the MF Norwegian School of Theology. Coordinator for the Egede Institute. Published several books and articles on journalism, communication, leadership and mission, including 'Equipping for Service: Leadership in Church and Society' (Regnum 2012). One of the editors of the Regnum Edinburgh 2010 Series.

Contributors

Babicova, Zuzana, Slovakia. MA from the University of Aberdeen, Comparative Literature and Thought. Chairperson of the World Student Christian Federation Europe since 2013. Programme management and development in the field of international. European and global ecumenical youth work, interfaith work development.

Bendor-Samuel, Paul, b. 1958. Brought up in Brazil, Ghana and Nigeria. MBBCH Welsh National School of Medicine, Cardiff, MRCGP London. Served in Tunisia in medical development work 1990–1995, then as Director of L'Association de coopération en Tunisie, 1995–2002. MBE 1999 for services to medicine in Tunisia. International Director of Interserve, 2003–2015, based in Kuala Lumpur, Malaysia. Since 2016, the Executive Director of the Oxford Centre for Mission Studies. Published chapters in several books, including Organisational Spirituality in Spirituality in Mission: Embracing the Lifelong Journey, and author of A Missão invertida (Ultimato 2013).

Buda, Daniel, b. 1977. MTh, PhD and Habilitation in Historical Theology from "Lucian Blaga" University, Sibiu, Romania. Further studies and research in historical theology and ecumenism in Heidelberg and Berlin (Germany), Bern (Switzerland) and New York (US). Archpriest in the Romanian Orthodox Church, theologian, church historian, translator, and specialist in ecumenical movement. Served as faculty member of "Lucian Blaga" University since 2003. Professor; associated research fellow at Faculty of Theology, Pretoria University; local organiser of the Third European Ecumenical Assembly, Sibiu, 2007; since 2008 programme executive and programme executive coordinator of Church and Ecumenical Relations and member of the Secretariat of the Commission on Faith and Order in the World Council of Churches, Geneva. Published several books and articles, especially in Romanian, English and German on historical theology, Antioch as a Christian centre, theory of church history, theology of history, patristic and ecumenism.

Dahle, Lars, b. 1961. Cand. Theol. from MF Norwegian School of Theology, PhD in Religious Studies from Open University (UK). Theologian, educator and apologist; has from 1991 served in various academic and leadership roles at NLA University College (Gimlekollen Campus), Norway. Currently Associate Professor in Systematic Theology and Apologetics at NLA, Director of Damaris Norway and Lausanne Catalyst for Media Engagement. Co-editor of "The Lausanne Movement: A Range of Perspectives" (Regnum 2014). Published various academic and popular articles, primarily on media and apologetics. Founding Editor of the Nordic apologetic journal Theofilos. Steering Committee Member, European Leadership Forum. Chair for Lausanne Europe 2020.

Davie, Grace is Professor emeritus in Sociology at the University of Exeter, UK and a Lay Canon of the Anglican Diocese of Europe. Her recent publications include Religion in Britain: A Persistent Paradox (Wiley-Blackwell 2015) and Religion in Public Life: Levelling the Ground (Theos 2017).

Kwiyani, Harvey is a Malawian mission scholar and practitioner working in Britain, teaching African theology at Liverpool Hope University. His current research interests focus on the faith of African migrants in Europe and North America. His published works include Sent Forth: African Missionary Work in the West (Orbis 2014) and Mission-Shaped Church in a Multicultural World, both of which explore the implications of migration in the context of African Christians' lived experiences in the Diaspora. He is a regular commentator on issues connected with African Christianity in the Diaspora and the emerging multicultural face of Christianity in Europe.

Mayer, Annemarie C., is Professor of Systematic Theology and the Study of Religions at the Faculty of Theology and Religious Studies of the Catholic University of Leuven. She is a member of the Research Unit of Systematic Theology and the Study of Religions. Her research interests focus on different approaches to inter-religious dialogue and the study of religions as well as on Christology and the doctrine of God, especially in the light of other monotheistic religions throughout the centuries, ecclesiology in an ecumenical context, especially the analysis of the changing ecclesial landscapes in Europe and elsewhere, and the correlation of mission and church. She has taught Dogmatic, Ecumenical and Fundamental Theology at the universities of Tübingen, Hildesheim, and Fribourg. She was the Catholic Consultant to the World Council of Churches in Geneva, being a member of the World Mission and Evangelism staff, served on the Reformed-Catholic International Dialogue and currently is a member of the Joint Working Group and the Commission Nationale Catholique pour l'Œcuménisme of the Belgian Bishops' Conference. She is one of the academic editors of Louvain Studies, Ephemerides Theologicae Lovanienses, and The International Journal for the Study of the Christian Church. Recent publications on the topic include *The Church in the Limelight of the Public Square: An Alternative Community? The Future of Interreligious Dialogue in the Light of Ramon Llull's Contribution to the Encounter of Religions. The ecumenical vision of Pope Francis: journeying together as fellow pilgrims – 'the mystery of unity has already begun'*.

Mombo, Esther, is a Professor of African Church history, Gender and theology at St. Paul's university in Limuru Kenya. She also serves as the Director of partnerships and alumni Relations in the same university. Her research and teaching interests span the fields of church history, interfaith relations, theological education, women and the church in Africa, poverty, HIV and AIDS among others. She serves in several ecumenical committees including the Commission of Education and Ecumenical formation of the World Council of Churches. Mombo works with religious groups on issues of gender, sexuality and patriarchy in as far as these three impact on people's full participation in church.

Noort, Gerrit, b. 1960, is an ordained minister of the Protestant Church in the Netherlands. He pursued his theological studies in Basel (Switzerland), Philadelphia (US), Amsterdam and Utrecht (Netherlands). After having served in a local reformed congregation in the Netherlands, he was a lecturer at the theological seminary of the Christian Church of Central Sulawesi (Indonesia) from 1991–1995. After repatriation he worked for the mission department of the Protestant Church in the Netherlands in both management and teaching positions. As of 2010 he is director of the Netherlands Mission Council, an ecumenical platform of churches and organisations involved in mission and evangelism. He is also a lecturer of missiology at Kampen Theological University and publishes regularly on mission and missiology. In 2016 he co-edited the WCC publication Sharing Good News. Handbook on Evangelism in Europe.

Petković, Tijana, b. 1991. MA from Faculty of Orthodox Theology, University of Belgrade, Alumni of Bossey Ecumenical Institute, University of Geneva, Erasmus exchange student at the FAU University Erlangen-Nürnberg. PhD candidate, University of Belgrade. Theologian. Published a few articles on bioethics.

Pustelnik, Pawel, b. 1988. MSc from Free University, Amsterdam, MSc from Cardiff University, PhD from Cardiff University, youth worker, entrepreneur and scholar. Pawel has been active in the youth ecumenical movement through the World Student Christian Federation (Editor-in-Chief of Mozaik) and Ecumenical Youth Council in Europe. He is a member of the World Council of Churches Working Group on Climate Change. Currently working for a private foundation taking care of education and care.

Reppenhagen, Martin, b. 1964. Dr theol. University of Greifswald, guest lecturer at Union Biblical Seminary Pune/India, parish and youth district pastor, research fellow and associate director of the research institute for evangelism and church development of Greifswald University, since 2014 dean of the Protestant Church of Baden. Supplemental chapter (together with Darrell L. Guder) to the 20th anniversary edition 2011 and editor of the German edition of David J. Bosch's Transforming Mission 2012, several publications on missional church.

Rolfsen, Raag, b. 1962. Major in Theology from Norwegian School of Theology, Minor in Philosophy from University of Oslo, Dr Philos from University of Oslo. Pastor and theologian. Local pastor in Drammen in Norway, Head of the Department for Study and Research in the Chaplaincy of the Armed Forces in Norway, and Director of Areopagos. Active locally and internationally in the ecumenical movement for many years. Published extensively in philosophical and theological journals.

Ross, Cathy, is Tutor in Contextual Theology at Ripon College Cuddesdon, MA Coordinator for Pioneer Leadership Training at CMS (Church Mission Society) and Lecturer in Mission at Regent's Park College, Oxford. Until 2016 she was the General Secretary of the International Association for Mission Studies. She has previously worked in Rwanda, Congo and Uganda with NZCMS. Her recent publications include Women with a Mission, Rediscovering Missionary Wives in Early New Zealand (Auckland: Penguin, 2006) and Mission in the 21st Century, Exploring the Five Marks of Global Mission (ed. with Andrew Walls); (London: DLT, 2008), Life-Widening Mission: Global Anglican Perspectives (Oxford: Regnum, 2012) and Mission in Context (with John Corrie, Ashgate, 2012), The Pioneer Gift (with Jonny Baker, London: SCM, 2014), Mission on the Road to Emmaus (with Steve Bevans, London: SCM, 2015), Pioneering Spirituality (with Jonny Baker, London: SCM, 2015). Her research interests are in the areas of contextual theologies, World Christianity, feminist theologies and hospitality.

Schlegel, Thomas, b. 1973 in Weimar, Dipl. theol from University of Jena, BTh (Hon) from University of Natal (RSA), got his PhD with a Dissertation on Karl Barth in Jena and Princeton Theological Seminary. After a time as pastor in Munich and Biberschlag (Thür) he was associate at the Research Institute for Evangelism and Church Development at the Greifswald University: Church in rural areas and the mechanisms of a shrinking church were in his research. His actual work deals with a missiology in Eastern Germany. One of the editors of Rural Theology and Theologische Beiträge. At the moment he is head of the "Congregation and Counselling" department and Kirchenrat at the Evangelical Church in Central Germany.

Wolters, Hielke, b. 1951, has been engaged for many years in ecumenical work and inter-religious dialogue and cooperation in the Netherlands as well as internationally. Wolters held positions ranging from working as a pastor in both rural and urban settings to director of the National Ecumenical Office for Industrial Mission. From 2000 until 2007 he was the director of the Stichting Oikos, an ecumenical institute that assisted churches in developing public awareness in the areas of international cooperation and sustainable development. Apart from these positions he served in various capacities as advisor to the Protestant Church in the Netherlands, the Dutch Council of

Churches and the Islamic University Rotterdam. In 2007 he began his work at the World Council of Churches as the Programme Director for Justice, Diakonia and Responsibility for Creation. Soon he became Associate General Secretary for programmes with a special focus on unity, mission and ecumenical relations. In that position he also was responsible for the Council's work on relations with member churches, just community of women and men, and inter-religious dialogue and cooperation. He retired in 2016. He holds degrees in information technology and in theology and received a Doctor of Theology degree from the Senate of Serampore College, India, in the area of Christian theology and social ethics on his research in the development of the thinking of the Indian theologian and ecumenical leader M. M. Thomas. He is author of a number of books and articles in the areas of missiology and social ethics, in particular in the context of transforming cultures and economies.